WASHINGTON, D.C.

In Lincoln's Time

Books by Herbert Mitgang:

FICTION

The Return

BIOGRAPHY

Abraham Lincoln: A Press Portrait
(Lincoln as They Saw Him)

The Man Who Rode the Tiger: The Life
and Times of Judge Samuel Seabury

CRITICISM

Working for the Reader: A Chronicle of Culture, Literature,
War and Politics in Books, 1950's to the Present

REPORTAGE

Freedom to See: Television and the First Amendment

Edited by Herbert Mitgang:
The Letters of Carl Sandburg
Spectator of America (by Edward Dicey)
Washington, D.C., in Lincoln's Time (by Noah Brooks)
America at Random: Topics of *The Times*
Civilians Under Arms: Stars and Stripes, Civil War to Korea

Noah Brooks
(c. 1886)

WASHINGTON, D.C.
in Lincoln's Time

BY NOAH BROOKS

Edited with New Commentary by
HERBERT MITGANG

CHICAGO

Quadrangle Books

1971

Library of Congress Catalog Card Number: 76-143573
SBN 8129-0171-1

A Note on the Text, and Acknowledgments

WHEN NOAH BROOKS distilled the best of his Lincoln and Civil War dispatches into this intimate view of the wartime President and of Washington, D.C., as a wartime camp, he had his memories and original newspaper reports at hand. He was a working journalist who had put in many years on papers from the Pacific Coast (the *Sacramento Union*) to the Atlantic (the *New-York Times*). His observations are surprisingly straightforward, even though personal journalism in that era often sounded partisan. His writing holds up today for its simplicity and authenticity. It has reportorial strength and more—a flair for the anecdotal and dramatic developed from his years as a storyteller. But always at the core of this book is the solid reporting found in his Washington dispatches.

The complete original text of *Washington in Lincoln's Time* has been followed in this publication of Noah Brooks's classic book. (For clarity, I have added "D.C." to the title.) Interpolations made by way of explanation appear in brackets; their purpose is to provide missing first names and titles, locate some remote place, or add relevant details for modern readers.

In addition to a biographical Introduction about Brooks, I have provided new commentary to set the scene for each of his chapters. The Appendix is a typical Washington dispatch written by Brooks to the *Sacramento Union,* showing how a newspaperman filed during the Civil War and what was considered newsworthy—from filibustering and patronage to the role of inactive army generals (early military-industrial complex?) and Congressional maneuvering.

Among those contributing scholarly advice and encouragement

were Carl Sandburg (whose biography of Lincoln, *The War Years,* mentions Brooks more than a hundred times); Ralph Newman of the Abraham Lincoln Bookshop, Chicago; and Edwin H. Carpenter, Jr., of the California Historical Society. In Castine, Maine, memories and mementos were generously shared by Francis Whiting Hatch, Noah Brooks Hooper, Margaret Ames, Frederick Dodge, Albert Frank Foye, and Barbara M. Trott. My wife, Shirley Mitgang, helped with the research during several wintry days in Brooks's Maine birthplace.

Contents

WASHINGTON, D.C.
In Lincoln's Time

INTRODUCTION

Of all the journalists and would-be confidants who sought passkeys to Abraham Lincoln's precious time in the White House, one newspaperman stood out as the favorite of the sixteenth President. Noah Brooks, a combination White House, Washington and war correspondent during the Civil War, was a friend from the Illinois prairie campaigns. He saw the President alone several times a week from December, 1862, to April 14, 1865, when "late in the afternoon I filled an appointment by calling on the President at the White House, and was told by him that he 'had had a notion' of sending for me to go to the theater that evening with him and Mrs. Lincoln; but he added that Mrs. Lincoln had already made up a party. . . ." Besides observing the President, Brooks saw the leading lights in the Cabinet and Congress; the chaos and bravery of the Army of the Potomac's generals and soldiers in the field beyond the capital; the fears and peculiarities and excitement of wartime Washington.

All this Brooks reported in a colorful series of 258 letters to his newspaper, the *Sacramento Union,* which was then the powerful press voice on the Pacific Coast. The heart of those letters, finely tempered by his postwar years of reflection and writing, he put into his major work, *Washington in Lincoln's Time.* As a contemporary portrait of the President and the capital city, it is outstanding for its intimacy and insight. The book is filled with incident and anecdote; many of these have been source material in the studies of Lincoln's life and actions in Washington. As Lincoln's law partner, William Herndon, re-created the early Illinois years (with allowances for opinion and prejudices) with a rawness unequalled for his time, so Noah Brooks in a personal way relived here the White House period.

The reader of this new edition of a long-out-of-print essential book on Lincoln and wartime Washington will make a pleasant discovery. Noah Brooks had, in addition to his access to the President, another important advantage over many of the journalists of his time: he could write with simplicity and eloquence. In his Civil War and Washington coverage Brooks helped to set the foundations for future national reporting in the United States. Much of the newspaper and magazine writing in the nineteenth century was long-winded, essayish and impersonal. But Brooks helped to break the pattern in his dispatches. There is present in his writing a human element which compares favorably to the best feature writing coming from Washington today.

"You speak of Lincoln stories," says Mr. Lincoln to Brooks in this book. "I don't think that is a correct phrase. I don't make the stories mine by telling them. I am only a retail dealer." There are dozens of Lincoln stories here "in the original"—before re-writing and reinterpretation by future biographers. Mr. Brooks was Mr. Lincoln's dealer.

Who was this journalist who could come and go freely into the White House? What was the relationship between the President and the newspaperman—one in his fifties, the other in his thirties? What elements were there in the background which enabled Brooks to write with such wit and authority about wartime Washington—indeed, what was Washington like when it was almost within range of the Confederacy's artillery?

To find out some of the answers, and to place this book in its proper perspective in the light of today's new interest in the time of which Brooks wrote, I went to the little town of Castine, on Penobscot Bay, in Maine. Historians and the journalists who admire Brooks know him by his pen name: "Castine." The signature "Castine" at the end of the letters to the *Sacramento Union,* the town of Castine and Brooks are linked closely. Here Brooks was born; here he spent happy boyhood years; here he returned after a newspaper career to reflect *Washington in Lincoln's Time* and live out his last years. Here one can still speak to friends who, as youngsters at the turn of the century, knew Brooks. Here one can see the small wooden house where he was born on October 24,

1830. It stands in a line on a lovely common with a monument to the Union boys in blue from the town "who offered their lives in the war for the preservation of the Union, 1861–65; With a great sum obtained we this freedom." Here is Noah's "Ark," as Brooks called it—the large house on upper Main Street where he lived and wrote in a special wing, lined with thousands of books and mementos of the Lincoln family and Washington. Here in the Witherle Memorial Library (George Witherle of Castine was a lifelong friend of Brooks) are the books which he kept in the "Ark," including a number on the Civil War period and the books which he himself wrote. Here in private homes are a number of famous California publications, including *The Overland Monthly,* for which Brooks, Bret Harte and Mark Twain, all friends, wrote. One can examine a privately held hand-written diary kept by young Brooks when he first went to seek his fortune in Boston, before moving on to Illinois and his chance encounter with the prairie campaigner who so strongly influenced his life. Here one can wander around an almost unchanged Maine salt-water town, and climb a hill to read the names of Noah Brooks, his wife and parents, on headstones overlooking Castine and its bay. The trail of Lincoln lore, seen from here, literally runs from Maine to California, with stopovers in Illinois and Washington.

Brooks spent the first seventeen years of his life in Castine. It is a town steeped in American history—the Indians, the French, the British and finally the Americans fought for this strategic bend in the Maine waters. Paul Revere commanded the artillery in a disastrous American attempt to assault Castine; a Revere bell hangs in the First Parish Meeting House. A diary kept by Brooks for July and August, 1848, in a hand-ruled notebook, reveals his affection for his home town: "Castine! I leave thee! Long, long must it be ere I gaze upon thy beauties, weary months must pass before again I shall tread the shore. . . ." The sentiments of youth go on for pages, but there are two interesting items in the diary which are clues to Brooks's personality and to his future course. The first is a score of games of chess played with his friend, George Witherle: "George, beat 26; myself beat 19; drawn games 3; total 48." The second is a series of drawings and notations: "columns, cornice, Corinthian, bridges." At eighteen, Brooks was a young intellectual with artistic and literary inclinations.

He went to Boston to learn the trade of a house painter, making his home in Chelsea, but by the age of twenty he had drifted into journalism. He wrote for the *Boston Atlas*, a Whig newspaper, and also the *Carpet Bag*, a small literary journal. He acquired the storytelling skills by contributing short sketches, essays and humorous pieces to the *Atlas*. At the same time he became aware of the political complexion of journalism, which colored every newspaper in the nineteenth century. It is an interesting coincidence that on Lincoln's first swing east on a tour for the Whigs, he stopped at the Tremont Temple in Boston and, as the *Atlas* reported it, "he spoke about an hour, and made a powerful and convincing speech, which was cheered to the echo." Only a few years after this was reported in the *Boston Atlas* of September 23, 1848, Brooks joined the staff. Lincoln received firm support later from the Boston paper, which exerted a wide influence throughout New England. This was one of the first of the links of friendship between the journalist and the President. As Brooks points out in this book, Lincoln had an extraordinary memory, and knew his newspapers; in private moments it is not unlikely that Lincoln recalled, with his politically aware young friend, his New England trip in support of the Whig campaign for Zachary Taylor.

The next stop for Brooks was Dixon, Illinois, where he went into the cabinet-ware trade. A number of people from Castine went to Dixon to try business and farming. Brooks was not successful as a tradesman—but there was a newspaper in Dixon, the *Telegraph,* and soon he was taking on writing jobs. It was in 1856, when Lincoln made many speeches for Frémont for President, that Brooks first covered Lincoln and spoke to him. The scene was a political rally in Oregon, Illinois, and this is how Brooks recalled the day:

"As one who dabbled a little in politics and a good deal in journalism, it was necessary for me to follow up some of the more important mass meetings of the Republicans. At one of these great assemblies in Ogle County, to which the country people came on horseback, in farm wagons, or afoot, from far and near, there were several speakers of local celebrity, among them being a Springfield lawyer who had won some reputation as a shrewd, close reasoner and a capital speaker on the stump. This was Abraham Lincoln, popularly known as 'Honest Abe Lincoln.'

"Lincoln led off, the raciest speakers being reserved for the later part of the political entertainment. I am bound to say that Lincoln did not awaken the boisterous applause which some of those who followed him did, but his speech made a more lasting impression. It was talked about for weeks afterward in the neighborhood, and it probably changed votes; for that was the time when Free-Soil votes were being made in Northern Illinois.

"I had made Lincoln's acquaintance early in that particular day; after he had spoken, and while some of the others were on the platform, he and I fell into a chat about political prospects. We crawled under the pendulous branches of a tree, and Lincoln, lying flat on the ground, with his chin in his hands, talked on, rather gloomily as to the present, but absolutely confident as to the future. I was dismayed to find that he did not believe it possible that Frémont could be elected.

"As if half-pitying my youthful ignorance, but admiring my enthusiasm, he said, 'Don't be discouraged if we don't carry the day this year. We can't do it, that's certain. We can't carry Pennsylvania; those old Whigs down there are too strong for us. But we shall, sooner or later, elect our President. I feel confident of that.'

" 'Do you think we shall elect a Free-Soil President in 1860?' I asked.

" 'Well, I don't know. Everything depends on the course of the Democracy,' [Lincoln replied]. 'There's a big anti-slavery element in the Democratic party, and if we could get hold of that, we might possibly elect our man in 1860. But it's doubtful—very doubtful. Perhaps we shall be able to fetch it by 1864; perhaps not. As I said before, the Free-Soil party is bound to win in the long run. It may not be in my day; but it will be in yours, I do really believe.' "

Shortly after this encounter with the man who would be elected President in '60, Brooks himself plunged into the battleground of Free-Soil. He had married Caroline Augusta Fellows, of Salem,

Massachusetts, and in 1857 they went to Kansas to homestead near Fort Riley. This was the frontier; the vortex of the struggle over expansion of slavery into the territories. By the time Lincoln and Douglas debated the issues during their historic contest for Illinois Senator in 1858, Brooks was back in the state—and reporting on the canvass for the *Dixon Telegraph*. Again he saw Lincoln on the stump.

The movement of the country was westward. The "Fifty-niners" were on the march, searching for new gold fields in Colorado and California. The not very successful tradesman-farmer-journalist decided to head for the West Coast with a company of emigrants crossing the plains by ox team. (Brooks later described his experiences in his most famous juvenile book, *The Boy Emigrants*, which first ran in the pages of *St. Nicholas Magazine*.) After an arduous journey, he arrived in California with "scarcely a rag to my back."

In Marysville, California, Brooks teamed up with Benjamin P. Avery, later United States Minister to China, to publish the *Marysville Daily Appeal*. Their competition, the *California Express*, was pro-Southern all during the war. But the new paper begun by Brooks and Avery helped to turn the tide for Lincoln even though it was the only paper outside of San Francisco which supported the Republican party. A few days before the 1860 election, Brooks wrote a long editorial portrait of his idol which helped to refute a slander begun after Lincoln's first appearances in public— when the *Springfield Register*, the Democratic newspaper in his home town, chided State Representative A. Lincoln for his "assumed clownishness." Brooks's editorial declared: "Lincoln is no vulgar ranter, no declaiming rail-splitter, devoid of the graces and dignity of manhood, lugging in the claptrap of honest labor to help on his ambitious schemes, but a manly, earnest, simple-hearted and courteous gentleman. We have been disgusted and mortified at the ignorant and unthinking enthusiasm of some of his supporters who would picture him as an unwashed and uncombed, long-legged, uncouth giant, bragging of his railing feats, and swinging his long arms over his discomfited opponents."

Now personal tragedy struck Brooks. At the age of thirty-five, his wife died. She apparently died in childbirth although the records do not reveal it. I walked around the cemetery in Castine and, on a rise of land, saw the Brooks family's headstones. Next to Noah Brooks's headstone was that of his wife: "Caroline Fellows, wife of Noah Brooks, Born in Salem, Mass., Died in Marysville, Cal., Aged 35 years. She hath done what she could." There is no written indication of a child—except in the memories of those who knew Brooks in Castine, before the turn of the century, when he returned here. I spoke to a Yankee gentleman, Noah B. Hooper, who was named after and remembers Castine's distinguished citizen; Hooper's father and Noah Brooks were old friends who shared Noah's "Ark" on Main Street. Mr. Hooper recalls that Noah Brooks had talked with his father and others in Castine about a son who had died with his wife. Some of Caroline's books can be found in the Castine library. In any event, Noah Brooks never remarried.

After his wife's death, Brooks seemed to lose interest in the Marysville newspaper. Caroline had died on May twenty-first; on November 1, 1862, Brooks left San Francisco on the steamer *Golden Age,* bound for New York. From there he went on to Washington to work for the *Sacramento Daily Union.* Together with the *Daily Alta California* of San Francisco, it was the main organ of news and opinion in the West. Brooks began his series of newsletters signed "Castine" and, by the end of the war, his far-reaching dispatches appeared under datelines from ten states, North and South.

In Washington, the new correspondent and the new President met again. Here is how Brooks recalled it: "Naturally, my first thought, on arriving in Washington in 1862, was to see how far the President resembled the Lincoln of Illinois before the war. The change in his personal appearance was marked and sorrowful. On the Sunday after my arrival in Washington I took a long look at him from the gallery of the New York Avenue Presbyterian Church. His eyes were almost deathly in their gloomy depths, and on his visage was an air of profound sadness. His face was colorless and drawn, and newly grown whiskers added to the agedness of his appearance. When I had seen him last in Illinois, his face, although always sallow, wore a tinge of rosiness in the cheeks, but now it was pale and colorless. Hearing from a friend that I was in the city, he immediately sent word that he would like to see me 'for old times' sake'; and nothing could have been more gratifying than the cordiality and bonhomie of his greeting when I called at the White House. 'Do you suppose I ever forget an old acquaintance? I reckon not,' he said, when we met."

From this point, Brooks begins his fascinating story. The Lincolns took the young newspaperman under their wing. Could one reason be that they sympathized with this widower? Without minimizing Brooks's personal charm, I believe this to be so. Ruth Painter Randall, the leading biographer of Mrs. Lincoln, who has looked behind the shutters of the Lincoln household in Springfield and Washington more intensively than any present-day scholar, gave me her view of the relationship: "To myself Brooks is the most appealing and lovable friend the Lincolns had in the White House. I think Lincoln really loved Noah Brooks."

The professional and social help given to Brooks was reciprocated. Brooks used his knowledge of California politics and personalities to help the President on a number of touchy matters and appointments. When Brooks followed the Union forces in the field, when he covered political stories and conventions, he would write private letters and later report to the President personally. Even Brooks's knowledge of Congress helped the President because he held a clerkship in the Thirty-eighth Congress when it was reorganized by the Republicans. (Other correspondents held office, too.) "Lincoln asked me to write him two or three private letters while I was there," Brooks recalled, concerning the Democratic national convention in '64, "to give him a better idea, as he thought, than he might get from the newspaper accounts of the interior spirit of the people I met." After the Republican convention in Baltimore, Brooks called at the White House and filled in the President. Brooks said that the President joked unmercifully about Brooks's failure to send him word of the nomination.

Brooks was destined to become one of Lincoln's private secretaries. "As early as January 1, 1865," Brooks wrote in the *Sacramento Union,* after the assassination, "our late President, the beloved Lincoln, told me that it had been decided not to renew the commissions of the Naval Officer and Surveyor of the Port of

San Francisco; that, as I was remaining away from California unwillingly, I had better take one or the other of these positions, unless I chose to remain at the Capital as his Private Secretary, in place of Mr. John G. Nicolay, who proposed to go to Europe." The promise of an appointment was fulfilled by President Andrew Johnson, who named Brooks Naval Officer of San Francisco on July 25, 1865. After a year and a half he was removed for political reasons.

Thereafter, Brooks returned to newspaper work. He became managing editor of the *Alta California* of San Francisco. He renewed friendships with Bret Harte and Mark Twain. In Castine, I saw copies of *The Overland Monthly*—sent "home" by Brooks to George Witherle after the Civil War—which was edited by Harte, aided by Brooks, and was one of the literate magazines in American journalism. Twain wrote a series of articles from Europe for Brooks's *Alta California,* later published as *The Innocents Abroad*. In 1871 Brooks moved to New York and became night editor of the *New York Tribune* at the request of Whitelaw Reid, another former Civil War correspondent. Brooks stayed with Reid until June, 1874, quit, took a short vacation in New England, and joined the staff of *The New York Times* as an editorial writer.

It was during his stay at *The Times*—where he worked for ten years—that Brooks became responsible for the witty "horse car poetry," often attributed to Mark Twain. It was while riding on a Fourth Avenue trolley car that Isaac H. Bromley, another journalist, exclaimed, "It's poetry, Brooks!" He pointed to the car notice: "The conductor when he receives a fare will immediately punch in the presence of the passenger, a blue trip slip for an eight-cent fare, a buff trip slip for a six-cent fare, a pink trip slip for a three-cent fare." Brooks reduced it to writing with some poetic changes, the verse was set to music, and printed in *Scribner's Monthly,* April, 1876. It spread around the country with many parodies. Twain wrote an article about the havoc created by the jingle, and changed the chorus of the verse to the way it is now quoted:

> Punch, brothers, punch with care!
> Punch in the presence of the passenjare!

On such minor matters fame often rests. Not much else is known about Brooks at *The Times*.

His next and final newspaper position was with the *Newark* (New Jersey) *Daily Advertiser,* where he served as editor, 1884–94, at the same time writing many magazine articles, popular juvenile books and minor historical works. Then he retired to his beloved Castine, there to write still more books and articles. He took an active part in improving the town and especially its public library. Still he managed to travel. He made a trip to the Mediterranean and visited the Holy Land briefly. He went to California, hoping to restore his failing health, and there, in Pasadena, on August 16, 1903, he died. But it is in Castine that the "Castine" of the *Sacramento Union* and Washington, D. C., is still green in memories. Here, at the turn of the century, he bought his namesake, Noah B. Hooper, his first and only bicycle. Between writing chores at the "Ark," he would take camping trips on a buckboard into the woods. In the warm weather he would hire a rowboat from Dennett's pier, take along one of the young men to pull the oars, and fish for flounder and tomcod in Penobscot Bay, in front of Castine's watery door. Sometimes he would talk of the President and the capital. They remember here that he loved to fish but did not like to hunt; he had heard the guns of the Army of the Potomac roar enough.

—Herbert Mitgang.

I

The Capital as a Camp

WASHINGTON at the beginning of the Civil War was still a relatively
small city. Its population was 61,122 in 1860, but in a matter of
months more than one hundred thousand people lived and were stationed there. The shacks of war began to rise and the capital assumed a temporary, transient look that it never lost. It was the "city
of magnificent distances" but without a magnificence in appearance.
The major public buildings of note were the White House, Capitol,
Treasury, Smithsonian Institution, Patent and Post Office. The
Army and Navy departments were housed inconspicuously in old
buildings near the Executive Mansion; these military offices were
within walking distance from the wooded lawn of the White House.
Foreign visitors, arriving on the Baltimore and Ohio Railroad,
were unimpressed by the unsightly sewage marshes at the foot of
the President's Park south of the old mansion. But the Capitol
building was impressive. It seemed to be identified with the growth
and war spirit of Washington; work continued on it all through and
after the war. The Capitol dominated the city, its dome half finished,
like the Union itself.

Washington began to look like an armed camp when five hundred Pennsylvania troops, the first to answer the President's call
for volunteers, entered the city on April 18, 1861. The next day
they were joined by the Sixth Massachusetts Regiment, and a few
days later the arrival of New York's Seventh infused optimism into
every department and corner of the city. Squads of cavalry took
possession of the Virginia end of the Long Bridge, at Washington,

13

and the Aqueduct Bridge, at Georgetown, as well as the Chain Bridge, four miles above Georgetown. Infantrymen patrolled the streets and public buildings. After Bull Run, schools, churches and public halls were converted into hospitals. By October, 1862, there were a quarter of a million Union soldiers encamped on both sides of the Potomac.

But the city still had a rural appearance. In the summer there was dust, in the winter mud. Endless lines of quartermaster wagons churned the roads. The first horse-drawn street cars began to operate, running from the Navy Yard to Georgetown. Pennsylvania Avenue, destined to be the capital's beautiful boulevard, was lined with rundown shacks; its cobbled pavement was broken and rutted. The contrasts were shocking. Negroes could be seen waiting outside the big hotels—Willard's on Fourteenth Street, the Kirkwood on Twelfth, the National and Metropolitan on opposite sides of Sixth Street—to remind startled Northerners newly arrived that slaves were held in the capital. At Willard's, breakfast included *pâté de foie gras* and fried oysters; the fifteen hundred underpaid Government clerks, living in shabby roominghouses, ate more modestly.

But the city wore the epaulets of an exciting war capital. Such was the scene when the new correspondent from California, "Castine," arrived.

I WENT to Washington in 1862 as correspondent of the *Sacramento Union,* then the great newspaper power of the Pacific coast. I remained there until after the close of the Civil War, and saw the beginning of the stormy presidential career of Andrew Johnson. During that momentous and interesting period of our national history I wrote newspaper letters nearly every day; and these, preserved in volumes of scrap-books, with other materials carefully kept, form the basis of the following reminiscences:

Several years before the war, while I was a resident of

Illinois, I had made the acquaintance of Abraham Lincoln, then regarded as a "rising prairie lawyer," and living in Springfield. I had met him at political assemblages, and he had occasional business errands to the town of Dixon, Lee County, where I lived. We formed an acquaintance which later grew into something like intimacy, although it should be said that Mr. Lincoln did not have intimate friends, unless we except a very few who, like Edward D. Baker, were among his earliest associates and companions.

Naturally, my first thought, on arriving in Washington in 1862, was to see how far the President resembled the Lincoln of Illinois before the war. The change in his personal appearance was marked and sorrowful. On the Sunday after my arrival in Washington I took a long look at him from the gallery of the New York Avenue Presbyterian Church. His eyes were almost deathly in their gloomy depths, and on his visage was an air of profound sadness. His face was colorless and drawn, and newly grown whiskers added to the agedness of his appearance. When I had seen him last in Illinois, his face, although always sallow, wore a tinge of rosiness in the cheeks, but now it was pale and colorless.

Hearing from a friend that I was in the city, he immediately sent word that he would like to see me, "for old times' sake"; and nothing could have been more gratifying than the cordiality and bonhomie of his greeting when I called at the White House. "Do you suppose I ever forget an old acquaintance? I reckon not," he said, when we met.

Washington was then a military camp, a city of barracks and hospitals. The first thing that impressed the newly arrived stranger, especially if he came, as I did, from the shores of the Peaceful Sea [Pacific Ocean], where the waves of war had not reached, was the martial aspect of the capital. Long lines of army wagons and artillery were continually rumbling through the streets; at all hours of the day and night the air was troubled by the clatter of galloping squads of cavalry; and the clank of sabers, and the measured beat of marching infantry, were ever present to the ear. The city was under military government, and the wayfarer was liable to be halted anywhere in public buildings, or on the outskirts of the city, by an armed sentry, who curtly asked, "What is your business here?" Army blue was the predominating color on the sidewalks, sprinkled here and there with the gold lace of officers. In the galleries of the Senate and House of Representatives, especially during the cold weather,—when the well-warmed Capitol was a convenient refuge for idle people,—great patches of the light blue of military overcoats were to be marked among more somber colors of the groups of visitors. It was contrary to army regulations to supply soldiers with liquors, and in most bar-rooms cards were conspicuous, bearing the legend, "Nothing sold to soldiers." At some of the drinking-places, as if to soften the severity of this dictum, was displayed an artistically painted group of the three arms of the military service, over which were printed the words, "No liquors sold to."

Now and again, just after some great battle near at hand, like that of Fredericksburg, or Chancellorsville, or Grant's long struggles in the Wilderness, the capital afforded a most distressful spectacle. Then, if at no other time, the home-staying citizen realized something of the horrors of war. The Washington hospitals were never empty, but at such times they were crowded with the maimed and wounded, who arrived by hundreds as long as the waves of sorrow came streaming back from the fields of slaughter. One occasionally met a grim procession of the slightly wounded coming up from the railway station at Alexandria or the steamboat landing from Aquia Creek [supply point on the Potomac River]. They arrived in squads of a hundred or more, bandaged and limping, ragged and disheveled, blackened with smoke and powder, and drooping with weakness. They came groping, hobbling, and faltering, so faint and so longing for rest that one's heart bled at the piteous sight. Here and there were men left to make their way as best they could to the hospital, and who were leaning on the iron railings or sitting wearily on the curbstones; but it was noticeable that all maintained the genuine American pluck in the midst of sorrow and suffering. As a rule, they were silent and unmurmuring; or if they spoke, it was to utter a grim joke at their own expense.

At the height of the war there were twenty-one hospitals in and about Washington. Some were in churches, public halls, the Patent Office, and other public buildings; but many were temporary wooden structures built for this special purpose. One of the representative hospitals was that of Harewood, erected by the government on the private grounds of [William] W. Corcoran [a Washington banker, who also had a home at Lafayette Square, across from the White House], in the outskirts of the city. There was a highly ornamented barn filled with hospital stores, clothing, and sanitary goods. A long row of cattle-sheds was boarded in and transformed into a hospital bakery. The temporary buildings constructed by the government were one story high, arranged in the form of a hollow square, row within row, and kept very neat and clean. At most of the hospitals the female nurses were supplied by the Roman Catholic Sisters of Charity and the Protestant Sisters of Mercy, working side by side.

At first the United States Sanitary Commission was charged with the duty of examining all nurses, male and female, before they were permitted to enter the service; but later a board of competent persons, organized by Miss Dorothea Dix, was authorized by the Secretary of War to perform this highly responsible duty.

The Sanitary Commission, whose labors can never be overestimated or overpraised, was supported by money and supplies from every local State in the Union. It organized an in-

dependent system of transportation, and was able, when a
sudden emergency arose on a battle-field, to anticipate the government service by many hours with medical stores, bandages,
lint, chloroform, and other requisites for the suffering wounded
whose primary operations were attended to on the field. This
was one of the many ways in which private enterprise and private means supplemented the authorities, whose machinery was
inadequate to the sudden needs of war. In the memorable week
after the battle of Antietam [September 17, 1862], twenty
thousand dollars of the gold of California were thus expended
for the relief of the men who suffered by the casualties of war.

In Washington we always looked for the regular and inevitable flood of strangers that poured into the city from the
North after any great battle fought in the fields of Virginia.
This was one of the fixed features of the strange life of the
national capital. These people came in quest of friends who
had been taken to the hospitals, or perhaps left dead on the
field. It was easy to recognize them by their anxious and distressed faces, their strangeness in the city, and their inquiries
for hospitals or the shortest routes to scenes made celebrated by
some life-destroying fight. Occasionally a detail of clerks was
made from some one of the executive departments of the government for the first aid to the wounded on battle-fields not too
far from Washington. These hospital stewards were volunteers,
sent to the front for fifteen days each, to get their first military
experience of army discipline and regulations.

Convalescents who had been discharged from the hospitals
and who were not fit for military duty were assembled at a
rendezvous in Alexandria, known as Camp Convalescent. This
camp eventually became so crowded with the vast numbers of
those who had been discharged from the hospitals or were
stragglers from the army, that its condition was properly characterized as "infamous." More than ten thousand men, some of
whom in the depth of winter were obliged to sleep on the cold

ground, under canvas shelter and without fire or suitable covering, were massed together there, in the company of healthy reprobates who were "bummers," deserters, and stragglers—the riffraff of the Federal and Confederate armies. There were two of these curious improvised institutions—Camp Convalescent and Camp Straggle—both of which were crammed full.

One of the most unique hospitals in Washington was that organized in the museum of the Patent Office. Each alcove was a well-ventilated and lighted ward. The tesselated marble floors were covered here and there with clean matting, and the general aspect of the place was pure and neat. The President and Mrs. Lincoln, accompanied by Mrs. Doubleday (wife of General Abner Doubleday) and myself, were once visiting the Patent Office hospital, and the two ladies, being a little in advance, left us lingering by the cot of a wounded soldier. Just beyond us passed a well-dressed lady, evidently a stranger, who was distributing tracts. After she had gone, a patient picked up with languid hand the leaflet dropped upon his cot, and, glancing at the title, began to laugh. When we reached him, the President said: "My good fellow, that lady doubtless means you well, and it is hardly fair for you to laugh at her gift."

"Well, Mr. President," said the soldier, who recognized Mr. Lincoln, "how can I help laughing a little? She has given me a tract on the 'Sin of Dancing,' and both of my legs are shot off."

President Lincoln, who loved to hear stories of the soldiers and their humorous pranks, told me of a soldier who was being carried to the rear in a severe engagement, seriously wounded, and likely to die. He espied a sutler [peddler following the Army] woman with leathery-looking pies, driving her trade on "the dubious verge of battle fought." The bleeding soldier grinned at the woman, and said: "Say, old lady, are those pies sewed or pegged?" [Lincoln—and Brooks—repeated this tale.]

The Washington of the war was a very different city from the present [1895, time of writing] stately capital. Before the war the city was as drowsy and as grass-grown as any old New England town. Squalid Negro quarters hung on the flanks of fine old mansions, and although in the centers of this "city of magnificent distances" there were handsome public buildings, with here and there a statue or some other work of art, the general aspect of things was truly rural. The war changed all that in a very few weeks. Temporary hospitals and other rude shelters arose as if by magic on every hand. The streets were crowded by night and day, and the continual passage of heavily loaded quartermasters' trains, artillery, and vehicles of kinds before unknown in Washington, churned the unpaved streets into muddy thoroughfares in winter, or cut them deep with impalpable dust in summer. It was a favorite joke of Washingtonians that "real estate was high in dry weather, as it was for the most part all in the air."

Over the flats of the Potomac rose the then unfinished white obelisk of the Washington monument, a truncated cone; and in the weather-beaten sheds around its base were stored the carved and ornamented blocks that had been contributed to the structure by foreign governments, princes, potentates, and political and social organizations. On its hill rose the unfinished dome of the Capitol, whose bare ribs were darkly limned against the sky. It was a feeling of pride, or perhaps of some tenderer sentiment, that induced the government to insist that work on the Capitol should go on in the midst of the stress and strain of civil war, just as though nothing had happened to hinder the progress of the magnificent undertaking. It is no metaphor to say that the sound of the workman's hammer never ceased on that building, even in the dark times when it was not certain that "Washington was safe." The completion of the pediments of the House and Senate wings went on without delay during all these perilous times. The colossal statue of Freedom which now adorns the apex of the central dome (designed by [Thomas] Crawford and cast in bronze by Clark Mills) was at first set up on a temporary base in the Capitol grounds, where it was an object of curiosity and interest to visitors.

When the bronze doors of the Capitol arrived, it was suggested by a Congressional humorist—[Samuel] S. Cox [of Ohio]—that they be strapped on the back of the Genius of Freedom, and the combination be known as a representation of a female Samson carrying off the gates of Gaza, which, he said, "would be scriptural, if not classic," and would dispose of two monumental works for which, apparently, no immediate use was possible.

As a matter of record, it may be said that the effigy of Freedom was finally put in its present place on the top of the lantern of the dome of the Capitol on December 2, 1863. The statue was constructed in sections, and the head and shoulders of the bronze figure in one section were drawn upward from the foot of the dome by a wire cable running through a lofty pulley; then, being swung lightly over the gleaming torso, it was settled into place, a few strokes of a hammer rang out on the air, and the thing was done. Then a star-spangled banner was hoisted to the top of a flag-staff that rose above the statue, and one hundred guns, fired from the East Park, near the Capitol, saluted the end of the work. The Capitol was finished. Thereupon an unbleached son of freedom sprang out from the crowd below and shouted, "Three cheers for the Goddess of Liberty!" which were given with a hearty good will. The function was simple enough; but the completion of the building which was begun in the time of Daniel Webster was a significant event in the history of the republic. Of course artists and artisans continued to labor on the Capitol during the war, and long afterward; but the figure of Liberty, designed and ordered during the administration of Jefferson Davis in the War Department [he served as Secretary, 1853–57, under President Pierce], was placed in position on the apex of the national Capitol while Davis was in arms against his government; and the sound of ax and hammer did not cease while the conflict lasted.

This was in the third year of the war, when the Confederate flag could no longer be seen waving from the Virginia heights across the Potomac; but for months before this the flag of the Union floating over the Capitol had been challenged by the stars and bars still visible on the other side of the river. And later in the war, when [Confederate Lieutenant General Jubal] Early came dashing up to our gates [his forces entered the suburbs of Washington, July 11, 1864], we saw for a brief season the same defiant colors.

The line of circumvallation [fieldworks] about Washington was eventually made very strong. Within the District of Columbia there were about forty forts, making a complete circle around the capital, their guns being trained to sweep every road or possible route leading into the city. Rifle-pits were cut from point to point, making a continuous line of defense. If the wayfarer or visitor desired a view of something of real war, other than that which might be had in the painful glimpses of dying and wounded brought from battle-fields, or of the grim lines of artillery and troops marching through Washington, a military pass, secured after many difficulties, would enable him to inspect the frowning line of fortifications that inclosed Washington as with a wall.

It is impossible in these days [Brooks, in 1895], so remote from the excitements of the Civil War, to give readers of this later generation any adequate idea of the uneasiness that pervaded Washington, or of the morbid sensationalism which characterized the conversation and conduct of the loyalists who were constantly haunted by suspicions of secret plotting all about them. One evening, while I was sitting with the President in his cabinet, Professor [Joseph] Henry, then in charge of the Smithsonian Institution, came in for a social chat with the President. The conversation ran upon various unimportant themes, and presently a card was brought in by the doorkeeper, who said that the man in waiting was extremely urgent to see the President, as he had matters of pressing importance to communicate. He was brought into the room, and proved to be a modest shopkeeper whose home was not far from the Smithsonian Institution. Glancing uneasily at the President's two visitors, whom he evidently did not know, he said his business was very important and should be kept secret. The President assured him that Professor Henry and myself were to be trusted with any business of state, however secret it might be; and he genially encouraged his visitor to speak out without fear of being betrayed in case the weighty matter which he carried in his mind was of an explosive character. The man then went on to say that he had frequently observed lights shown from one of the towers of the Smithsonian Institution late at night. He had noticed that these lights invariably made their appearance about the same time (at midnight), and he was confident that the person displaying them was carrying on a contraband correspondence with the rebels by means of signals. The President, with great gravity, closely examined the witness, but elicited nothing more from him than the fact that the lights were actually shown.

The President said, "Do you suspect anybody in the Smithsonian Institution?"

"No," replied the witness, "I do not know anybody inside of that institution. But I have heard that Professor Henry is a Southern man and a rebel sympathizer."

With that the President turned to Professor Henry, and, with admirable command of countenance, said, "This is Professor Henry; perhaps he will be able to answer for himself." The look of dismay on the countenance of the visiting witness was so comic that the President could not restrain his laughter. Professor Henry, who was somewhat disturbed by this expression of suspicion on the part of the well-meaning but mistaken

Unionist, very briefly disposed of his tale. He explained that the scientific instruments used to ascertain the direction and force of the wind, temperature, etc., were examined at certain hours of the day and night for the purpose of taking their record, and that the supposed signal-light in the Smithsonian tower was the lantern carried to the observatory at midnight by the attendant who made those observations. Somewhat crestfallen, the visitor withdrew, the President thanking him for his vigilance and well-meant promptness in reporting this incident, and adding, as the man departed, "If you should see any indications of a rebel conspiracy in Washington, you will do the country real service by reporting at once to headquarters."

The frequent appearance in Washington of paroled rebel officers, who usually wore their own uniform with evident pride and pleasure, and sometimes with a swagger, generally threw loyalists into a fever of excitement. More than once I saw ultra-loyal newsboys or boot-blacks throw a lump of mud, or a brickbat, at the passing Confederate. One of these officers, a Lieutenant Garnett, being on parole, sent in his card to Representative [Charles A.] Wickliffe, of Kentucky, and was by him introduced upon the floor of the House, where he attracted attention, as well as indignation, from the members present. Presently a wave of excitement seemed to sweep over the galleries, the spectators being visibly affected by the appearance of an officer in full Confederate uniform sitting on one of the sofas of the House of Representatives. This was intensified when a doorkeeper spoke to the visitor, who rose from his seat, gave a profound and sweeping bow, and withdrew to the outer corridor. It appeared that the doorkeeper had told the Confederate that it was contrary to the rules of the House for him to be present.

One of the most interesting side incidents of the war during the winter of 1862–63, in Washington, was the court-martial that tried General Fitz-John Porter for alleged disobedience of orders. [He was found guilty and turned out of the Army.] Another interesting and attractive military tribunal was that convoked at the request of General [Irvin] McDowell to inquire into the conduct of that officer after General [George B.] McClellan assumed command of the Army of the Potomac. The mean little room in which the court of inquiry was held was usually crowded whenever any prominent general officer was summoned before it. About the middle of December, 1862, General McClellan, who not long before had been relieved from command of the Army of the Potomac, was a "star witness" before the court. There was a great rush of sightseers, anxious to see "'Little Mac," to hear his voice, and to feel the magnetism of his presence. So great was the crowd of visitors that the single orderly who kept the door was at his wit's end to provide a channel of ingress for the ex-commander-in-chief of the Army of the Potomac. When he finally arrived, McClellan, who wore an undress uniform and a short military cloak, slipped in through the crowd without attracting much attention, and great was the disappointment of the mob at the door to find that they had missed seeing him. General McClellan was rather dapper, trimly built, with round, full outlines of face and figure, light hair and mustache, and an easy and gracious manner. He answered the questions put to him in a quick, clear, low voice, keeping his light-gray eyes intently fixed upon the questioner; and his mouth almost constantly wore a pleasant and winning smile. Every one in the crowded and uncomfortable court-room seemed to feel the attractiveness of his face and manner, and it was curious to note the admiring, half-loving, half-pitying expression which moved over the unconscious countenances of the intently gazing spectators as they bent forward to catch the slightest look and intonation of the ex-commander. The progress of business in the McDowell court of inquiry was tediously slow. McDowell wrote each of his questions on a slip of paper. The clerk took

it from him, and read it to the witness, who answered it; then
the clerk wrote down the answer, and question and answer were
wafered on a sheet. McDowell, who sat opposite McClellan, had
a full face, a commanding military figure, and certainly was
"the General," so far as looks were concerned, compared with
McClellan. McDowell's manner was dignified, decisive and at
times almost solemn. [McDowell was exonerated.]

Just before the battle of Chancellorsville, I visited the
Army of the Potomac, its headquarters being then at Falmouth
[above Fredericksburg], in President Lincoln's company. We
were detained on the way by a storm, and spent one night on
board the steamer anchored in the Potomac. In the course of
conversation that evening, the President was communicative
and in a confidential mood, and discussed the military situation with much freedom. Speaking of McClellan, he said, "I
kept McClellan in command after I had expected that he would
win victories, simply because I knew that his dismissal would
provoke popular indignation and shake the faith of the people
in the final success of the war." Very soon after the battle of
Chancellorsville, and before the battle of Gettysburg was fought,
the old rumor of McClellan's recall once more got upon its
legs, to the great consternation of many of Lincoln's friends
in Washington. This report was more than usually vigorous
and plausible. Hooker's failure at Chancellorsville, and the
blow which his military prestige had suffered in consequence,
gave public opinion a decidedly sharp fillip. One evening, while
this rumor was gaining strength, I chanced to be in the family
sitting-room at the White House, where the President, Mrs.
Lincoln, and several callers were assembled, when an indiscreet
young lady directly attacked Lincoln with the extraordinary
question: "Mr. President, is McClellan going to be recalled to
the command of the Army of the Potomac?" The President
good-naturedly parried this home-thrust, but gave no satisfactory answer. Afterward joining in the conversation, I in-

timated to the President that as he had not settled the matter, there probably might be some ground for the general suspicion that McClellan would be recalled. Lincoln, who sat near me, assumed a very severe look, and turning, said in an undertone, "And you, too?" I instantly recalled our conversation on the steamer [*Carrie Martin,* kept at the Washington Navy Yard], and apologized for my lack of faith. He then added, "I see you remember the talk we had on the *Carrie Martin.*"

It is curious to note how the names of many of the men who were prominent in the political history of the Civil War have now well-nigh vanished from the minds of our people. Thaddeus Stevens, of Pennsylvania, at his post of chairman of the House Committee of Ways and Means, was for a long time the leader of the House, and the most conspicuous figure of the Republican party in that branch of Congress. He was the oldest and the ablest man in congressional life. He was sturdy, well built, with dark-blue and dull-looking eyes, overhanging brow, thin, stern lips, a smooth-shaven face, and he wore a dark-brown wig. He walked with a limp, one of his feet being deformed. "Thad" Stevens was never tender-hearted, winning, or conciliatory. He was argumentative, sardonic, and grim. When he rose to speak, it was his usual custom to lock his hands loosely before him, making but few gestures. He spoke with great calmness and deliberation, dropping his sentences as though each one weighed a ton; his voice was low, but distinct, and he launched his anathemas at his opponents as coolly as if he were bandying compliments. While he wore "the very front of Jove himself," he had a certain repose of manner that was particularly exasperating to his adversaries. Nor did he spare his own political associates if they happened to differ with him. On one occasion, a New York representative, who had a curious way of dividing himself on each side of nearly every question, irritated Mr. Stevens by his perverse conduct, and was thus rebuked by the old leader:

"The gentleman from New York has more privileges here than belong to him. He has the advantage of being able to pair off with himself on every question." On another occasion, Mr. Stevens, being temporarily in the seat of [Representative C. L.] Vallandigham, heard a Republican member make an appeal to the Constitution of the United States. Rising with grim humor in the place of the distinguished Copperhead from Ohio, Stevens said: "How dare you, sir, mention the Constitution of the United States in this House?"

Henry Winter Davis was another eloquent and able man, but, except for his record as a persistent and violent critic of Lincoln's reconstruction policy, he has not left any lasting trace of his public career. At that time he was about forty-five years of age, light in complexion, with a round, boyish head, sandy hair and mustache. He had a high, clear, ringing voice, and a manner of speaking which was peculiar in its sharpness and firmness. He was a brilliant speaker, but not a ready debater; and he had a compact and direct way of putting things which always commanded close attention whenever he spoke. Garfield once said of him that his eloquence was "clear and cold, like starlight." In the Thirty-sixth Congress Davis gave the casting vote which dissolved a tie, and elected Pennington, of New Jersey, Republican Speaker of the House.

Clement L. Vallandigham of Ohio was the leading spirit in the mischievous Peace faction on the Democratic side of the House. He was well built, and was then about forty years of age, with a small head, regular and somewhat delicate features, and dark hair slightly sprinkled with gray. His complexion was fresh and fair, and his manner was agreeable and prepossessing. He dressed with great neatness, and, as he sat at his desk, turning over his papers, occasionally smiling at the petty discussions raised by [William S.] Holman [Republican from Indiana], the small jokes of Cox, or the grumblings of Wickliffe of Kentucky, he was altogether a personable man.

He was a good speaker—smooth, plausible, and polished; and in private life he was a most agreeable and delightful talker. I think of him now, with real regret (notwithstanding his political record), as a genial and pleasant companion, a steadfast friend, and a man well versed in literature, history, and politics; he died in the prime of his manhood. When he made a set speech he often became greatly excited, his face wore an expression at times almost repulsive, and his voice rose with a wild shriek; his hands fluttered convulsively in the air, and the manner of the man underwent a physical transformation. His power over his party in the House was complete when "fillibustering" tactics were going on. At a word from him, or a wave of his hand, the Peace Democrats would incontinently scud into the lobbies or cloakrooms; or his signal would bring them all back when they were needed in their seats.

Fernando Wood succeeded to the leadership of the Peace Democrats in the Thirty-eighth Congress, Vallandigham not having been returned to the House. A more marked contrast between two men can hardly be imagined. Wood was always calm, cool, and collected. His hair and moustache were dyed black, and his thin, spare face, elegant manners, and precise method of speech, gave him the appearance of a refined and scholarly man. He never lost his temper, was always agreeable, polite, and even courtly. He did not like Vallandigham, and on more than one occasion he held long conversations with President Lincoln in regard to the then notorious Ohio Copperhead. He was especially anxious that the President should not make a martyr of Vallandigham, of whom he expressed a most contemptuous opinion, and of whom he said that, if he were let alone, he would speedily sink out of sight.

Another conspicuous Representative was James A. Garfield [the U. S. President inaugurated and assassinated in 1881], who came into the House at the beginning of the first session of the Thirty-eighth Congress. He had been chief-of-staff to General [William S.] Rosecrans, and the day before he was sworn in, when he was introduced to his future associates, he wore a brigadier-general's uniform. The next day he appeared in citizen's garb, and took his seat in the House. His disposition to literary and bookish allusions is well known. Once in a while his colleague, Samuel S. Cox (who then also represented an Ohio district), would rally Garfield on his pedantry, or sarcastically allude to him as "the learned gentleman from Ohio." Garfield's manner was rather boyish, even when in public view. He would sometimes wind his arm round the waist of one of his associates in the House, and walk him up and down in the space behind the seats of the members, apparently oblivious to the fact that hundreds of people were regarding him with amusement.

Schuyler Colfax was a prime favorite with the members of the House, and with the newspaper men. He had a youthful face and manner, and was somewhat under the medium height. Colfax was versatile, indefatigably industrious, and was one of the readiest debaters on the Union side. He was light-haired and blue-eyed, and usually wore an expression so engaging and genial that unpleasant people sometimes called him "Smiler" Colfax. Before he was elected Speaker, he was chairman of the House Committee on Post Offices, and in that place he exercised a great influence in the readjustment of the mail service of the country after the secession of the Southern States. It is impossible for any one who knew Colfax intimately to recall his long and prosperous career as a public man without a pang of regret. As I have said, he was a general favorite, and his affability, his readiness to do a good turn for friend and foe alike, his skill and ability in parliamentary usages, commended him to the admiration and esteem of thousands of people. In an evil hour for him, his reputation was clouded, and his personality disappeared from public life. His manner as a presiding officer left something to be desired. He was too rapid to be dignified, and his devotion to the public business often betrayed him into neglect of the proprieties. Ben Perley Poore [a journalist], the cynical observer of Congress, said that Colfax presided over the House "like an auctioneer"; and it was a cause of mortification to some that when the President's private secretary appeared at the door of the House with a message, he was invariably addressed by the Speaker as "Mr. Sekkertary." Colfax was greatly beloved by his constituents, and was frequently honored with complimentary testimonials of his popularity. He was entertained at a banquet by the newspaper correspondents in Washington on his election to the Speakership, and, at another time, a handsome service of silver was presented to him by his Indiana friends in Washington.

No sketch of the House of Representatives of those days would be complete without a note concerning Thaddeus Morris, the Speaker's special page. When Mr. Orr, of South Carolina, was Speaker, he discovered in this young man, then a mere boy, a remarkable knowledge of parliamentary law combined with an extraordinary memory for names and dates. Orr at once attached Morris to the Speaker's chair, where he kept his place until his death in March, 1864. Probably few strangers ever noticed the tall, slim young man who leaned negligently on a corner of the Speaker's marble desk, apparently but slightly interested in the proceedings of the House, but really regarding all that passed with the most watchful vigilance. The youngster kept track of the mazy confusion of business, and could disentangle for the sometimes bewildered Speaker the most labyrinthine complication. Whenever a knotty question of parliamentary law or precedence arose, Morris would solve the difficulty with amazing facility. While the Speaker was addressing the House in a perfunctory way, stating the question at issue in order to consume the time needed by Morris to gather his authorities, the young man would silently place before the Speaker reference-book after reference-book, with chapter and verse duly marked, perhaps taken from the records of the earliest years of the government, and collated for use as precedents in just such a case as that under consideration. The mute prompter's hand was the compass that enabled the tempest-tossed Speaker to steer clear of rocks and shoals on which he might have wrecked his reputation as a presiding officer. Morris's death was a real loss to the House, but possibly some of the hair-splitting debaters who had failed to trip the Speaker when they "rose to a question of order" did not regard with unmitigable grief the place left vacant at the corner of the Speaker's desk.

In the Senate, of course, were many men whose names are as intimately connected with the history of those times as any in the House of Representatives. On the Republican side, Henry Wilson, of Massachusetts, was conspicuous as the Chairman of the Senate Military Committee. He was stout, florid, dark-haired, and of a portly figure. In manner he was entirely unlike his colleague, Mr. [Charles] Sumner. Wilson was rather loose and ramshackle in his manner of speech; his enunciation was not distinct, his delivery was slipshod, and he was neither precise nor fortunate in his choice of words to express ideas. He impressed one as a man of great mental force not well schooled. Sumner, on the other hand, was a model of forensic elegance, scholarly culture, and precision. His manner of statement was emphatic, even oracular. Some of his unfriendly critics said he was dogmatic; and he spoke with a certain fastidiousness in the choice of language which provoked injurious comments. Speaking to me of these comments, which had reached his ears, Sumner once said that when he addressed the Senate, even on matters of mere routine, he thought he ought to be as accurate and as fastidious as if he were engaged in high debate; and he cited an anecdote of Daniel Webster, who, when asked concerning his custom of wearing his best and most elaborate dress on the public platform, reproachfully asked his interlocutor if he should not present his best thoughts, his best manner, his best garb, when he addressed his fellow men.

Wilson was always genial, conciliatory; Sumner's bearing was apt to be dictatorial and unduly impressive, even on occasions of slight importance. Sumner's figure was tall, well-knit, and handsome. He had a noble head, a profusion of dark-brown hair, which was arranged with an appearance of studied negligence, and his presence was always commanding and dignified. He was one of the few men whom visitors to the Senate galleries first asked to have pointed out for them.

He affected a picturesque style of dress, wearing colors brighter than those which predominated in the senatorial togas of the period. His favorite costume was a brown coat and light waistcoat, lavender-colored or checked trousers, and shoes with English gaiters. His appearance in his seat in the Senate Chamber was studiously dignified. He once told me that he never allowed himself, even in the privacy of his own chamber, to fall into a position which he would not take in his chair in the Senate. "Habit," he said, "is everything." This being repeated to jolly Senator [James W.] Nesmith of Oregon, he said: "I wonder how Sumner would look in his night-shirt?" During the greater part of my stay in Washington I occupied the rooms on New York Avenue which had previously been tenanted by Mr. Sumner. Mr. D. A. Gardner, the aged custodian of the house, whom we facetiously dubbed "The Ancient," once told me that his family always knew when Sumner was preparing to make a set speech in the Senate, weeks before it was known to the general public. In the rear of Sumner's apartment was a gallery from which the interior of the rooms could be viewed. The younger members of the Gardner family, with a curiosity natural to youth, would be attracted by the sound of the Senator's magnificent voice rehearsing his speech, and from the gallery they could look in and see him before a pier-glass, fixed between the front windows, studying the effect of his gestures by the light of lamps placed at each side of the mirror. It is very likely that this entirely natural practice of the Senator became known to his enemies, who magnified it, sneeringly saying that "the Senator from Massachusetts was in the habit of rehearsing his speeches before a looking-glass, with a nigger holding a lamp on each side of him."

"Bluff Ben Wade" of Ohio, as he was familiarly known to his friends and admirers, was one of the most notable figures in the Senate during the war times. He was in person the embodiment of the high qualities that he possessed—manliness, courage, vehemence, and a certain bulldog obduracy truly masterful. His figure was stout, sturdy, and muscular, a little above the medium height, and indicative of great physical endurance. His iron-gray hair, sharp bright eyes, and firm-set jaw were characteristic of the alert and combative statesman that he was. Nevertheless, Wade was a tender-hearted, gracious, and lovable man. His impatience with the apparent sluggishness of Lincoln's administration betrayed him into frequent exhibitions of bad temper, and his intense radicalism too often hurried him into complications with the more conservative Union politicians in Washington; and he did not always extricate himself from these entanglements with credit to himself.

William Pitt Fessenden of Maine was Chairman of the Senate Committee on Finance during the greater part of the war and up to the time of his translation to the chair of the Treasury Department, made vacant by the sudden resignation of Secretary Chase. Fessenden was a tall, spare man, with angular features and figure, and a pale, intellectual face, from which the iron-gray hair was carefully brushed backward. His manner was cold, dry, and severe. His humor was acrid and biting. Remonstrating with a member of the House who had championed a bill for the abolition of the franking privilege, but who wanted it quietly strangled in the Senate, Fessenden grimly said: "My dear fellow, you can't make the reputation of a statesman with fourpence-ha'penny tricks like that." Another politician—a gentleman from Nevada—approached Fessenden to secure his aid in putting through the Senate a bill appropriating money to establish a United States branch mint in Carson, Nevada. Among other arguments to move the Senator's objection that the Territory was too young and too small to amount to anything, the Nevada man said: "All that the Territory needs to make it a good State is a little more water, and a little better society." "That's all that hell wants," was the Maine Senator's discouraging reply.

"Zack" Chandler of Michigan, tall, saturnine, at times grim and at times jocular, was one of the Senators who attracted the attention of visitors to the Capitol; his bold and sometimes reckless audacity, his perfect self-control, and his wonderful familiarity with the ins and outs of politics, made him a most interesting personality in the Senate.

Occasionally a cabinet minister would stray into the sacred precincts of the Senate, or Hooker, Burnside, or Meade would be seen sitting in the corner of the chamber consulting with Senator Wilson, or some other Republican leader identified with the conduct of the war.

Secretary [of State, William H.] Seward was slight and small in stature, light-haired, and oddly hostile to all attempts at taking his likeness. His manner in public was elegant and courtly, and he was one of the few men I ever knew in Washington who made a practice of bowing to apparent strangers who looked at him as if they knew who he was. He usually wore a dark-colored frock-coat and light trousers, and his figure was erect and alert. He was affable and courteous in address, and was seldom excited or outwardly ruffled. Like Lincoln, he was fond of good stories, and he was himself a capital story-teller as well as a good smoker; and his cigars were famous for their high quality. Rightly or wrongly, he was popularly regarded as friendly to McClellan, and for that and other reasons was disliked by Mrs. Lincoln, who would have been glad if the President had put Mr. Seward out of the State Department, and put in his place Mr. Sumner, whom she greatly admired.

Once I saw Secretary Seward engaged in a case before the United States Supreme Court. This was probably his only appearance before that tribunal during his term of office in the State Department. It was in the celebrated Albany bridge case, which had been carried over from a period before Mr. Seward's appointment. His manner at that time was not impressive. He spoke with great deliberation; he frequently fumbled with a big red silk handerchief that lay on the table before him, and occasionally he blew a tremendous blast on his very large nose, as if he were in the habit of taking snuff.

Secretary Stanton was not often seen outside the War Department building. He apparently spent his days and nights in that musty old barrack. His customary position in his office was standing at a high, long desk, facing the principal entrance to the room, and open to all who had the right of audience; for he shunned every semblance of privacy in office. From that awful tribunal, so well remembered by all who had occasion to approach the great War Secretary on matters of public importance, were issued many orders of supreme moment. He was opinionated, almost immovable in his judgments; yet absolutely just, when not led astray by his impetuous temper, as he was apt to be at times in the prodigious rush of official cares. Unlike nearly all his associates in the cabinet, Stanton was never accused of having any ambitions for a higher place than his own. He lived in handsome style, entertained generously, and was desperately hated by the newspaper men, some of whom appeared to regard him as a fiend incarnate. Certainly, Stanton's terrific earnestness in the prosecution of the war and the maintenance of the discipline of the military service, made him regardless of many of the minor graces of life which might

have endeared him to a generation of men who held him in
the highest respect for his patriotism, great public services, and
wonderful talent for administration. His spectacled face, with
full black whiskers grizzled with gray, and a peculiar silvery
streak on the chin, is familiar to thousands of Americans who
have seen his portrait on the paper currency of the nation.

Lincoln appeared to have not only a great respect for
Secretary Stanton's abilities, but a certain diffidence about any
attempt to thwart the Secretary in any way. I doubt very much
if he ever said—as was reported of him—that he "had no influence with this administration," the War Department being
especially referred to; but I know that he disliked to con-
tradict or interfere with the Secretary if it could be avoided.
On more than one occasion, however, the Secretary's iron will
had to give way before a decisive order. An amusing, yet striking, illustration of the qualities of mind of the President and
Secretary was afforded in the case of Captain [Thomas] T.
Eckert, then superintendent of the military telegraph bureau
that had been created in the War Department (and now [1895]
president of the Western Union Telegraph Company). Captain
Eckert was a man of indomitable industry, an incessant worker,
and he was so over-burdened with labor that he seldom left his
narrow quarters, where he was "cribbed, cabined, and confined" near the War Department building, even for needful
rest and sleep. Much to Eckert's amazement and chagrin,
Captain [Edward S.] Sanford, also attached to the military
service as a special officer (and afterward well known as president of an express company), was detailed to take his place
as superintendent of the bureau. Captain Sanford was reluctant
to displace Captain Eckert, especially as he was not familiar
with the practical working of the telegraph. Accordingly, Sanford took occasion to let Eckert know that he was to be relieved
"for neglect of duty," by the order of the Secretary of War.
An allegation so unjust wounded and surprised the hard-work-

ing and harassed officer, who was conscious that he had done his full duty by the Government. The upshot of the business was that Captain Eckert, after he had succeeded in sending in his resignation before an order of dismissal could reach him, was permitted to face the War Secretary for the first time since he had been on duty. It appeared that Captain Eckert had originally been ordered to report to General McClellan, and those orders had never been changed or revoked. Stanton had forgotten this, or did not know it; and he had charged to the remissness of Captain Eckert's bureau the currency on the streets of Washington of military intelligence, which had really leaked out from McClellan's headquarters. The Secretary learned for the first time, in reply to questions propounded by him with almost brutal sternness, that Captain Eckert's orders required him to report to General McClellan, and not to the Secretary of War, nor even to the President. While this harsh catechism was going on, the tall form of the President appeared in the doorway behind the captain, and Lincoln, lingering for a moment as he entered, heard some portions of the talk. Then, striding forward, he cheerily addressed Eckert (who, by the way, had been appointed from Ohio) with, "How now, my Buckeye friend, what's the trouble here?" When he was told that the captain was on the point of being discharged for neglect of duty, the President expressed his amazement, and said that he had long been in the habit of going to Captain Eckert's office for news from the front, for encouragement and comfort when he was anxious and depressed. He had gone there, he said, at all hours of the day and night,—two o'clock in the day, and two o'clock in the morning, at midday, day-break, and sunrise,—and he had never found the captain absent from his post of duty; and that he should be guilty of neglect of duty was simply incredible. The grim Secretary relaxed his attitude of stern reproach, and Captain Eckert was directed to return to his post with the rank and pay of major, reporting thereafter to the Secretary and the President. In due course of time, Major Eckert was appointed Assistant Secretary of War, and before he resigned his commission at the close of the war, he bore the rank and title of brevet brigadier-general. It was this faithful officer, by the way, who was chosen to carry to the Confederate commissioners at Hampton Roads, later in the war, the President's reply to their appeal, before the President made up his mind, at Grant's suggestion, to go there in person. Lincoln's arrival on the scene when the captain was "having it out" with the headstrong Secretary was in the nature of a special providence.

Captain Gustavus V. Fox, a man cast in the mold of the indefatigable Secretary of War, but agreeably affable and winning in his manner, was the Assistant Secretary of the Navy, and its informing spirit. Once the President requested me to go to the Navy Department, and see what could be done for a young friend of mine who had been in the army, and who desired to get into the navy, in order to keep his promise not to go back into the military service. And as I was discussing the ways and means, the President said, "Here, take this card to Captain Fox; *he* is the Navy Depatment." Captain Fox, although a hard worker, was rotund and rosy, the very picture of a good liver who took life easy. But he was capable of performing prodigious feats of labor, and he was a complete encyclopedia of facts and figures relating to the naval service and its collateral branches, and was ready to take up and dispose of any of the multitudinous details of the Navy Department at a moment's notice. He was a marvelously self-poised and ready man; he was the life and soul of the department.

Secretary Welles was not readily accessible to anybody, civilian or military, and his gentle and courteous manner, when he was reached, was rather disappointing to the visitor. He appeared to be vague and shadowy. One energetic and business-like Senator ([John] Conness of California) was wont to declare that the Secretary did not have a tangible shape, and that one's arm could sweep through his form. It is hardly necessary to add that the Secretary of the Navy was disliked by the newspaper people, and that he suffered accordingly. One of the craft fancied that he saw in Mr. Welles's face and profile a likeness to the ill-fated consort of Louis XVI., as she is painted by one of the Düsseldorf artists, on her way to execution. And "Marie Antoinette" the Secretary was called by the irreverent newspaper men, who had a nickname for every public man.

President Lincoln dearly loved a good story at the expense of any one of the dignitaries of the time, and he was accustomed to relate with much amusement a tale that was told of the Secretary of the Navy by one of the humorous scribes brought forth by the literary opportunities of the war—"Orpheus C. Kerr." The story ran that a dying sailor in one of the Washington hospitals said he was ready to go if he could see his old grandmother at home before he died; and the attendant at his bedside, being directed to ask Secretary Welles if he would personate that relative, the Secretary replied that he would do it with pleasure—but he was then busy examining a model of Noah's ark with a view of introducing it into the United States Navy. One autumnal evening, while the President and his family were lingering at the Soldiers' Home, near Washington, where the summer had been passed, a little party from the city was being entertained. [The Home was Mr. Lincoln's summer White House. It was three miles beyond the crossing of the city boundary and Seventh Street. The home, in part, was founded by the tribute which General Winfield Scott had levied on Mexico City.] Among these was Mr. A—— T——, of New Hampshire. The President, standing with his back to the fire and his legs spread apart, recited from memory the aforementioned invention, appropriately illustrating it with gestures, much to the amusement of those present. When he had finished, he turned to me and said: "Now don't let the

Secretary know that I have been telling these stories on him; for he would be dreadfully mortified if he knew it." Probably I showed some surprise and vexation at this implied and unmerited rebuke; and when we were preparing to retire for the night, the other visitors having departed, Lincoln took occasion to explain that he did not for a moment suppose that I would violate any confidence, but he had used me as a friend over whom to hit Mr. T——, who, as he expressed it, was a "leaky vessel," and might go away and tell all that he had heard, unless warned.

Of the other members of the cabinet, Attorney-General [Edward] Bates was a gentleman of the old school, short in stature, gray-haired, rather shy and reserved in manner, and not much seen in Washington society. Mr. Bates was of a philosophic turn of mind and a close observer of man and nature; and, when one had made his intimate acquaintance, he was found to be a most delightful talker. In his old-fashioned courtliness he resembled Mr. Seward. Montgomery Blair, Postmaster-General, was rated as the best-read man in Lincoln's cabinet, and he was well versed in literature ancient and contemporaneous; but his manners were awkward and unattractive. In politics he was a restless mischief-maker, and, like his brother Frank, he was apparently never so happy as when he was in hot water or was making water hot for others. He was the stormy petrel of the Lincoln administration. Although Caleb B. Smith of Indiana, Secretary of the Interior, was one of the original members of Lincoln's cabinet, his immediate successor, John P. Usher, from the same State, is generally regarded as the representative man in the Interior Department during that administration: he held office from the time of Smith's resignation in the autumn of 1862 to near the end of Lincoln's life. Secretary Usher was a fair, florid, well-nourished and comfortable man, an able lawyer, a great worker, and generally accessible to the newspaper men, who for that reason always

had a good word for the good-natured and kindly disposed
Secretary of the Interior. This habit of the gentlemen of the
press, who classed public men rather by their personal qualities
than by their actual merits, appears to have survived the shock
of war.

During the time of his occupying the post of confidential
military adviser to the President, General [Henry W.] Halleck
had his office in the Winder building, near the War Department,
and his residence was on Georgetown Heights. [Halleck, commander of the Department of the Mississippi, first was appointed general-in-chief of the Union armies; in March, 1864,
he became chief-of-staff, a non-combat post, and remained
as the President's adviser.] General Halleck's figure was tall
and well proportioned, though somewhat inclined to portliness.
His face was exceedingly grave and saturnine, his complexion
sallow and dark, and his habitual bearing was that of a man
sure of himself and distrustful of everybody else. But in the
privacy of his own house he could relax to geniality; he liked
a good story, and could tell one with gusto. Halleck was a close
student of human nature, and while his smoothly shaven face
was a complete mask for his own emotions and thoughts, his
large dark penetrating eyes looked through one with searching
thoroughness. It is not true that President Lincoln was ruled
completely by General Halleck, as so many ill-informed people
used to say. Lincoln liked to "talk strategy" with Halleck, but
was never very much under the general's influence even in military matters. He had opinions of his own, and was often impatient with Halleck's slowness and extreme caution.

One evening in the early summer of 1863, just after the
failure of the naval attack on Fort Sumter, the President asked
me to go with him to Halleck's headquarters for a chat with
the general. Soon after our arrival, the President and General
Halleck fell into a discussion as to the possibility of landing
a strong force of artillery and infantry on Morris Island,

Charleston Harbor, under cover of the gunboats, to coöperate with the Navy in an attack upon the rebel fortifications on Cummings Point. The President said he thought that Fort Sumter might be reduced in this way, and that, by gradual approaches, we could get within range of the city of Charleston. He illustrated his theory of gradual approaches by means of three or four lead-pencils and pen-handles, which he arranged in parallels, shifting them from time to time to show how, according to his notion of military strategy, our lines could be advanced in the desired direction. Halleck would not say that it was impracticable to land troops on the southeast end of the island, but he insisted that they could do nothing after they got there; and he made a strong point of the statement that the strip of land between Fort Wagner and the place of landing was so narrow that the zigzag parallel lines laid out by the President, according to scientific rules, could not be made. Assistant-Secretary Fox of the Navy Department came in during the conference, and the President appealed to him for his opinion. Captain Fox agreed with Lincoln that the movement could be made, but whenever the President pressed his view upon Halleck, the general invariably replied: "If it were practicable it would have been done; but the plan would be utterly futile for the reason that there is not room enough for the approaches which must be made." Halleck, although he treated the suggestions of Lincoln with great respect, evidently entertained profound contempt for his military knowledge. When he went away Lincoln (whose common-sense view of the sitation appeared to me, an amateur, to be sensible and feasible) expressed himself as discouraged with what he called "General Halleck's habitual attitude of demur."

That night, as we walked back to the White House through the grounds between the War Department buildings and the house, I fancied that I saw in the misty moonlight a man dodging behind one of the trees. My heart for a moment stood still,

but, as we passed in safety, I came to the conclusion that the
dodging figure was a creature of the imagination. Nevertheless,
as I parted from the President at the door of the White House,
I could not help saying that I thought his going to and fro in
the darkness of the night, as it was usually his custom, often
alone and unattended, was dangerous recklessness. That night,
in deference to his wife's anxious appeal, he had provided himself with a thick oaken stick. He laughed as he showed me this
slight weapon, and said, but with some seriousness: "I long ago
made up my mind that if anybody wants to kill me, he will do
it. If I wore a shirt of mail, and kept myself surrounded by a
body-guard, it would be all the same. There are a thousand ways
of getting at a man if it is desired that he should be killed. Besides, in this case, it seems to me the man who would come after
me would be just as objectionable to my enemies—if I have
any."

The oaken stick to which I have just referred was fashioned
from a bit of timber from one of the men-of-war sunk in the
fight at Hampton Roads; the ferrule was an iron bolt from the
rebel ram *Merrimac,* and another bolt from the *Monitor* furnished the head of the cane. After Mr. Lincoln's death, Mrs.
Lincoln gave me the stick, which had been presented to the
President by an officer of the Navy.

II

Glimpses of Lincoln in War Time

PRESIDENT LINCOLN brought full meaning to his Constitutional role of Commander-in-Chief. He had to. He envisioned the task of the Army of the Potomac as pursuing and defeating the Army of Virginia and capturing Richmond. But "McClellan has the slows," Lincoln said quaintly, while waiting for his Army commander to get cracking and stop rehearsing and marching. Nor was Lincoln's flank at "Headquarters of the Army, Washington," fully protected—at first he was burdened by General-in-Chief of the Army Winfield Scott, "Old Fuss and Feathers" himself, who had led the Army in the Black Hawk War way back in the 1830's, in which Abraham Lincoln served as a captain and later as a private. Now Lincoln was Commander-in-Chief. The search for a general who would fight with audacity and without excuses continued until 1864 when Lincoln finally found his man in Grant.

Lincoln's method was to check constantly with the military telegraph bureau in the War Department for latest word from the front. And he would visit the Army in the field, driving around the encampments on horseback and by carriage. Through field-glasses he could observe enemy pickets; and the Stars and Bars flying. Sometimes on these almost-pleasant forays to the front away from politically divided Washington he would be accompanied by Brooks. On one occasion when Lincoln went off to the troops, he left a message for Brooks to call on him at the White House the next day—for the President's personal report. "I shall never forget that picture of despair," Brooks recalled, after the President had

45

heard news of another defeat. "He gave me the telegram, and in a voice trembling with emotion, said, 'Read it—news from the Army.'"

In between the war reports, Brooks reported the Washington scene before him. In a dispatch to the *Sacramento Union,* March 28, 1863, he described the looks of the capital: "Washington is probably the dirtiest and most ill-kept borough in the United States . . . the streets are seas or canals of liquid mud . . . conglomerations of garbage, refuse and trash, the odors whereof rival those of Cologne, which Coleridge declared to be 'seventy separate and distinct stinks.'"

And there was always sidebar news involving the Lincoln family. Brooks reveals the improbable story of the spiritual medium employed in the White House, who had beguiled Mrs. Lincoln— and his own role in exposing the séance.

IT would be impossible to give to one who was not near the front in time of war a vivid idea of the excitement that prevailed at the national capital during the fighting around Fredericksburg, Virginia, in December, 1862. And the depth of the gloom that succeeded that disastrous attack is equally indescribable. Although everybody appeared to have kindly and generous feelings for General [Ambrose E.] Burnside, there was not much confidence expressed in Washington when his movement against Fredericksburg began. It seemed to us, uninformed and ignorant civilians, a most difficult and hazardous undertaking; and it is worthy of remembrance that almost everybody had a conviction that there was to be a supporting movement, somehow and somewhere, when Burnside should cross the Rappahannock and assault the heights of Fredericksburg. I have never learned why such a belief was common at the capital; but such was the fact. There was no such supporting or coöperating movement.

Burnside's troops began crossing the river at dawn on the eleventh of December, 1862. The great fight came on the thirteenth, when the Union forces faced that dreadful hill, near the town, whose declivity was a compact mass of artillery and musketry served by a brave and determined enemy. The Union troops marched to certain death. The Union loss in killed and wounded was 10,884. After one or two spasmodic and ineffectual attempts to renew the fight and carry the heights, the Army was withdrawn to the northern side of the river in the midst of a storm which prevailed during the evening of December fifteenth.

UNCHEERFUL HOLIDAYS

Several days passed before anybody in Washington, outside of government circles, actually realized that we had suffered a great and bloody defeat. We hoped against hope; for by that time we had begun to learn that the news of a Union victory was never long delayed nor ever understated in detail. When ill news came, it leaked out in driblets. This was when the direful accounts of the Fredericksburg repulse slowly filtered through the lines. And, so strict was the censorship in Washington, the general public outside of that city did not receive all the truth until it had been known and discussed in the national capital for at least twenty-four hours.

Although there was some fighting on the twelfth of the month, and a sanguinary struggle on the thirteenth, the last of the wounded were not received at the Washington hospitals until the twenty-ninth. The least severely wounded came first, and it was remarked that a major portion of these were disabled by wounds on the upper part of their bodies—heads and shoulders suffering most. They had been shot at while climbing a hill.

Most uncheerful were the so-called holidays of that season.

The city was filled with wounded and dying men; and multitudes of people from the North, seeking lost, missing, or wounded relatives, crowded the hotels. Nevertheless, with all these signs of woe on every hand, and with the great heart of the nation oppressed with discouragement and anxiety, the customary and conventional festivities of Christmas and New Year's day must be observed. I made the rounds of the official residences in company with a California representative in Congress, and we were struck with the artificiality of the show. One or two of the members of the President's Cabinet did not receive calls on New Year's, but there was much elegance and profuseness of hospitality at the house of the Secretary of War, and Mr. Stanton's face wore no sign of the worry that must have distressed him on that anxious, unfestive day.

Not so with the President. He received the diplomatic corps at eleven o'clock in the forenoon, and when these shining officials had duly congratulated him and had been bowed out, the officers of the Army and Navy who happened to be in town were received in the order of their rank. At twelve, noon, the gates of the White House grounds were flung wide open, and the sovereign people were admitted to the mansion in instalments. I had gone to the house earlier, and now enjoyed the privilege of contrasting the decorous quiet of the receptions at the residences of lesser functionaries with the wild, tumultuous rush into the White House. Sometimes the pressure and the disorder were almost appalling; and it required no little engineering to steer the throng, after it had met and engaged the President, out of the great window from which a temporary bridge had been constructed for an exit.

In the midst of this turmoil the good President stood serene and even smiling. But as I watched his face, I could see that he often looked over the heads of the multitudinous strangers who shook his hand with fervor and affection. "His eyes were with his thoughts, and they were far away" on the bloody and snowy field of Fredericksburg, or with the defeated and worn Burnside, with whom he had that very day had a long and most depressing interview. In the intervals of his ceremonial duties he had written a letter to General Halleck which that officer construed as an intimation that his resignation of the office of general-in-chief would be acceptable to the President. It was not an occasion for cheer.

But when Congress reassembled in January, 1863, after the holiday recess, the air was somewhat clarified, and the hearts of Union Senators and Representatives were cheered by military news from the Southwest, where Rosecrans and Sherman had gained important victories; new ardor was infused into the drooping spirits of Unionists at the capital. The autumn elections of 1862 had been interpreted by the Peace Democrats as a rebuke of the so-called "abolition policy" of the Lincoln administration, and the last previous session of Congress (the Thirty-seventh) had met in December, 1862, under circumstances of great depression. But in January the effect of good news from the front was clearly discernible on the faces of returning legislators. It was easy to see that they were far more cheerful than they were when they adjourned for the holiday recess.

One of the early incidents of the January session was a strong war speech from Senator [J. A.] Wright, of Indiana, who occupied the seat vacated by the expulsion of Jesse D. Bright from the United States Senate. He was a War Democrat, and took high ground in favor of the President's policy of emancipation. Among other things, to the great delight of the Unionists, he said that he hoped to see the time when a hundred thousand slaveholders would be running one way and two millions of slaves would be running in the opposite direction. In spite of the hammering of the gavel of the presiding officer, the galleries broke forth into thunderous applause; and this was renewed when, later on in his speech, the Indiana Senator said that he was glad to know that there was at least one general who was not fighting for the Presidency; and he had been heard of at the head, not the rear, of his army, and had had two of his staff shot down by his very side. This was an allusion to [Major General William S.] Rosecrans, who was then the favorite of the hour, and the applause that followed was so deafening and indecorous that Senator [Lazarus W.] Powell, of Kentucky, white with wrath and shaking his fist at the galleries, demanded that those seats be cleared. The Senator was seconded in his motion by [Willard] Saulsbury, of Delaware; but the hilarious crowd in the galleries, I am bound to say, received these warnings with undisguised contempt, and actually laughed at the speakers below. The President of the Senate, however, solemnly admonished the spectators that the rules of the Senate must be enforced, and that a repetition of their offense would be followed by a clearing of the galleries; and the speech-making went on without further interruption.

Once more, when Burnside began his famous "mud march," January twenty-first, Washington was excited with the high hopes which were inspired by that hapless movement. Civilians came hurrying to the capital to be on hand when the news of victory should arrive; and congressmen who were believed to be within the inner circle of governmental confidence were sure that great things were soon to be forthcoming. Vain hope! After a short and costly struggle with the elements, the rain and the mud conspiring to hinder the least progress of the Army, an attempt to cross the Rappahannock at Banks's Ford was abandoned, and the Army of the Potomac returned to its place of encampment.

But, although the fond expectations of the people had been dashed by this renewed failure, the disappointment was not nearly so great as that caused by the Fredericksburg disaster. There was an element of the grotesque in the "mud march" which diverted attention from its serious consequences. The

loss of material in that brief and inglorious campaign was very
large.

Burnside's usefulness as an Army commander was conceded to be over, and when he was replaced, a few days later,
by "Fighting Joe Hooker," popular hope, so often disappointed,
again rose high. At last, it was felt, the man had come. The
hour could not be far off.

REVIEWING HOOKER'S ARMY

Early in April, 1863, I accompanied the President, Mrs.
Lincoln, and their youngest son, "Tad," on a visit to the Army
of the Potomac—Hooker then being in command, with headquarters on Falmouth Heights, opposite Fredericksburg. Attorney-General Bates and an old friend of Mr. Lincoln—Dr.
A. G. Henry of Washington Territory—were also of the party.
The trip had been postponed for several days on account of un-
favorable weather, and it began to snow furiously soon after
the President's little steamer, the *Carrie Martin,* left the Washington Navy Yard. So thick was the weather, and so difficult
the navigation, that we were forced to anchor for the night in a
little cove in the Potomac opposite Indian Head, where we remained until the following morning. I could not help thinking
that if the rebels had made a raid on the Potomac at that time,
the capture of the chief magistrate of the United States would
have been a very simple matter. So far as I could see, there
were no guards on board the boat, and no precautions were
taken against a surprise. After the rest of the party had retired
for the night, the President, Dr. Henry, and I sat up until long
after midnight, telling stories and discussing matters, political
or military, in the most free and easy way. During the conversation after Dr. Henry had left us, Mr. Lincoln, dropping
his voice almost to a confidential whisper, said, "How many
of our ironclads do you suppose are at the bottom of Charleston

harbor ?" This was the first intimation I had had that the long-talked-of naval attack on Fort Sumter was to be made that day; and the President, who had been jocular and cheerful during the evening, began despondently to discuss the probabilities of defeat. It was evident that his mind was entirely prepared for the repulse, the news of which soon after reached us. During our subsequent stay at Hooker's headquarters, which lasted nearly a week, Mr. Lincoln eagerly inquired every day for the rebel newspapers that were brought in through the picket-lines, and when these were received he anxiously hunted through them for information from Charleston. It was not until we returned to Washington, however, that a trustworthy and conclusive account of the failure of the attack was received.

Our landing-place, when en route for Falmouth, was at Aquia Creek, which we reached next morning, the untimely snow still falling. "The Creek," as it was called, was a village of hastily constructed warehouses, and its water-front was lined with transports and government steamers; enormous freight-trains were continually running from it to the Army encamped among the hills of Virginia lying between the Rappahannock and the Potomac. As there were sixty thousand horses and mules to be fed in the Army, the single item of daily forage was a considerable factor in the problem of transportation. The President and his party were provided with an ordinary freight-car fitted up with rough plank benches, and profusely decorated with flags and bunting. A great crowd of Army people saluted the President with cheers when he landed from the steamer, and with "three times three" when his unpretentious railway carriage rolled away. At Falmouth station, which was about five miles east of the old town, two ambulances and an escort of cavalry received the party, the honors being done by General Daniel Butterfield [formerly of the 12th New York militia], who was then General Hooker's chief of staff.

At Hooker's headquarters we were provided with three

large hospital tents, floored, and furnished with camp bed-
steads and such rude appliances for nightly occupation as were
in reach. During our stay with the Army there were several
grand reviews, that of the entire cavalry corps of the Army
of the Potomac, on April sixth, being the most impressive of
the whole series. The cavalry was now for the first time massed
as one corps instead of being scattered around among the various
army corps, as it had been heretofore; it was commanded by General [George] Stoneman. The entire cavalry force was rated at
seventeen thousand men, and Hooker proudly said that it was
the biggest army of men and horses ever seen in the world,
bigger even than the famous body of cavalry commanded by
Marshal Murat.

The cavalcade on the way from headquarters to the re-
viewing-field was a brilliant one. The President, wearing a
high hat and riding like a veteran, with General Hooker by his
side, headed the flying column; next came several major-generals, a host of brigadiers, staff-officers, and colonels, and lesser
functionaries innumerable. The flank of this long train was
decorated by the showy uniforms and accoutrements of the
"Philadelphia Lancers," who acted as a guard of honor to the
President during that visit to the Army of the Potomac. The
uneven ground was soft with melting snow, and the mud flew
in every direction under the hurrying feet of the cavalcade. On
the skirts of this cloud of cavalry rode the President's little
son "Tad," in charge of a mounted orderly, his gray cloak
flying in the gusty wind like the plume of Henry of Navarre.
The President and the reviewing party rode past the long lines
of cavalry standing at rest, and then the march past began. It
was a grand sight to look upon, this immense body of cavalry,
with banners waving, music crashing, and horses prancing, as
the vast column came winding like a huge serpent over the hills
past the reviewing party, and then stretching far away out of
sight.

The President went through the hospital tents of the corps that lay nearest to headquarters, and insisted upon stopping and speaking to nearly every man, shaking hands with many of them, asking a question or two here and there, and leaving a kind word as he moved from cot to cot. More than once, as I followed the President through the long lines of weary sufferers, I noticed tears of gladness stealing down their pale faces; for they were made happy by looking into Lincoln's sympathetic countenance, touching his hand, and hearing his gentle voice; and when we rode away from the camp to Hooker's headquarters, tremendous cheers rent the air from the soldiers, who stood in groups, eager to see the good President.

The infantry reviews were held on several different days. [There were six corps of infantry; a cavalry corps; an artillery force.] On April eighth was the review of the Fifth Corps, under [George] Meade; the Second, under [Darius N.] Couch; the Third, under [Dan] Sickles; and the Sixth, under [John] Sedgwick. It was reckoned that these four corps numbered some sixty thousand men, and it was a splendid sight to witness their grand martial array as they wound over hills and rolling ground, coming from miles around, their arms shining in the distance, and their bayonets bristling like a forest on the horizon as they marched away. The President expressed himself as delighted with the appearance of the soldiery, and he was much impressed by the parade of the great reserve artillery force, some eighty guns, commanded by Colonel De Russy. One picturesque feature of the review on that day was the appearance of the Zouave regiments, whose dress formed a sharp contrast to the regulation uniform of the other troops. General Hooker, being asked by the President if fancy uniforms were not undesirable on account of the conspicuousness which they gave as targets to the enemy's fire, said that these uniforms had the effect of inciting a spirit of pride and neatness among the men. It was noticeable that the President merely touched his hat in return salute to the officers, but uncovered to the men in the ranks. As they sat in the chilly wind, in the presence of the shot-riddled colors of the Army and the gallant men who bore them, he and the group of distinguished officers around him formed a notable historic spectacle. After a few days the weather grew warm and bright; and although the scanty driblets of news from Charleston that were filtered to us through the rebel lines did not throw much sunshine into the military situation, the President became more cheerful and even jocular. I remarked this one evening as we sat in Hooker's headquarters, after a long and laborious day of reviewing. Lincoln replied: "It is a great relief to get away from Washington and the politicians. But nothing touches the tired spot."

On the ninth the First Corps, commanded by General [John] Reynolds, was reviewed by the President on a beautiful plain at the north of Potomac Creek, about eight miles from Hooker's headquarters. We rode thither in an ambulance over a rough corduroy road; and, as we passed over some of the more difficult portions of the jolting way, the ambulance driver, who sat well in front, occasionally let fly a volley of suppressed oaths at his wild team of six mules. Finally Mr. Lincoln, leaning forward, touched the man on the shoulder, and said: "Excuse me, my friend, are you an Episcopalian?"

The man, greatly startled, looked around and replied: "No, Mr. President; I am a Methodist."

"Well," said Lincoln, "I thought you must be an Episcopalian, because you swear just like Governor Seward, who is a churchwarden." The driver swore no more.

As we plunged and dashed through the woods, Lincoln called attention to the stumps left by the men who had cut down the trees, and with great discrimination pointed out where an experienced axman made what he called "a good butt," or where a tyro had left conclusive evidence of being a poor chopper. Lincoln was delighted with the superb and inspiriting

spectacle of the review that day. A noticeable feature of the
doings was the martial music of the corps; and on the following
day the President, who loved military music, was warm in his
praise of the performances of the bands of the Eleventh Corps,
under General [Oliver O.] Howard, and the Twelfth, under
General [Henry W.] Slocum. In these two corps the greater
portion of the music was furnished by drums, trumpets, and
fifes, and with most stirring and thrilling effect. In the division
commanded by General [Carl] Schurz was a magnificent array
of drums and trumpets, and his men impressed us as the best
drilled and most soldierly of all who passed before us during
our stay [most were German troops, part of the Eleventh Corps].

I recall with sadness the easy confidence and nonchalance
which Hooker showed in all his conversations with the President and his little party while we were at his headquarters.
The general seemed to regard the whole business of command
as if it were a larger sort of picnic. He was then, by all odds,
the handsomest soldier I ever laid my eyes upon. I think I see
him now: tall, shapely, well dressed, though not natty in appearance; his fair red and white complexion glowing with
health, his bright blue eyes sparkling with intelligence and
animation, and his auburn hair tossed back upon his well-
shaped head. His nose was aquiline, and the expression of his
somewhat small mouth was one of much sweetness, though
rather irresolute, it seemed to me. He was a gay cavalier, alert
and confident, overflowing with animal spirits, and as cheery
as a boy. One of his most frequent expressions when talking
with the President was, "When I get to Richmond," or "After
we have taken Richmond," etc. The President, noting this,
said to me confidentially, and with a sigh: "That is the most
depressing thing about Hooker. It seems to me that he is over-
confident."

One night when Hooker and I were alone in his hut, which
was partly canvas and partly logs, with a spacious fireplace

and chimney, he stood in his favorite attitude with his back to
the fire, and, looking quizzically at me, said, "The President
tells me that you know all about the letter he wrote to me when
he put me in command of this Army." I replied that Mr.
Lincoln had read it to me; whereupon Hooker drew the letter
from his pocket, and said, "Wouldn't you like to hear it again?"
I told him that I should, although I had been so much impressed by its first reading that I believed I could repeat the
greater part of it from memory. That letter has now become
historic; then it had not been made public. [The letter, written
by the President on January 26, 1863, began, "I have placed
you at the head of the Army of the Potomac," and ended, "Be-
ware of rashness, but with energy, and sleepless vigilance, go
forward, and give us victories."] As Hooker read on, he came
to this sentence:

You are ambitious, which, within reasonable bounds, does good
rather than harm; but I think during Burnside's command of the
Army you took counsel of your ambition, and thwarted him as
much as you could, in which you did a great wrong to the country
and to a most meritorious and honorable brother officer.

Here Hooker stopped, and vehemently said: "The President is mistaken. I never thwarted Burnside in any way, shape,
or manner. Burnside was preëminently a man of deportment:
he fought the battle of Fredericksburg on his deportment; he
was defeated on his deportment; and he took his deportment
with him out of the Army of the Potomac, thank God!" Re-
suming the reading of Lincoln's letter, Hooker's tone immediately softened, and he finished it almost with tears in his eyes;
and as he folded it, and put it back in the breast of his coat, he
said, "That is just such a letter as a father might write to his
son. It is a beautiful letter, and, although I think he was harder
on me than I deserved, I will say that I love the man who wrote
it." Then he added, "After I have got to Richmond, I shall give

that letter to you to have published." Poor Hooker, he never got to Richmond; but the letter did eventually find its way into print, and, as an epistle from the Commander-in-chief of the Army and Navy of one of the greatest nations of the world, addressed to the newly appointed general of the magnificent Army intended and expected to capture the capital of the Confederacy and to crush the rebellion, it has since become one of the famous documents of the time.

A peep into the Confederate lines while we were with the Army was highly entertaining. "Tad" having expressed a consuming desire to see how the "graybacks" looked, we were allowed, under the escort of one of General Hooker's aides and an orderly, to go down to the picket-lines opposite Fredericksburg and to take a look at them. On our side of the [Rappahannock] river the country had been pretty well swept by shot and by the axmen, and the general appearance of things was desolate in the extreme. The Phillips House, which was Burnside's headquarters during the battle of Fredericksburg, had been burned down, and the ruins of that elegant mansion, built in the olden time, added to the sorrowful appearance of the region desolated by war. Here and there stood the bare chimneys of houses destroyed, and across the river the smoke from the camps of the enemy rose from behind a ridge, and a flag of stars and bars floated over a handsome residence on the heights, just above the stone wall where our men were slain by thousands during the dreadful fight of December, 1862. The town of Fredericksburg could be thoroughly examined through a field-glass, and almost no building in sight from where we stood was without battle-scars. The walls of the houses were rent with shot and shell, and loose sheets of tin were fluttering from the steeple of a church that had been in the line of fire. A tall chimney stood solitary by the river's brink, and on its bare and exposed hearthstone two rebel pickets were warming themselves, for the air was frosty. One of them wore with a jaunty swagger a United States light-blue army overcoat. Noting our appearance, these cheerful sentinels bawled to us that our forces had been "licked" in the recent attack on Fort Sumter; and a rebel officer, hearing the shouting, came down to the river-bank, and closely examined our party through a field-glass. On the night before our arrival, when Hooker had vainly looked for us, a rebel sentry on the south side of the Rappahannock had asked if "Abe and his wife" had come yet, showing that they knew pretty well what was going on inside the Union lines. The officer inspecting our party, apparently having failed to detect the tall form of President Lincoln, took off his hat, made a sweeping bow, and retired. Friendly exchanges of tobacco, newspapers, and other trifles went on between the lines, and it was difficult to imagine, so peaceful was the scene, that only a few weeks had passed since this was the outer edge of one of the bloodiest battle-fields of the war.

One of the budgets [pouches] that came through the lines while we were at Hooker's headquarters inclosed a photograph of a rebel officer addressed to General [William W.] Averill, who had been a classmate of the sender. On the back of the picture was the autograph of the officer, with the addendum, "A rebellious rebel." Mrs. Lincoln, with a strict construction of words and phrases in her mind, said that the inscription ought to be taken as indicating that the officer was a rebel against the rebel government. Mr. Lincoln smiled at this feminine way of putting the case, and said that the determined gentleman who had sent his picture to Averill wanted everybody to know that he was not only a rebel, but a rebel of rebels —"a double-dyed-in-the-wool sort of rebel," he added.

One day, while we were driving around some of the encampments, we suddenly came upon a disorderly and queer-looking settlement of shanties and little tents scattered over a hillside. As the ambulance drove by the base of the hill, as if by magic the entire population of blacks and yellows swarmed out.

It was a camp of colored refugees, and a motley throng were the various sizes and shades of color that set up a shrill "Hurrah for Massa Linkum!" as we swept by. Mrs. Lincoln, with a friendly glance at the children, who were almost innumerable, asked the President how many of "those piccaninnies" he supposed were named Abraham Lincoln. Mr. Lincoln said, "Let's see; this is April, 1863. I should say that of all those babies under two years of age, perhaps two thirds have been named for me."

AFTER HOOKER'S DEFEAT

The President returned to Washington not only invigorated and refreshed by his short outing, but somewhat cheered and comforted by the general appearance of the army and the indications that the coming battle, when it should be fought, would result fortunately for the cause of the Union. The world now knows how great was the new disappointment that fell upon him and upon the nation when the battle was actually fought and lost at Chancellorsville, a few weeks later.

I was at the White House on Wednesday, May 6 [1863], and the President, who seemed anxious and harassed beyond any power of description, said that while still without any positive information as to the result of the fighting at Chancellorsville, he was certain in his own mind that "Hooker had been licked." He was only then wondering whether Hooker would be able to recover himself and renew the fight. The President asked me to go into the room then occupied by his friend Dr. Henry, who was a guest in the house, saying possibly we might get some news later on.

In an hour or so, while the doctor and I sat talking, say about three o'clock in the afternoon, the door opened, and Lincoln came into the room. I shall never forget that picture of despair. He held a telegram in his hand, and as he closed the door and came toward us I mechanically noticed that his face, usually sallow, was ashen in hue. The paper on the wall behind him was of the tint known as "French gray," and even in that moment of sorrow and dread expectation I vaguely took in the thought that the complexion of the anguished President's visage was almost exactly like that of the wall. He gave me the telegram, and in a voice trembling with emotion, said, "Read it— news from the Army." The dispatch was from General Butterfield, Hooker's chief of staff, addressed to the War Department, and was to the effect that the Army had been withdrawn from the south side of the Rappahannock, and was then "safely encamped" in its former position. The appearance of the President, as I read aloud these fateful words, was piteous. Never, as long as I knew him, did he seem to be so broken, so dispirited, and so ghostlike. Clasping his hands behind his back, he walked up and down the room, saying, "My God! my God! What will the country say! What will the country say!"

He seemed incapable of uttering any other words than these, and after a little time he hurriedly left the room. Dr. Henry, whose affection for Lincoln was deep and tender, burst into a passion of tears. I consoled him as best I could, and while we were talking and trying to find a gleam of sunshine in this frightful darkness, I saw a carriage drive up to the entrance of the White House, and, looking out, beheld the tall form of the President dart into the vehicle, in which sat General Halleck, and drive off. Immediately after, an attendant came to tell us that the President and General Halleck had gone to the Army of the Potomac, and that Mr. Lincoln would return next day, and would like to see me in the evening.

The wildest rumors were at once set on foot; but it was known that the President and General Halleck had gone to the front, taking a special steamer at the Navy Yard at four o'clock that afternoon. It was commonly believed that Hooker was or would be put under arrest; that Halleck would be placed in command of the Army of the Potomac; that Stanton had resigned; that Lee had cut Hooker to pieces, and was approaching Washington by the way of Dumfries; that McClellan was coming on a special train from New York, and that [Franz] Sigel, [Benjamin] Butler, [John] Frémont, and several other shelved generals, had been sent for in hot haste. The crowd at Willard's Hotel that night was so great that it was difficult to get inside the doors. The friends of McClellan, and the Copperheads generally, sprang at once into new life and animation, and were dotted through the gloomy crowds with smiling faces and unsuppressed joy.

Of course these fantastic stories speedily passed away like mists before the sun. Hooker was not removed, and although he never again commanded the Army of the Potomac in any great battle, his withdrawal from his high post was accomplished later on without any such disgrace as would have attended his dismissal at that time. When he was finally relieved of the command of the Army of the Potomac, a few days before the battle of Gettysburg, and while Lee was on his march to invade Pennsylvania, Hooker went to Baltimore to wait for orders, very much as McClellan had gone to Trenton to wait when he had relinquished his baton of command. No orders went to Hooker, and, becoming impatient, he came to Washington to ask for orders. He sent his card to my rooms, and I called on him at his headquarters on Pennsylvania Avenue, opposite Willard's Hotel. He did not in the least exhibit that chastened spirit which I expected to see in him, but evidently regarded himself a greatly abused man. He could not speak in moderation of any one of his generals; and as for Halleck and Stanton, no words at his command could express his hatred and contempt for these men, whom he regarded as the authors of all his misfortunes. He asked me what the President had said about him. I hesitated, but when he pressed for a reply, said that Lincoln had told me that he regarded Hooker very much as a father might regard a son who was lame, or who had some other incurable physical infirmity. His love for his son would be even intensified by the reflection that the lad could never be a strong and successful man. The tears stood in Hooker's eyes as he heard this curious characterization of himself; but immediately rallying, he said, "Well, the President may regard me as a cripple; but if he will give me a chance, I will yet show him that I know how to fight." The next day Hooker was arrested on an order from the War Department for having visited Washington without leave, contrary to existing rules and regulations. This certainly was a most ungracious and needless bit of oppression; it would have been very easy to have warned Hooker that he was liable to arrest, and to have given him an opportunity to get away from Washington without discredit.

I never saw Hooker again until long after the war, when he was living at the Brevoort House, New York, where I was then in the habit of dining. [Brooks, in the 1870's, worked on the *Tribune* and *Times,* then located downtown. Hooker died in 1879.] His mind had become somewhat shaken by sickness, and the long and painful strain of years of strenuous service. Apparently he never saw me without a quickening of his memory of Chancellorsville, the President, and what came after. In a loud voice, which astonished the quiet diners at the Brevoort, he would at once discourse of his misfortunes and wrongs, and speak of certain public men, civil and military, in the most violent and abusive terms. After a while, so habitual was this lecture, which poor Hooker seemed to address to the company in general, I was obliged to take a table in a corner of the dining-room as far as possible from him. He has long since passed off the stage of action, but no one who knew him in his prime can fail to recall him to mind as one of the most picturesque per-

sonalities of the war; one of the brightest figures in that long
and fast-fading panorama that reached from the firing on Fort
Sumter to the burial of Lincoln at Springfield.

EXCLUSIVE INFORMATION

In spite of a rigorous censorship of the wires, military
matters did sometimes get out of Washington in the most in-
explicable manner, eluding the stern authority in the telegraph
office. When it was decided to reinforce Rosecrans, in 1863, with
the Eleventh and Twelfth Corps of the Army of the Potomac,
an officer of the War Department went to every newspaper
correspondent in the city, and requested them, at the special
desire of the President and the Secretary of War, not to make
any mention of the proposed movement. The correspondents
all agreed to this, and telegraphed or wrote to their newspapers
not to refer to the matter, should it come to their knowledge in
any way. But one night (September twenty-sixth) everybody
was astonished by news from New York that the *Evening Post,*
an unconditional supporter of the Administration, had published full particulars of the reinforcement of Rosecrans by
the Eleventh and Twelfth Army Corps under Hooker. [The
New York Evening Post was edited by William Cullen Bryant.
Bryant and Henry J. Raymond of *The New York Times* were
the President's steadfast friends in the New York press.] The
Washington Sunday morning papers copied the intelligence,
and a Philadelphia paper, saying that the news was "contraband," suggested that the editors of the *New York Evening Post*
should breakfast in Fort Lafayette. It is a curious illustration
of the muddled condition of things at that time, that the Monday morning papers in Washington discreetly held their peace,
and printed not a word of news or comment concerning the
whole affair. The *Evening Post* explained its position by saying that its Washington correspondent was not responsible for

the "rumors" which had appeared in its Saturday edition, and that the paper had been imposed upon by others. When this comical imbroglio began, the Washington correspondents were in despair. Stanton raged like a lion, and Lincoln, I am bound to say, was exceedingly angry.

The *Evening Post,* in its zeal to secure the earliest information, more than once got itself or its correspondents into trouble. When it was known that the President had written a letter to the Republican mass-meeting to be held in Springfield, Illinois, September 3, 1863, there was a great stir among the newspaper men in Washington, every correspondent being anxious to get an advance copy of so important a document. The Peace Democrats of Illinois, and indeed throughout the West, were then in a state of furious and threatening wrath. Senator [William A.] Richardson of Illinois had addressed a meeting at Springfield that summer in a most hysterical and blood-curdling manner, and the meeting adopted resolutions denouncing "misrule and anarchy," and declaring in favor of "peace upon the basis of restoration of the Union." [Senator Richardson was an old Douglas Democrat.] That the President of the United States should consent to write a letter to a convocation gotten up in his own State by way of a counterblast to this traitorous demonstration was enough to stimulate to the highest pitch the desire of every journalist to secure an early copy of the document. But to all importunities the President and his secretaries were deaf; and the paper, which was dated August 26, 1863, was sent out of the White House, it was said, by a private messenger. Nevertheless, several days before the meeting of the Springfield assemblage, the letter appeared in full in the *New York Evening Post,* and to our great amusement was telegraphed back to Washington, and printed in that city before it could be publicly read in Springfield. This was the famous letter [addressed to Hon. James C. Conkling], which has since become a political classic, in which occurred the unique phrase [for the Navy], "Uncle Sam's web-feet," and in which the good President said, "The signs look better," "The Father of Waters again goes unvexed to the sea," etc.

So far as I know, the method by which the *Evening Post* got possession of a copy of that letter has never been made public. It was not an offense against military law, of course, to print it, as it was a political and not military piece of information, but I remember that Lincoln said he was "mad enough to cry." He had refused a copy of his letter to the Washington agent of the Associated Press, explaining that although solemn promises not to publish had repeatedly been given, he found that the practice of furnishing advance copies of anything to the newspapers was a source of endless mischief. He was sorry to say that he could not always depend upon even the most impressive promises of those who besieged him for "early and exclusive" information.

AN INTERRUPTED SÉANCE

The most terrifying threat that could be held over a zealous war-correspondent was that of arrest and confinement in the old Capitol prison. Every person who spent much time in Washington during the war will recall with mingled amusement and dread the freedom with which this threat was bandied about among people who were not by any means authorized to promote the rapid transit of anybody to that malodorous Bastille. Let me give an instance in which, though one of the unauthorized, I made use of this fear-compelling threat. A seamstress [Mrs. Keckley] employed in the White House had induced Mrs. Lincoln to listen to the artful tales of a so-called spiritual medium who masqueraded under the name of Colchester, and who pretended to be the illegitimate son of an English duke. The poor lady at that time was well-nigh distraught with grief at the death of her son Willie. By playing on her motherly sor-

rows, Colchester actually succeeded in inducing Mrs. Lincoln
to receive him in the family residence at the Soldiers' Home,
where, in a darkened room, he pretended to produce messages
from the dead boy by means of scratches on the wainscoting and
taps on the walls and furniture. Mrs. Lincoln told me of these
so-called manifestations, and asked me to be present in the
White House when Colchester would give an exhibition of his
powers. I declined; but meanwhile I received an invitation to
invest one dollar and attend "a Colchester sitting" at the house
of a Washington gentleman who was a profound believer in
this pretentious seer. To gratify my curiosity, I paid the entrance fee, and, accompanied by a trusty friend, went to the
séance. After the company had been seated around the table in
the usual approved manner, and the lights were turned out,
the silence was broken by the thumping of a drum, the twang-
ing of a banjo, and the ringing of bells, all of which instruments had been laid on the table, ready for use. By some hocus-
pocus, it was evident, the operator had freed his hands from
the hands of those who sat on each side of him, and was himself making "music in the air." Loosening my hands from my
neighbors', who were unbelievers, I rose, and, grasping in the
direction of the drum-beat, grabbed a very solid and fleshy hand
in which was held a bell that was being thumped on a drum-
head. I shouted, "Strike a light!" My friend, after what appeared to be an unconscionable length of time, lighted a match;
but meanwhile somebody had dealt me a severe blow with the
drum, the edge of which cut a slight wound on my forehead.
When the gas was finally lighted, the singular spectacle was
presented of "the son of the duke" firmly grasped by a man
whose forehead was covered with blood, while the arrested scion
of nobility was glowering at the drum and bells which he still
held in his hands. The meeting broke up in the most admired
disorder, "Lord Colchester" slipping out of the room in the
confusion. His host subsequently brought down word from the

discomfited seer to the effect that Colchester was "so outraged by this insult" that he refused to reappear!

A day or two after this, I was astonished by a note from Mrs. Lincoln requesting me to come to the White House without a moment's delay, on a matter of the most distressing importance. On my arrival, the lady, somewhat discomposed, showed me a note from "Colchester," in which he requested that she should procure for him from the War Department a pass to New York, and intimated that in case she refused he might have some unpleasant things to say to her. We made an arrangement by which Colchester came to the White House at a specified hour the next day, and after I had been formally introduced to the charlatan, Mrs. Lincoln withdrew from the room. Going up to Colchester, I lifted the hair from the scar on my forehead, yet unhealed, and said, "Do you recognize this?" The man muttered something about his having been insulted, and then I said: "You know that I know you are a swindler and a humbug. Get out of this house and out of this city at once. If you are in Washington to-morrow afternoon at this time, you will be in the old Capitol prison." The little scamp pulled himself together and sneaked out of the house, and, so far as I know, out of Washington. I never saw or heard of him afterward.

SOCIAL INCIDENTS

The White House did not witness many brilliant festivities during the war, after that famous party which was given by the President and Mrs. Lincoln early in the first year of the Lincoln administration. But Mrs. Lincoln's afternoon receptions and the President's public levees were held regularly during the winters. Nothing could be more democratic than these gatherings of the people at the White House. They were usually held twice a week during the winter, those on Tuesday evenings being so-called dress receptions, and the Saturday levees being less formal in character. A majority of the visitors went in full dress: the ladies in laces, feathers, silks, and satins, without bonnet; and the gentlemen in evening dress. But sprinkled through the gaily attired crowds were hundreds of officers and private soldiers, the light-blue army coat of the period being a conspicuous feature of the moving panorama. Here and there a day-laborer, looking as though he had just left his work-bench, or a hard-working clerk with ink-stained linen, added to the popular character of the assembly. Usually the President stood in the famous Blue Room, or at the head of the East Room; and those who wished to shake hands made their entrance, one by one, and were introduced by the functionary detailed for that occasion. So vast were the crowds, and so affectionate their greetings, that Mr. Lincoln's right hand was often so swollen that he would be unable to use it readily for hours afterward; and the white kid glove of his right hand, when the operation of handshaking was over, always looked as if it had been dragged through a dust-bin. Much of the time, I think, the President never heard with his inner ear the names of persons presented to him by Secretary [John G.] Nicolay, Commissioner [Benjamin B.] French [officer in charge of Washington buildings], or United States Marshal [Ward Hill] Lamon [of the District of Columbia]. His thoughts were apt to be far from the crowds of strangers that passed before him. On one occasion, bringing up a friend, I greeted the President as usual, and presented my friend. The President shook hands with me in a perfunctory way, his eyes fixed on space, and I passed on, knowing that he had never seen me or heard the name of my friend; but after I had reached a point seven or eight persons beyond, the President suddenly seemed to see me, and, continuing the handshaking of strangers while he spoke, shouted out: "Oh, Brooks! Charley Maltby is in town, and I want you to come and see me to-morrow." Maltby, it may be said, was an old friend of Mr. Lincoln's then living in California, and about whose petition for a Federal appointment the President wished to talk with me. Lincoln's sudden outburst, naturally enough, astonished the people who heard it.

While the President and his party were with the Army of the Potomac at the time previously referred to, pleasant collations were occasionally served at the headquarters of the various corps commanders whose troops were being reviewed. At a luncheon given by General Sickles at his headquarters, among the ladies present was the Princess Salm-Salm, whose husband was a staff-officer in the Army. This lady attracted much admiration by her graceful and dashing riding in the cavalcade that attended the reviews. Before her marriage she was a Miss Joyall of Philipsburg. It was this remarkable woman who astonished the President, on his entering General Sickles's headquarters, by flying at him, and imprinting a bouncing kiss on his surprised and not altogether attractive face. As soon as he could collect himself and recover from his astonishment, the President thanked the lady, but with evident discomposure; whereupon some of the party made haste to explain that the Princess Salm-Salm had laid a wager with one of the officers that she would kiss the President. Her audacious sally won her a box of gloves.

I have called the princess remarkable; and her career certainly deserves a parenthetical note, for she was a conspicuous figure in some social circles of Washington during Lincoln's time. Her parents were of humble origin, living in Philipsburg, at the Canadian end of Lake Champlain, called Missisquoi Bay. The girl earned her living by service among the neighboring farmers, but subsequently became an actress in a strolling company of players. From this time her life was picturesque and varied. It was said that her well-known skill and deftness in the care and management of horses were acquired when she was a circus-rider; at that period of her checkered career she

was billed as "Miss Leclerq." Prince Salm-Salm served as a
volunteer staff-officer during our war, after which he and his
wife went to Mexico, where they identified themselves with the
failing cause of the Emperor Maximilian. The lady narrated her
remarkable adventures in Mexico in a bright book, and the
couple returned to Austria, whence the prince had been previously expelled on account of his profligate habits, but where he
was now made welcome and was given a pension and a post in
one of the royal palaces near Vienna. It was subsequently reported that this American princess joined herself to the French
forces under the Geneva cross, in the Franco-Prussian war, and
that her husband was killed while fighting on the same side at
the battle of Gravelotte.

During the war the proportion of civilians to those who
wore the trappings of the Army and Navy was so small that
men felt it almost a distinction to wear the ordinary evening
dress. An order from the War Department forbidding military
officers to come to Washington without leave did not by any
means abate what was felt to be a great nuisance. Too many officers haunted the lobbies of the Capitol in search of political
aid to secure for them the promotions that they desired, or the
passage of bills in which military or naval officers had special
interest. I saw a curious example of military absenteeism one
night at Ford's Theater, where I had accompanied the President
to see Edwin Booth in "The Merchant of Venice." The President had sent word late in the afternoon that he would like to
have a box for himself and a friend; but when we arrived at
the theater, going in by the stage entrance, we were met by
the manager, who said that the boxes had all been taken before
the President's message had been received, but he would use his
efforts with a party of officers, as soon as they arrived, to induce
them to give up a box which they had engaged. While he was
speaking, an usher came behind the scenes, and said that the
officers had very willingly relinquished their box for the pleas-

ure of the President. Between the acts the manager came to pay his respects to the President, and to inquire for his comfort, and Lincoln asked for the names of the military gentlemen who had so kindly given up their evening's entertainment in his behalf. The manager replied that he did not know, but he afterward quietly told me that he knew that one half of the number were officers absent from the Army without leave, and that they considered it a good joke that they could escape the President's observation at the cost of relinquishing their box at the theater. The manager shrewdly guessed that the President had asked for their names in order to discover if they were in Washington on leave; but that was not Lincoln's way.

President Lincoln's theater-going was usually confined to occasions when Shakespeare's plays were enacted; for, although he enjoyed a hearty laugh, he was better pleased with the stately dignity, deep philosophy, and exalted poetry of Shakespeare than with anything that was to be found in more modern dramatic writings. But I remember a delightful evening that we once spent at the old Washington Theater, where we saw Mrs. John Wood in John Brougham's travesty of "Pocahontas." The delicious absurdity and crackling puns of the piece gave the President food for mirth for many days thereafter. At another time we saw Edwin Forrest in "King Lear," and the President appeared to be more impressed by the acting of John McCullough, in the role of Edgar, than with the great tragedian's appearance as the mad king. He asked that McCullough might come to the box between the acts; and when the young actor was brought to the door, clad in his fantastic garb of rags and straw, Mr. Lincoln warmly, and yet with diffidence, praised the performance of the scene in which he had just appeared.

It was Mr. Lincoln's delight to sally forth in the darkness, on foot, and, accompanied only by a friend, to visit some theater to which notice of his coming had been sent only just before his setting out. When we consider that it was popularly believed that Washington at that time was infested with spies and midnight assassins, we may well wonder at his temerity. But perhaps it was the unexpectedness and lack of advertisement of his movements that may have induced him to undertake these little excursions. It was the wide publicity given to his intention to go to the play that wrought his own undoing in 1865. Those who are disposed to consider that Lincoln exhibited a frivolous side of his character by his play-going should reflect that the theater was almost the only place where he could escape from the clamor of office-seekers, and for a moment unfix his thoughts from the cares and anxieties that weighed upon his spirit with dreadful oppressiveness. Official etiquette forbids the President of the United States the social pleasures outside of his house which a less exalted functionary or a private citizen may enjoy. In Lincoln's case, more than in that of any other who has held the presidential office, there was abundant justification of his seeking for opportunities to escape from the stately prison-house of the official residence.

PUBLIC EXERCISES AT THE CAPITOL

One of the most charming figures in semi-public life in Washington during the war was Miss Anna Dickinson, then in the first flush of her success as an eloquent speaker. [She was an Abolitionist, and a sort of girl orator of her time.] Her first appearance in January, 1864, was a grand triumph for a young woman just beginning her long and picturesque career. She was invited by a host of distinguished men (at the head of the list being Vice-President Hamlin and Speaker Colfax) to address the people in the Hall of Representatives. The great room was crowded, and the house never looked gayer than it did that evening, bright as it was with the velvets, flowers, and brilliant colors of a great company of society women. Miss Dickinson was accompanied to the platform by the Vice-President and the

Speaker, and was introduced by the former, who likened her to Joan of Arc. Dressed in black silk, with a touch of color at her throat, her wavy black hair in short redundant curls, Anna Dickinson made a figure long to be remembered as she slowly paced to and fro on the platform, dropping her well-formed and compact sentences upon the people below. Lincoln was present, and incidentally the fair orator introduced a striking and encomiastic allusion to the chief magistrate, and the vast audience applauded with tremendous enthusiasm. In the following March, however, the lady changed her mind, as ladies may, and in a speech delivered at Grover's Theater "raked the Lincoln administration fore and aft." But later on she experienced a change of heart, and forsook Frémont, who had been her idol for a time, and paid a very beautiful tribute to the new administration of Lincoln. Her last appearance in the House of Representatives was very soon after Lincoln's second inauguration. Those who were present on that 4th of March, 1865, may remember that just as the President took the oath of office, the sun, which had been obscured by clouds, burst forth, and its golden beams fell upon the distinguished group assembled on the Capitol steps. Lincoln next day asked me if I had noticed the sunburst, and then went on to say that he was just superstitious enough to consider it a happy omen. In the address above referred to, Miss Dickinson also referred to the breaking of the clouds, and in touching and inspiring words pictured the dispersion of the gloom that lowered over the country. The President sat directly in front of the platform from which Miss Dickinson spoke. Before she began, he had recognized me as I sat in the reporters' gallery over the platform; and when the speaker alluded to the sunburst, he looked up at me and deliberately winked.

The National Capitol witnessed a novel sight in the early spring of 1863, when a wedding was solemnized in the great Hall of the House of Representatives. So far as I know, this was the only bridal ceremony ever conducted within the walls of the legislative chamber. It took place on a Sunday. The high contracting parties were Miss Rumsey and Mr. Fowler, two members of the choir that led the singing in the House of Representatives for the religious services held in the House during the old war days. That was a "star" occasion; for the Rev. Dr. [Thomas H.] Stockton (a half-brother of Frank R. Stockton, the author) on that day closed a long term of service as chaplain of the House, and preached a farewell sermon full of interesting historical reminiscences. Dr. Stockton had held the post of chaplain of the House during the administrations of Andrew Jackson and Martin Van Buren, and his reminiscent discourse was a valuable contribution to the history of Washington in earlier years. The bride and bridegroom were well known as the managers of one of the most admirable beneficences of the time—the Soldiers' Free Library—and the Hall of the House was crowded to its utmost capacity, and hundreds went away disappointed of entrance. The bride wore upon her corsage a big knot of red, white, and blue ribbons, and after the ceremony had been concluded, some inconsiderate patriot loudly called for "The Star Spangled Banner." The newly made bride graciously consented, and the audience joined in the chorus with tremendous effect until the vast Hall rang with music and enthusiasm. Even in those fiery days, song-singing and loud cheering in the national Capitol were a novelty. The Hall of the House was much more readily given for purposes other than legislative than it has been since.

LINCOLN'S MEMORY

A notable meeting was held in the hall of the House of Representatives in January, 1865, when the United States Christian Commission held its anniversary exercises. Secretary Seward presided, and made a delightful address. As an example of Mr. Lincoln's wonderful power of memory, I noticed that a few days after that meeting in the Capitol he recalled an entire sentence of Mr. Seward's speech, and, so far as I could remember, without missing a word. This faculty was apparently exercised without the slightest effort on his part. He "couldn't help remembering," he was accustomed to say. One would suppose that in the midst of the worries and cares of office his mind would become less retentive of matters not immediately related to the duties of the hour. But this was not the fact. Although the memories of long past events, and words long since read or heard; appeared to be impossible of obliteration, more recently acquired impressions remained just as fixed as the older ones. One of my cousins, John Holmes Goodenow, of Alfred, Maine, was appointed minister to Turkey early in the Lincoln administration, and was taken to the White House, before his departure for his post, to be presented to the President. When Lincoln learned that his visitor was a grandson of John Holmes, one of the first Senators from Maine, and a man of note in his day and generation, he immediately began the recitation of a poetical quotation which must have been more than a hundred lines in length. Mr. Holmes [Goodenow], never having met the President, was naturally astonished at this outburst; and as the President went on and on with this long recitation, the suspicion crossed his mind that Lincoln had suddenly taken leave of his wits. But when the lines had been finished, the President said: "There! that poem was quoted by your grandfather Holmes in a speech which he made in the United States Senate in ——" and he named the date and specified the occasion. As John Holmes's term in the Senate [began in 1820 and] ended in 1833, and Lincoln probably was impressed by reading a copy of the speech rather than by hearing it, this feat of memory appears very remarkable.

Lincoln's power of memory was certainly very great; if he had been by any casualty deprived of his sight, his own memory would have supplied him with an ample and varied library. He used to say that it was no evidence of his partiality for a bit of literature that he remembered it for a long time. For example, he once recited to me a long and doleful ballad, the production of a rural Kentucky bard, composed in the vein of "Vilikins and his Dinah," and when he had finished, he added, with a deprecatory laugh, "I don't believe I have thought of that before for forty years."

Mr. Lincoln's manner toward enlisted men, with whom he occasionally met and talked, was always delightful in its bon-homie and its absolute freedom from anything like conde-scension. Then, at least, the "common soldier" was the equal of the chief magistrate of the nation. One day in the latter part of March, 1863, I was at the White House with the President, and he told me to tarry for a while, as a party of Ohio soldiers who had been lately exchanged after many harassing experi-ences were coming to see him. It appeared that these were the survivors of what was then known as the Marietta raid. Twenty-one men from Ohio regiments of the command of General O. M. Mitchel, then in northern Alabama, were sent on a dangerous mission to destroy the railroad communications of Chattanooga to the south and east. The expedition failed, and of the original number only six returned to Washington, after incredible hard-ships and suffering,—one third of the party having escaped, and another fraction having been hanged as spies, the rebel au-thorities deciding that the fact that these men wore citizen's clothes within an enemy's lines put them in that category.

The men, who were introduced to the President by Gen-eral E. A. Hitchcock, then on duty in Washington, were Mason, Parrott, Pittenger, Buffum, Reddick, and Bensinger. Their names were given to the President, and, without missing the identity of a single man, he shook hands all round with an un-affected cordiality and good-fellowship difficult to describe. He had heard their story in all its details, and as he talked with

each, asking questions and making his shrewd comments on
what they had to say, it was evident that for the moment this
interesting interview was to him of supreme importance. At
that time we had great difficulty in effecting exchanges of
prisoners, and General Hitchcock had compiled a series of
papers of startling importance bearing on the question. The
stories of these long-suffering men, and the cheerful lightness
with which they narrated their courageous and hazardous deeds,
impressed Mr. Lincoln very deeply. Speaking of the men afterward, he said, with much feeling, that their bearing, and their
apparent unconsciousness of having taken their lives in their
hands, with the chances of death all against them, presented an
example of the apparent disregard of the tremendous issues of
life and death which was so strong a characteristic of the American soldier.

One of Lincoln's favorite poems was [Oliver Wendell]
Holmes's "The Last Leaf"; and one November day we were
driving out to the Soldiers' Home, near Washington, when the
aspect of the scene recalled the lines to his mind. Slowly and
with excellent judgment he recited the whole poem. Enlarging
upon the pathos, wit, and humor of Holmes, I found that the
President had never seen a copy of the genial doctor's works, so
far as he could remember, although he was not certain that he
had not. I offered to lend him my copy of the poems, a little
blue-and-gold book; and the next time I went to the White
House I took it with me. About a week after leaving the book
with the President, I called at the house one evening, and, finding him alone, we settled down for a quiet chat. He took from a
drawer in his table the blue-and-gold Holmes, and went over
the book with much gusto, reading or reciting several poems
that had struck his fancy. He expressed his surprise at finding
that some of the verses which he admired most had been drifting about in the newspapers without the name of the author
attached to them; and it was in this way, he said, that he had

found "The Last Leaf," although he did not know that Dr. Holmes was the author. Finally he said that he liked "Lexington" as well as anything in the book, "The Last Leaf" alone excepted, and he began to read the poem; but when he came to the stanza beginning:

"Green be the graves where her martyrs are lying!
Shroudless and tombless they sunk to their rest,—"

his voice faltered, and he gave me the book with the whispered request, "You read it; I can't." Months afterward, when several ladies were in the Red Parlor one evening, calling upon Mrs. Lincoln, he recited that poem without missing a word, so far as I could remember it. And yet I do not believe that he ever saw the text of "Lexington" except during the few busy days when he had my book.

I have still in my possession the blue-and-gold Holmes [Brooks's books in Castine, Maine, include library editions of Holmes published by the Cambridge Press, but not the edition described here], Ticknor & Fields edition, 1862, with the leaf folded lengthwise, as Lincoln folded it to mark the place where he found "Lexington." In a preface written in 1885 Dr. Holmes said that "good Abraham Lincoln had a liking for 'The Last Leaf,'" and that Governor [John] Andrew [of Massachusetts] had told the author that Lincoln repeated the poem to him.

III

After the Battle of Gettysburg

THE background to the Civil War's most celebrated battle was best summed up in a hand-written letter, dated Washington, D. C., June 10, 1863, from A. Lincoln to Major General Hooker. "If left to me," Lincoln said, exercising his role as a strategist, "I would not go south of the Rappahannock upon Lee's moving north of it. If you had Richmond invested today, you would not be able to take it in twenty days; meanwhile, your communications, and with them, your Army would be ruined. I think Lee's Army, and not Richmond, is your true objective." Then Lincoln, after the battle, when the Army of Northern Virginia had escaped, chided General Meade in a letter he never sent, and expressed his feelings again to General Oliver O. Howard, who commanded a corps at Gettysburg: "I was deeply mortified by the escape of Lee across the Potomac, because the substantial destruction of his Army would have ended the war."

Noah Brooks hoped to see the big battle. Lincoln provided the necessary documents and passes. Brooks took off for Williamsport, Md., to cover Meade's headquarters, and from there went on horseback up to the lines. His front-line coverage, in a long dispatch on August 10, 1863, to the *Sacramento Union,* was graphic: "Up the last hill I rode, and looking across the turbid Potomac, could see, amid the rolling, woody hills on the Virginia side, the numerous ascending colors of smoke which marked where the rebel encampments now lie. On a bare hill, about a mile away, are lines of earthworks hastily thrown up, and from these a few

80

rebel sharpshooters pepper away at anything which shows its head on the clear space around the hither end of the rude bridge." Lee's forces, he saw, had escaped again, and when Brooks reported this to Lincoln, he recalled, the President's "grief and anger were something to behold."

After viewing the scene, Brooks rode back to the rail station at Frederick and caught a two-o'clock train to Washington. His companion was Vice-President Hamlin—a trusted radical Republican, former Governor and Senator, and an old neighbor from the Penobscot Bay area of Maine.

UNDER the influence of the good news that reached us in the early weeks of July, 1863, Washington was a cheerful place to live in. There had been many months of wearying discouragement; people had waited with hope often deferred for tidings of victory to the Union arms, and these never came. The battle of Gettysburg, fought so near the national capital, as it seemed to us, was a prodigious event; for, although it was not then regarded, as it is now, as the turning-point in the war, even the most cautious and conservative of observers began to think that it might prove that "beginning of the end" which the more sanguine had seen so many times and so many times had despaired of realizing.

But from the southwest came tidings of great joy to every patriotic heart. During the first two weeks of July we heard of the fall of Port Hudson, the surrender at Vicksburg, the opening of the Mississippi River, the renewed attack on Charleston, and other less important successes, which, under ordinary conditions, would have been eagerly grasped at as of pith and moment. The single drop of bitterness in our cup of joy was the unexpected flight of Lee's Army across the Potomac after the battle of Gettysburg; this, it was felt, was another postponement of a long-looked-for event—the final crippling of the army of invasion that had so many times threatened Washington. The first news of the capitulation of Vicksburg, by the way, was received at the Navy Department, about noon, July seventh, in a despatch from Admiral [David D.] Porter. Secretary [Gideon] Welles astonished everybody who knew him by putting on his hat and solemnly proceeding to the White House to tell the news to President Lincoln. It was said at the time that the Secretary, on arriving at the executive chamber, executed a double shuffle and threw up his hat by way of showing that he was the bearer of glad tidings. This was a mere invention; but Lincoln did say that he never before nor afterward saw Mr. Welles so thoroughly excited as he was then.

Soon, however, Washington was straining its attention toward Maryland, where, it was popularly supposed, the Army of the Potomac, under the command of General Meade, had at last "corralled" Lee and all his forces, supplies, and guns in an elbow of the Potomac, between Williamsport and Falling Waters. After the battle of Gettysburg, railroad communication was again resumed between the Relay House [below Baltimore], on the Baltimore and Washington line, and the town of Frederick [west of Baltimore], Maryland. This last-named place then became the Union base of supplies, and immense quantities of stores were forwarded at once. We were in almost hourly expectation of a great battle which should be fought on Maryland soil and result in the annihilation of the Army of Virginia and the hastening of the collapse of the rebellion. Like many others, I was anxious to see the expected end of the rebellion and witness the effectual crushing of the army that had so frequently threatened Washington and so persistently protected the rebel capital. President Lincoln sympathized with my natural desire to see the great fight, and he not only furnished me with passes to the front, but gave me letters to General Meade and Adjutant-General Seth Williams of the Army of the Potomac. I was intimately ac-

quainted with General Rufus Ingalls, Chief-Quartermaster of
the Army of the Potomac, and armed with these credentials,
I pressed forward to the headquarters of the army by the way
of Frederick. On the train, meeting with two old friends from
California, we formed a plan to hire horses in Frederick and
so make our way up to the devious verge of the battle which
now seemed imminent. All along the route, we passed immense
trains of supplies of all kinds, miles and miles of freight-cars
standing on the track loaded with forage, ammunition, rations,
horses, contrabands, soldiers, and all the other means and appliances which an active army requires.

The streets of Frederick were alive with cavalry, infantry,
supply-trains and ambulances. Squads of staff officers were
pushing their way through the throngs, and here and there
the flag of some division commander denoted temporary headquarters. The road to Middletown was crowded with numerous
wagon-trains and troops moving forward to the front. With
considerable difficulty we threaded our way through the masses
of men, wagons, and horses, and finally reached Middletown,
between the Catoctin and South Mountain ranges. At the foot
of South Mountain was a huge park of supply-trains, which
formed a depot of commissary stores and was the base between
the Army and the main base at Frederick. As we galloped along
the open spaces which intervened between the city of Frederick
and an Army division standing at rest, we descried the body
of a man dangling by a noose from a limb of a tree—a ghastly
sight. This was a spy, who had been in the Army of the Potomac
for several months peddling maps and singing army songs.
On his person had been found, when he was arrested, a number
of minute drawings of the fortifications around Washington,
a statement of the forces in the forts, etc., and about thirty
thousand dollars in greenbacks. He was tried, condemned, and
hanged as a spy.

The comfortable houses along the roads were besieged

by Union soldiers begging for fresh bread, milk, eggs, and such other articles as would naturally excite the desire of men long used to the hard fare of the army. There were, however, no complaints as to any disorderly conduct on the part of these hungry and importunate men. They offered money in payment for anything which they received, and the Maryland farmers, be it said to their credit, were invariably generous and liberal to their unwelcome guests. It was, however, notorious that some of the Marylanders who hung out Union flags, and waved their handkerchiefs, in welcome to the blue-coated soldiers of the Army of the Potomac, had been quite as enthusiastic, not many days before, when the gray-coated veterans of Lee had passed that way. At a house where we stopped for the night, the ladies of the family were ardent in their protestations of loyalty to the Union and their delight at the rebel defeat at Gettysburg; but a Union sergeant from a detachment of troops stationed near by expressed to me his strong desire to search the house for ten or twelve Confederate flags, which he and his comrades said had formerly decorated the piazza and roof of the domicile. But, for the most part, Unionism was sincere and outspoken throughout all the region of Hagerstown, Boonsboro, and Middletown. We met here one Dick Schackles, who was well known for his loyalty throughout Western Maryland. He avowed himself a "Henry Clay Whig," and thanked God that he had never been anything else. He was jubilant that the time was coming, as he said, when the "blasted Locofocos who had baited the rebels across the line would be down, down, down where they belonged." He said: "We do not call them Copperheads up here; we call them Locofocos, and they are the meanest, dirtiest snakes that ever crawled." The profanity and abuse with which he assaulted "the Locofocos and Northern rebels" was something startling. Dick Schackles had good reason to speak ill of the rebels, for, having heard of him and his aggressive Unionism, they were by no means considerate of his property rights, or his comforts, while they were in that part of the country. But the hurrying and confusion of marching and countermarching made it impossible for either army to punish soldiers guilty of outrages.

The ruin and destruction that marked the footsteps of the armies were heartrending to behold. Fences were torn down, and grain ready for the reaper was trodden under foot, and ground into the rain-drenched soil by army wagons, artillery, and the hoofs of cavalry. All along the roadside, as we approached the headquarters of the Army of the Potomac, were stragglers and "bummers [parties of foragers]," some of them barefoot, many without guns, and hundreds of them asleep in the grass or under the lee of outbuildings. The rebel captives, whom we occasionally met in droves, were generally good-looking and well-clad men, not at all like the scarecrows we had usually seen sent up to Washington as prisoners, when our Army was in Virginia. We found General Meade's headquarters in a magnificent grove of giant oaks about a mile south of Boonsboro, near Antietam Creek. Meade was a tall, spare man, a little past his prime, but still straight and wiry; he wore spectacles almost constantly, had a sallow face, dark eyes, and dark hair plentifully sprinkled with gray. He was very plainly dressed, affable but not genial in his manners, and usually reserved in speech. I noticed that when he mounted or dismounted he moved very stiffly, without any of that elasticity of motion characteristic of the other officers of the Army.

There was about Meade's headquarters a certain suppressed excitement, which was the natural result of an expectation of another battle to be fought. It was known that General Meade had received several pressing messages from General Halleck, which, of course, were inspired by President Lincoln, warning him that the rebel Army might escape across the Potomac unless the Union forces should speedily take the aggressive. There had been several days of tremendous rain, and the Potomac and its tributary streams at this point were filled to overflowing. On the Sunday night before our arrival at headquarters, a council of war had been held, and, as usual in such cases, the vote was against an attack. It is a military tradition that a council of war never fights. This one was no exception to the rule. Meade's staff officers were considerably disgruntled by the so-called Washington "interference." Halleck had sent an order to Meade in which he directed the attention of the commander of the Army of the Potomac to the fact that it was currently believed in Washington that Lee had received pontoons from the south of the Potomac and was preparing to cross; and he concluded his order by saying: "The War Department would again urge upon the commanding general the importance of attacking the enemy as soon as practicable, using that energy and decision of action which alone can accomplish so desirable an end, the complete crippling of the insurgent army in Maryland." This despatch of Halleck's had been printed in a special order issued to the corps and division commanders of the Army of the Potomac before our arival, and was then in their hands. The staff officers regarded the publication of Meade's order as a piece of satire, because it not only reproduced portions of Halleck's instructions, but enjoined upon them "such due vigor and energy in action as would result in securing the end desired by the country, and alluded to in the despatch from the War Department."

This is the exact language of a printed circular given to me at General Meade's headquarters, and quoted by me in a newspaper letter written by me, dated July 14, 1863. No such order can now be found. The nearest approach to it is the following. See Official Records [Brooks refers here to the U. S. War Department's seventy-volume records of the Union and

Confederate Armies, Government Printing Office, Washington],
Vol. XXVII, part III, page 605:

HEADQUARTERS ARMY OF THE POTOMAC, July 8, 1863.

The following copies of a despatch from the President to the
Major-General commanding, and of the reply to the same, are com-
municated to corps commanders, in the earnest hope that they will
use their best efforts to assist the commanding general in meeting
the wishes of the President.

By command of Major-General Meade,

S. WILLIAMS,
Assistant Adjutant-General.

[*Inclosures.*]

WASHINGTON, July 8, 1863. 12:30 P. M.
MAJOR-GENERAL MEADE:

There is reliable information that the enemy is crossing at
Williamsport. The opportunity to attack his divided forces should
not be lost. The President is urgent and anxious that your army
should move against him by forced marches.

H. W. HALLECK,
General-in-Chief.

The general feeling at headquarters was that General Meade
(who was convinced that Lee's Army could not escape across the
Potomac at that time) had scored rather a good point on the
Washington authorities from the President downward.

Sharing in this general feeling of exultation and expectation, I accepted General Ingalls's offer of a cavalry horse and
an orderly, and pushed forward across the fields which lie between Antietam Creek above Boonsboro and Sharpsburg and
the Hagerstown pike. This was about noon, July fourteenth,
and all that morning there had been rumors of a retreat of the

enemy across the Potomac. General Ingalls was positive that
the Confederate Army had made good its retreat to Virginia,
and some of the younger men at headquarters did not hesitate
to say that Meade had been "most egregiously fooled." About
twelve o'clock noon, heavy cannonading was heard from the
front in the direction of Williamsport, on the Potomac, and
opinions differed as to whether this was the beginning of a general engagement or was the firing of [Gen. Judson] Kilpatrick's
and [Gen. John] Buford's cavalry on the retreating flanks of
the rebels. About two miles from Antietam Creek, we came
upon the Federal line of intrenchments (now abandoned),
and found the Third Corps drawn up in line of battle; the
Second and Fifth having pushed on ahead. We soon overtook
those troops, marching in three columns over fields of grain,
through thrifty orchards, clover-fields and gardens. The ground
was soft and the country roads were in a dreadful state of mire.
The movements of the troops, however, were regardless of roads,
and in their forward advance they manœuvered precisely as
they would through a savage country. It was rather entertaining, on the whole, to come into the abandoned rebel lines, as
we soon did. Here were rifle-pits and other hastily constructed
earthworks; but not a picket or a sentry was to be seen. All
had "skedaddled" incontinently, leaving behind them the refuse of their camps. Here and there I found letters half-written,
which the rebel soldiers were inditing to friends at home and
had thrown away, apparently, in the sudden haste of their departure. The relic-hunter could have collected a museum of
military curios in these deserted camps. Fragments of army
equipage and wearing-apparel, abandoned horses, broken artil-
lery-wagons, and other debris, were dropped about in picturesque confusion. All along the route toward Falling Waters
were disabled caissons, wrecked ambulances and army forges,
muskets, knapsacks, and a few country wagons, left by the flee-
ing enemy. The cannonading we had heard at headquarters

ceased, but a few volleys of musketry were fired in the vicinity
of Falling Waters, four miles below Williamsport, on the Potomac. Striking into the woods near Falling Waters, we came
upon squads of rebel prisoners in hundreds or more, lying on
the ground and guarded by a few Union cavalry. These poor
fellows were ragged, wet, and muddy, many of them having
been caught while in the river attempting to ford the stream.
The roads were choked with cavalry, and here and there were
parks of artillery at rest, brought out on a bootless errand, the
drivers sleeping under the caissons.

Now we learned that the rebels had drawn in their lines
at about six o'clock that morning, the main body of the army
having previously crossed the .stream by means of bridges
hastily thrown across. The approach to the little village of
Falling Waters, Maryland, was over a hill which rose sharply
from the grain-fields around it. Having mounted this hill, one
saw that the roads passed over gentle undulations gradually
sloping down to the river. On the top of the hill, which commanded all these roads leading to the river crossing, and parallel
to the stream, were a series of light earthworks which the rebels
had occupied with a rear-guard of four thousand men, [Gen.
Jubal A.] Early's division of the rebel Army. Behind the works
were still passing out the last of the rebels when our forces
came up at noon that day. Lee had finished here, on the previous
Saturday, a pontoon-bridge across the Potomac, and the structure, eked out with scows, boats and lumber seized in the
vicinity, was standing when we arrived. It was a very good
piece of engineering and trestle-work. Here and there on the
floor of the bridge lay a dead soldier, and occasionally a gray-
coated body could be seen half in and half out of the water that
lapped the shore. The rebels who were protecting the retreat
of their Army in the breast-work on the hill, had received our
cavalry as they charged up the hill with a volley which laid low
about twenty of our men and wounded many more; at the same

time, a considerable force of rebel infantry was deployed on their right where the hills sloped down into a wheat-field, in which the shocks of grain stood in scattered cocks. But the onslaught of the Union cavalry was so furious that the Confederates could not stand before it, and began a fighting retreat. The cannonading which we had heard two hours before, when we were on the Sharpsburg pike, was the firing of the Union light artillery, brought to bear upon the enemy as they fought bravely through the flowery lanes and grain-fields of Falling Waters on their way to the temporary bridge.

In the meantime, another cavalry force had surrounded the small squads of rebels who were trying to escape across on the floating scows which had been used at Williamsport, and had been brought down to this point. About three hundred and fifty of them were taken prisoners, and these, with sixteen hundred who were cut off at the end of the bridge, were all that were found here of Lee's Army, which was to have been "bagged" while it was securely caged in the elbow formed by the bend of the Potomac at this point. All, did I say? There were a score or more lying there with the Union soldiers in the wheat-fields among the sheaves which their fight had overturned, their faces toward the sky, gray-backs and blue-backs sleeping the sleep that knows no waking. To one unused to the gory sights of battle-fields, the picture presented there was strangely fascinating. The dead soldiers, blue-clad or gray-clad, lay in various positions scattered over the grain-field and in the clover meadow; but most of them had been turned over on their backs since they fell. The expressions on the countenances of these poor fellows were usually peaceful. One rebel soldier attracted my attention by the attitude in which he lay still in death, his head upon his arm, just as I remembered that David Copperfield saw his friend, the drowned Steerforth, lying on the beach, as he had "often seen him lie at school."

In a military hospital that had been hastily improvised

in a barn, at the head of a leafy lane, were gathered the wounded of both armies, under the charge of Federal surgeons, of whom I occasionally caught glimpses with their bare hands and arms reddened with the gore of the poor fellows, whose cries and groans sounded lugubriously within. The men captured in this little fight were from the 40th, 47th, and 55th Virginia, and 55th North Carolina regiments. They were commanded by Brigadier-General [James J.] Pettigrew. They made a courageous stand and a brave fight against the Union cavalry. They were gallantly charged by the Michigan Brigade, composed of the 1st, 5th, 6th, and 7th Michigan Cavalry, aided by a detachment of the 8th New York, fifteen hundred men in all, remnants of several regiments decimated by death, and commanded by General George A. Custer. Among these who did not survive their wounds at Falling Waters was the rebel General Pettigrew, who was then lying in a barn at Falling Waters, but was next day taken across the river under a flag of truce from Lee's army. He died at Bunker Hill, Virginia, two days later (July seventeenth). The spoils of war included three regimental battle-flags; one brass field-piece, and a large rifled cannon which was found concealed in the woods on the banks above the pontoon-bridge.

Turning my horse's head in the direction of Meade's headquarters, I looked across the swollen and turbid Potomac where I could see the smoke of rebel camps rising in the thick Virginia woods on the other side of the stream. It is impossible now to describe—almost impossible to recall—the feeling of bitterness with which we regarded the sight. Lee's Army was gone. In spite of warnings, expostulations, doubts, and fears, it had escaped, and further pursuit was not even to be thought of.

I remember the anxiety, almost anguish, with which Lincoln had said before I left Washington that he was afraid that "something would happen" to prevent that annihilation of

Lee's Army, which, as he thought, was then certainly within
the bounds of possibility. But the last hope of the Confederacy
had not failed them yet. The desperate venture of an invasion
of Pennsylvania and Maryland had failed, it was true. But
the fatal blow which seemed to hang in the air when I left
Washington did not fall. As I rode down the hill and through
the undulating fields beyond, the blue-coated soldiers, jolly
and *insouciant,* greeted the solitary civilian horseman with
jocose remarks about the "Johnny Rebs" who had so cunningly
run away from them. Many of these men had enlisted "for the
war," and when I stopped to exchange salutations, they good-
naturedly said, "Well, here goes for two years more." I noticed
a curious effect of whispering speech as I rode through the
woods. Two or three thousand men waiting for orders were
scattered over the ground among the bushes, beguiling their
time by eating, drinking, and talking in low tones. The curious
fluttering noise of this wide conversation of so large a body of
men was something like that undistinguishable chorus which
we have heard in one of Gilbert and Sullivan's operas, when
the girls on the beach sit down and "talk about the weather";
but this was a prodigious chorus—it was the gabble of two or
three thousand men, all talking at once, and producing an undulating volume of sound like the noise of birds seeking their
roosts at night.

Meade's headquarters, on my return, presented a chop-
fallen appearance; probably the worst was known there before
I had left on my own private and special reconnaissance. Here
I met Vice-President Hamlin, who was also a visitor at Meade's
headquarters, and who had been taken out to see the fight
(which did not come off), at a point nearer Williamsport. As
we met, he raised his hands and turned away his face with a
gesture of despair. Later on, I came across General [James
S.] Wadsworth, who almost shed tears while he talked with
us about the escape of the rebel Army. He said that it seemed

to him that most of those who participated in the council of war had no stomach for the fight. "If they had," he added, "the rebellion, as one might say, might have been ended then and there."

Vice-President Hamlin and myself were despatched by General Meade in an ambulance under the charge of a young lieutenant of cavalry by the turnpike road to Frederick, where we took a train for Washington. Columns upon columns of army wagons and artillery were now in motion toward Frederick, crossing the fields, blocking the roads, and interlacing the face of the whole country with blackened tracks which heavy wheels cut in the rich, dark soil of Maryland, saturated with days of rain. Here and there one passed a knot of wagons inextricably tangled or hopelessly mired by the roadside. At one point, I was amused by seeing an eight-mule team thus stalled in a marshy piece of ground, every animal being on its back with its four legs motionless in the air. Whenever a teamster essayed to touch any part of the harness, all those thirty-two legs would fly with the speed and regularity of a tremendous machine, and the unfortunate meddler would bounce high in the air and come down again angry and swearing. It is no exaggeration to say that the Boonsboro pike that day was a blue streak of profanity from Meade's headquarters to Frederick. At one point, our driver was urged by the lieutenant to cut in between two trains which had suddenly parted and showed a long clear space ahead. As he was whipping up his horses, the wagon-master in charge of the tangled teams came out ahead of us and, shaking his fist, shouted in stentorian tones, "Get out of that!" Whereupon our lieutenant stood up on the dashboard and shouted in reply, "I have the Vice-President of the United States in this wagon, and he must get the two o'clock train from Frederick." [The rail line went from here to Relay House, below Baltimore, thence to Washington.] The wagon-master, nothing daunted, cried back, "I don't care if you have got the Saviour of mankind in that wagon, you can't come up here." Even the tired and dejected Vice-President was forced to smile grimly at the resolute wagoner's reply.

Nevertheless, we did catch the two o'clock train from Frederick; and the next day, according to the President's request, I reported to him all that I had seen and heard. It is enough to say that although he was not so profoundly distressed as he was when Hooker's Army recrossed the Rappahannock after the battle of Chancellorsville, his grief and anger were something sorrowful to behold.

IV

Lincoln, Chase, and Grant—
Among the Law-Makers

CONGRESSIONAL developments, legislation and the personalities of the Representatives and Senators occupied the attention of the roving Washington correspondent. The behavior of the California delegation was watched closely; so was Western legislation on such pertinent matters as land rights and railroads and faster mail. Lincoln consulted Brooks behind the scenes on California patronage. There was one particularly tough case when Lincoln's political rival within the Cabinet, Secretary of the Treasury Chase, made touchy changes in the Treasury setup in California.

In his personal style, Brooks did not overlook the news of the correspondents themselves on the Hill. Although opinionated, at least they were outspoken on the Members of Congress. The Civil War marked the beginning not only of rapid war dispatches but intensive Congressional coverage. Here is how Brooks told his readers in the Far West about the capital correspondents at a House Session: "The gallery where we sit has its full complement of reporters, who are busy taking notes, or exchanging weighty opinion upon the questions of the day, as their relative positions on the different newspapers may demand; Gobright, who makes up the dispatches for the Associated Press, and so is responsible for all of the reports which go to the country from this branch of Congress, is busy keeping track of the debate, and is writing his 'long-hand' sketch from his 'short-hand' notes; he is flanked on either hand by the *New York Herald* and *World,* while your special correspondent [Brooks's "Letter from Washington" was followed by the line "From Our Special Correspondent"] comes next on the left." Brooks also noted the presence of "the two *Tribunes,* one from Chicago and one from New York, with the *San Francisco Journal, Missouri Democrat,* and other 'Jacobins' in the rear. Other reporters are dotted in around us, and many circulate on the floor of the House, where they have managed to be smuggled in as Committee Clerks to the disgustful envy of their less fortunate or less pushing brethren."

Lincoln's amazing patience with Chase—and then Lincoln's greatness in naming his obdurate Secretary of the Treasury to the Supreme Court as Chief Justice—is fortified by the incidents related by Brooks here. Brooks quotes Lincoln as saying, "But I shall nominate him for the Chief Justice, nevertheless." The President had refused to accept Chase as an enemy; thirty years afterward, Brooks felt constrained to show Chase in a less wholesome light.

THE numerous exciting topics brought up in the debates of Congress during the war made the Capitol a point of exceeding interest to people in Washington in search of a new sensation. Nobody could tell when an animated and acrimonious, or very important, discussion would spring up in either branch of Congress. The bill to indemnify civil officers of the government for the consequences of their exercise of extraordinary functions during the suspension of the privileges of the writ of habeas corpus, the bill to authorize the enlistment of colored soldiers, the proposition to divide the State of Virginia, the Conscription Bill, and similar so-called war measures, were all prolific causes of numerous political wordy tilts in Congress. And in all such cases there would be a field-day at the Capitol, and hurrying crowds would overflow the galleries allotted to visitors, and the doors of the chamber would be besieged by men who craftily pleaded their special privilege of entrance. It was difficult to account for the celerity with which the news that an exciting debate was going on would be circulated through the city of Washington. When the House, for example, met at noon and listened perfunctorily to the prayer of the chaplain and the equally perfunctory reading of the minutes of the previous day's session, there would apparently be no cloud on the congressional sky. [Not all the Capitol chaplains were perfunctory. The Reverend Byron Sunderland, one day in April, 1864, invoked: "O Lord, give us that Thou wilt in thine infinite wisdom vouchsafe to our rulers and legislators in this Congress assembled more brains—more brains, Lord."] The progress of legislation would go droning on with a dreary monotony that lulled the few drowsy spectators, and gave the newspaper men an opportunity to bring up their arrears of work; and then there would suddenly spring up a breeze of debate that would eventually sweep through the Hall like a gale. Almost immediately every seat on the floor would be filled; absentees would come flocking in from corridors and committee rooms, and as if by magic, before an hour passed, the galleries were empty no longer. Or it often happened that an excited debate which had been interrupted by adjournment, would end then and there; and, although the multitudes would stream up to the Capitol, next day, to hear "the rest of the story," proceedings would open tamely, and the subsequent discussion would as tamely drift off into congressional platitudes and be heard of no more.

There were several field-days in Congress when attempts were made to censure or expel some of the more reckless and indiscreet Copperheads. One of the most impressive of these was in the Thirty-eighth Congress, when Speaker Colfax left his seat, and, amidst profound silence in the House, offered a resolution to expel Alexander Long, one of the Ohio representatives, who had declared himself in favor of acknowledging the independence of the rebel States. Long's offense had been committed the day before, and he had been replied to by Garfield, who compared him to Benedict Arnold, and had said that he (Long) proposed to surrender his country's flag and honor and integrity into the hands of its rebel enemies. Colfax supported a resolution of expulsion in a speech of much solemnity and impressiveness.

His voice trembled with emotion while he said that he had a double duty to perform; first, as presiding officer of the House, and second, as the representative of more than one hundred thousand voters in his own congressional district of Indiana. It was in the latter capacity, he said, that he called for the expulsion of Long. Colfax was rather severely criticized, even by some of the Union members, for his taking it upon himself to offer this resolution without consulting any of his associates. The debate ran along with fluctuations of excitement through several days, and was participated in by all the leading members on both sides of the House. The discussion, as usual, took a wide range—the right of revolution, the status of the so-called rebel States, and a multitude of other questions being lugged in without much regard to the original cause of the long and tedious discussion. It was at this time that General Garfield came most prominently to the front as one of the readiest debaters and most impressive speakers in Congress.

Curiously enough, while this skirmishing was going on, another Peace Democrat, Benjamin G. Harris, of Maryland, got into trouble by not only indorsing everything that Long had said, but by announcing himself to be a believer in a peace which, he said, could only be obtained by a recognition of the Southern Confederacy. There was a general outcry from the Union members, who called him to order. He defiantly yelled, "You've got to come to it," and went on to say that he had been a slave-owner before the Abolitionists stole all his slaves away

from him, and had borne in silence the insults which had been
heaped upon him as a slave-owner by those who called slavery
"the sum of all villainies." Finally he cried, "The South asks
you to let them alone; but no, you say you will bring them into
subjection; that is not yet done, and God Almighty grant that
it may never be; I trust you will never subjugate the South."
Instantly the House was in the wildest confusion, and a score
of members were on their feet shouting to the Speaker and
endeavoring to be recognized. Out of the tumult finally rose
the stentorian voice of E. B. Washburne, of Illinois, who called
Harris to order "for words spoken in debate," and demanded
that the language of the member should be taken down and read
from the clerk's desk. After much confusion, this was finally
done, and the words objected to were read by the clerk in the
midst of profound silence, whereat Harris airily exclaimed:
"That's all right; that's what I said." Then Washburne moved
a vote of expulsion, and the House was well tangled up by the
two motions—one to expel Long, of Ohio, and the other aimed
at Harris, of Maryland. Fernando Wood, apparently envious
of the sudden reputation which his political associates had
acquired, tried to slide in a little speech in which he said that
if Long were expelled, he (Wood) might as well go with him,
as he indorsed every word that the Ohio gentleman had said.
At this Washburne, pale with rage, shook his fist at Wood and
shouted, "We'll put you out, too."

The most picturesque incident of this acrimonious debate
was Long's final speech in his own defense. He was a tall, well-
formed man, with a small head, a noticeably red face, and
fiery auburn hair. He had been distinguished throughout the
session for his quiet and reserve, and the speech which provoked
this terrific storm was almost his maiden effort in Congress; he
said it had been written four weeks before its delivery and kept
in his desk waiting for an opportunity to launch it upon the
House. In the course of his defense, he said that copies of his

so-called treasonable speech had been largely subscribed for by
Republican members who were anxious to sow treason among
their constituents. He referred satirically to W. D. Kelley, of
Pennsylvania, who, he said "played Forrest here for the benefit
of the House." The most impressive speech of this famous debate was made by "Thad" Stevens, who came into the House
from his sick-bed, and, though pale and wan, arose like a column
of iron in his place to say that he had learned that during his
absence from the House somebody on the other side had attempted to compare his position on the status of the so-called
rebel States with that of the two gentlemen now under censure.
With a grim smile, he said: "It has been said by members upon
this floor, that those who would recognize the so-called Southern Confederacy by treaty occupy the same position as myself."
S. S. Cox, whose remarks were evidently in the mind of Stevens,
attempted to reply, but the stern old Pennsylvanian waved him
down by the motion of his hand, and said "that whoever would
link me [Stevens] with the infamous creatures now before
the consideration of the House was a fool or a knave, perhaps
both." The debate began on the eighth of April [1864], and did
not end until the fourteenth. The upshot of the matter was
that the two thirds vote necessary to expel a member could not
be secured in the case of Long, and he was censured by a vote
of ninety-three to eighteen. The same correction overtook the
loquacious Marylander by a vote nearly identical.

"Garrulous Garrett Davis" got into trouble about the
same time when he attacked the Amnesty Proclamation [Jan-
uary 1, 1863] of President Lincoln in a series of resolutions
offered by him in the Senate. After his usual fashion, he had
embodied a long stump speech in his resolutions, in the course
of which he said: "Verily, the people North and the people
South ought to revolt against their war leaders and take this
great matter into their own hands, and elect members to a
national convention of all States to terminate a war that is

slaying its hundreds of thousands. Officers, plunderers, and spoilsmen in the loyal States threaten the masses of both sections with irretrievable bankruptcy and indefinite slaughter." On this, a resolution to expel Davis from the Senate was offered by Senator Wilson, of Massachusetts; and there was a great rush to the Senate galleries when Davis's so-called trial began. Wilson opened for the prosecution, and made a strong and sensible speech, and was replied to by Davis, who began by taking off his neckerchief, unbuttoning his waistcoat, and generally getting ready to "wade in." Davis, before he had fairly got under way, drove pretty much everybody out of the Senate, and the galleries were empty. He insisted upon reading nearly all of the long sections of the old Fugitive Slave Law, and other statutes and documents which he thought bore upon the matter under discussion. The proposition to expel him dragged along for weeks and months, and was not finally disposed of until the public had lost all interest in it. While the matter was pending, Davis was even more than usually defiant. At one time he proposed his celebrated scheme to divide the Northern States so that Massachusetts and New Hampshire should be one State, Vermont, Connecticut, and Rhode Island another, and Maine be left to take care of itself.

At another time Davis proposed to amend the Constitution by providing that no person whose mother or grandmother had been a Negro should be a citizen of the United States, or be entitled to any privileges of citizenship. This latter scheme provoked the galleries to a tremendous burst of laughter, which excited the rage of the little old Kentuckian, and was sternly rebuked by the presiding officer. At another time, when he was conducting a bitter fight against the establishment of the Freedmen's Bureau, the garrulous senator made a vituperative speech against Lincoln, whom he compared to George III. He said that Lincoln was "a man of weak mind and inordinate vanity, who thought himself a great man and a statesman, as he played his fantastic tricks before high Heaven." When, in course of debate, [Senator Charles] Sumner reminded the shrieking Kentuckian that Madison had said that the Revolutionary War was in behalf of the rights of humanity, Davis replied that Madison by "humanity" meant "white men only," at which everybody laughed; and Davis himself, dropping into his seat, fairly chuckled with mirth. The motion to expel Davis was finally dropped, and the combative little man kept up his fusillade of violent speeches as long as he remained in the Senate.

A great deal of heat was wasted on the proposition to enact a law to indemnify the President and other public officers for any responsibility which they might have incurred in suspending the privileges of the writ of habeas corpus in the so-called arbitrary arrests. During the progress of the bill a long and exceedingly bitter debate went on in the House, where [Representative Daniel W.] Voorhees made a cantankerous speech against it. As the passage of the measure was already assured (it was on a proposition to amend the bill after its first passage that Voorhees's speech was made), there was no disposition to make any reply to "the Tall Sycamore of the Wabash"; accordingly, Mr. [S. C.] Dailey, a Territorial delegate from Nebraska, was coached and put forward to make a speech in rejoinder, by way of derision. Dailey was what was called a "smooth-bore" speaker, and he had no sooner begun to pour out his disjointed sentences than the mortified Voorhees fled in dismay; but Dailey succeeded in stirring up the House. He spoke to the galleries, where there chanced to be a regiment of soldiers, and paid a glowing tribute to the "brave boys in blue"; whereupon the brave boys in blue gave him a round of applause. At this Vallandigham sprang out into the aisle, trembling with rage, and insisted that the galleries should not be permitted to show their approval or disapproval to "the actors on this floor." It was a long time before the sparring between

members which followed this sally was brought to a close, and
Dailey was permitted to finish his speech. The bill (as we all
know) eventually passed.

Probably no measure brought before the War Congress
excited so much debate and political feeling as the Conscription
Bill and its subsequent amendment known as the Negro Soldier
Bill. The bill to authorize the draft was debated pro and con,
amended and generally fought over, for nearly a year before
it finally became a law. It was bitterly opposed by the Peace
Democrats, Vallandigham being at the head of the opposition
in the House. During the earlier debates, the feeling of wrath
among the Peace Democratic members of the House was manifested at every step of the way. One day Representative Campbell of Pennsylvania referred to the Peace Democrats as "domestic traitors"; whereupon Vallandigham, who had given a
few minutes of his allotted time to Campbell, wrathily bounced
up and said that he had yielded the floor to a gentleman and
not to a blackguard. Campbell retorted: "The gentleman is
himself a blackguard," apparently not seeing the incongruous-
ness of calling a man a gentleman and a blackguard in the same
breath. This sally provoked the mirth and the applause of the
galleries, which were, as usual, crowded with soldiers; and
several of the Peace Democrats loudly and angrily demanded
that the galleries be cleared. One of the speakers, Representative [James C.] Robinson of Illinois, said that "Congress had
been too often insulted by Army contractors and Government
plunderers." This offensive remark caused the blue-coated
sovereigns in the gallery to laugh in chorus with derision; but
some of them uttered angry exclamations, and for a moment
there were serious signs of mutiny. S. S. Cox remarked that he
hoped that the galleries would not be cleared, as only a few
persons had joined in the demonstrations, and "the fool-killer
would be able to take care of *them.*" Good humor was restored by
this time, and the impending storm was averted.

The Conscription Bill passed through many and curious phases before it became a law, and whenever it appeared in either branch of Congress, there was a signal for a racket to begin. Even after the law had gone into the statute-books, Secretary Stanton attempted to construe the clause allowing exemption from the draft on a payment of three hundred dollars in such a way as to increase the burdensomeness of the law; but he was overruled by the solicitor of the War Department and the attorney-general. One of Fernando Wood's amusing amendments proposed to the pending bill was that "all persons who, from conscientious disbelief in the humanity, necessity, or eventual success of the war, were opposed to its further progress, should be exempted from the draft."

The bill to enlist Negroes in the Army was opposed with tremendous energy by Peace Democrats, who affected to look on the proposition as an attempt to excite a servile war. [Lincoln called early for the use of Negro troops. Between Emancipation and the end of the war, 180,000 Negroes enlisted and fought under the Union flag.] This was the view of the case, it will be remembered, that was taken by the Confederate authorities; and Representative Wickliffe of Kentucky made himself ridiculous by offering a resolution inquiring as to the truthfulness of the report that fugitive slaves were being mustered into the service of the United States, contrary to law. Wickliffe was speedily silenced when, in due course of time, there came back from the Army, through the War Department, the explanation that "colored Americans had been enlisted in the military service in the absence of their fugitive masters, who had fled southward." This ludicrous finale for a time quelled even the querulous and perpetually complaining gentleman from Kentucky. Later on, when it was found that colored substitutes would be accepted in place of drafted white men, there was a great rush on the part of the authorities of several of the Free States to fill up their quotas by enlisting Negroes from the Border States and the District of Columbia. The War Department stopped this by compelling all enlisting agents to give bonds that men taken outside of their own State lines should not be used as recruits in the Army. The United States Government, so Secretary Stanton said, wanted to employ these colored men in its own work, and would not tolerate interference from any of the States. Upon this, Senator Wilson, of Massachusetts, proposed to amend the conscription law by allowing the agents of loyal States to go into all of the seceded States where Union lines had been reëstablished, and to enlist men, black or white, for their own State organizations. This was intended to facilitate the enlistment of black soldiers in the South; but the proposition came to Stanton's ears, and he and Wilson had a hot discussion, in the course of which the Secretary told the Senator that no agents of Free States had any right in Southern States raking up able-bodied colored men, who would be put in the poorly officered State regiments, instead of being placed in the more thorough and vigorous organizations of colored troops then being undertaken by the Government of the United States. Becoming somewhat excited by this discussion, Secretary Stanton told Senator Wilson that if the Wilson amendment became a law, the War Office would be seeking a secretary on the very next day after. It is needless to add that Wilson's amendment was heard of no more.

The value of Negro substitutes for drafted white men was quaintly hit off by "Petroleum V. Nasby," in one of his inimitable papers written from "Confedrit Crossroads." [David R. Locke, using the "Nasby" pen name, was senior editor for the *Bucyrus* (Ohio) *Journal.*] In a previous paper the parson had poured out the vials of his wrath upon the wicked project to use colored men as soldiers in the war; but when he discovered that colored substitutes could be made available to save the precious lives of the unwilling residents of the Border States, he sounded an impassioned cry to "rally" all the colored people that were drifting about the region of his Crossroads. This letter attracted the attention of President Lincoln, who never missed an opportunity to read Nasby's then famous papers. The President, by frequent reading, was able to repeat this particular "rally" from memory, and for a long time he humorously illustrated the inconsistency of the Copperhead position on the question of Negro enlistments by reciting the letter with great effect, invariably ending his recitation with a hearty laugh.

One evening, long after the Nasby letter had been printed, and while the Lincoln family were at their summer house, the Soldiers' Home, I went out with the President to stay overnight. Several visitors came in, and the conversation fell upon the condition of the freedmen in the Border States. The President, standing before the fire-place, recited the whole of Nasby's letter, then displaced in the public mind by later productions. The last part, which Lincoln said was specially good, ran thus: "Arowse to wunst! Rally agin Conway! Rally agin Sweet! Rally agin Hegler! Rally agin Hegler's family! Rally agin the porter at the Reed House! Rally agin the cook at the Crook House! Rally agin the nigger widder in Vance's addishun! Rally agin Missis Umstid! Rally agin Missis Umstid's children by her first husband! Rally agin Missis Umstid's children by her sekkund husband! Rally agin all the rest uv Missis Umstid's children! Rally agin the nigger that kum yisterday! Rally agin the saddle-kulurd gal that yoost 2 be hear! Ameriky fer white men!" Lincoln used to quote these rallying-cries, at intervals, after other men had read and forgotten them.

In the winter of 1862, the dismemberment of Virginia by the admission of the western counties of the Old Dominion as the new State of West Virginia was the subject of a long and interesting debate. The congressional elections of the previous November had resulted somewhat unfavorably for the Administration. Lincoln's emancipation policy, the removal of

McClellan, and other important events, as it was alleged, had so aroused the popular indignation that the Republican majority in the next succeeding House of Representatives was somewhat diminished. This gave pause to some of the more timorous Unionists, who hesitated at taking a step so radical as that proposed in the division of Virginia. Among those who voted against the passage of the West Virginia bill were such Republicans as Roscoe Conkling of New York, John B. Alley of Massachusetts, James M. Ashley of Ohio, and Martin F. Conway of Kansas. This last-named gentleman, however, was an erratic and radical politician, whose objection to the bill was that it provided for gradual, and not immediate, emancipation of the slaves in the proposed new State. Conway subsequently secured notoriety by his preposterous scheme to divide the Northern States into new confederacies. Later on he made an insane speech in the House, in which he attacked the Lincoln administration for its "pro-slavery character," asserting that Lincoln was trying to build up a pro-slavery party, and had filled the departments and the Army with pro-slavery sympathizers with the rebellion. Conway was a small, red-topped, pale-faced man, with an excitable temperament and vehement manners. Once, while he was in the midst of an incendiary harangue, the limit of his time expired, and when he asked permission to go on, he was stopped by Owen Lovejoy with an objection; whereupon Conway, darting his finger at the burly radical from Illinois, screamed, "And you too, Brutus!" This was not the only exciting episode in which Conway was a conspicuous figure. It was charitably believed that his reason had been unsettled by his intense attention to the political issues that were then so prominent.

One of the most notable incidents in Congress in the winter of 1862–63 was the remarkable speech of Vallandigham, in which he defined his position and made his reëlection to Congress an impossibility so long as a respectable majority of his own party had any influence at the polls. It was an important occasion, and the rumor that he would at that time define his position brought a great concourse to the House; and when he began to speak the members from the opposite side of the chamber clustered around the nearest adjoining seats, and listened with intentness to what he had to say. It was a singular spectacle, this rapt attention by relentless patriots to the studied but vehement address of a man who was soon to be sent across the rebel lines by a Union officer as a traitor to his country. But the eagerness of the Republican listeners to hear Vallandigham's speech was inspired rather by the hope that he would say something that would damage the cause of the Peace Democrats than by their admiration of his oratory. In brief, his was an argument in favor of the right of the revolution. He said that George Washington was a rebel, and that we were all descended from rebels. He referred very frequently to some form of compromise; and the ghost of "peaceful compromise" was continually hovering in the background while he spoke. He ventured somewhat into the domain of prophecy when he said, "History will record the utter, disastrous, and most bloody failure of the experiment of an attempt to coerce the Southern States." He also said that if the war was prolonged, and the South should establish its independence, "the great Northwest would go with the South, and would not be a mere appanage to the Atlantic States, without a seaboard."

One of the most vigorous and pungent speeches of that session was made in reply to Vallandigham by John A. Bingham, of Ohio. Judge Bingham was one of those curiously constituted men who never excel in a formal speech, and who require provocation, contradiction, and interruption to arouse them to real eloquence. The more frequently he was interfered with and baited in the discussion, the more vigorous was his logic, and the more brilliant and forcible his rhetoric. On this occasion he was a remarkable figure. He was a small nervous man, with a pale, thin face, and long, tawny, fine hair, an excitable manner, and lambent, light-blue eyes. Again and again he "brought down the House" with his apt rejoinders to Vallandigham, who lost ground whenever he ventured to interrupt Bingham.

Another speaker who replied to Vallandigham's speech was Representative Hendrick B. Wright, of the Luzerne Congressional District, Pennsylvania. Mr. Wright was an elderly, white-haired man, a War Democrat, and his commanding figure rose high above the mob of congressmen who eagerly clustered around him to hear what he might say. He had recently lost his eldest son, a captain in "Rush's Lancers," who had died at the age of twenty-five, of fever contracted in the marshes of Virginia; and a second son, only sixteen years old, was then standard-bearer in another Pennsylvania regiment. Eloquently referring to the complaint of the Peace Democrats that the war required a great sacrifice of blood and treasure, he said that it was better that we should offer three hundred thousand more of the best men of the nation, and so end the rebellion, than bequeath its horrors to a generation to come, and let it meet the terrors that we had not the courage to grapple with and conquer. There were moist eyes in the throng of heroes round this noble Roman father as he thus concluded: "The war has cost me its trials and tribulations. I can truly close my remarks with a quotation from an ancient philosopher, uttered over the body of his son, slain in battle:

> " 'I should have blushed if Cato's house had stood
>   Secure and flourished in a civil war.' "

It would be needless here to refer to Vallandigham's subsequent career. We may recall his incendiary speeches in Ohio later in that year, his arrest by General Burnside, his deportation beyond the rebel lines, and the flames of discord that flared up in the North when these events took place. Although Presi-

dent Lincoln was greatly surprised and dismayed by Burnside's treatment of Vallandigham, he wrote several documents
pertinent thereto which have passed into history as political
classics. With a single stroke of his pen he revealed the kernel
of the contention when he asked, "Must I shoot a simple-minded
soldier boy who deserts, while I must not touch a hair of the
wily agitator who induces him to desert?" [Lincoln to Governor
H. Seymour, June 12, 1863.]

When Vallandigham, passing through the Confederacy,
had, by a detour seaward, finally returned to the United States
through Canada, I had occasion to mention his name to Lincoln,
remarking that he had been speaking in Ohio. "What!" exclaimed the President, looking at me quizzically, "has Vallandigham got back?" Somewhat puzzled, I explained that everybody knew that. "Dear me!" said Lincoln, with preternatural
solemnity. "I supposed he was in a foreign land. Anyhow, I
hope I do not know that he is in the United States; and I shall
not, unless he says or does something to draw attention to him."
Presently he went to his table, and, drawing out some loose
sheets of paper, said that he had there the rough notes of an
interview which he had lately had with Fernando Wood. This
was in August, 1864. It appeared that Wood had said to the
President: "We Peace Democrats are the only Democrats; all
others are bastards and impostors; there is no such thing as a
War Democrat, for that is a contradiction in terms. We don't
expect to elect our candidate for President this fall: the people
of the North are not yet ready for peace. But peace must come
sooner or later; and when it does, the Democratic party will
be the party which will act and assimilate with the dominant
party in the South, and so we shall again have our rightful
ascendancy. Now, Mr. President, you cannot find fault with
that; it is not going to hurt you any."

Lincoln then said that he had told Wood that he was disposed to be generous; and he asked if Vallandigham's alleged

return was any part of this program. Wood replied that it was not, and added: "You may not believe me, but I assure you that I never knew or expected that he would return, though I acknowledge that I have had a letter from him since he got back. He has had already more notoriety than he deserves, and I warn you that the true policy is that he be severely let alone." To this the President replied, according to his own account: "I don't believe that Vallandigham has returned; I never can believe it until he forces himself offensively upon the public attention and upon my attention. Then we shall have to deal with him. So long as he behaves himself decently, he is as effectually in disguise as the man who went to a masquerade party with a clean face."

LINCOLN AND CHASE, AND THEIR POLITICAL FRIENDS

Secretary Chase was inordinately jealous of any apparent invasion of the appointing power of his office. His warmly supported theory was that each head of an executive department should exercise exclusive control of all the appointments and removals in his branch of the public service. This, of course, would leave the President absolutely shorn of all power in the matter of making appointments, whether important or unimportant. If the Secretary of the Treasury were to be supreme in the choice of an officer to fill the most considerable place in his department, then the Secretary of State should also be the sole authority in respect of selecting foreign ministers to represent our government abroad. Secretary Chase not only held to this view, at least so far as his own department was concerned, but he also resented the interference of congressmen, and more than once brushed aside President, Senators, and Representatives in his determination to make important appointments without their consent or approval.

A curious illustration of this usage of the Secretary came

to my knowledge in March, 1863. There had been a thorough overhauling of the chief federal offices in San Francisco, conducted by a special agent of the Treasury Department—Thomas Brown—who was a confidential friend of Secretary Chase. On his report, it was determined in the interior councils of the Treasury Department to make "a clean sweep." Secretary Chase intimated this determination to the three California congressmen—A. A. Sargent (afterward United States Senator, and subsequently minister to Germany), F. F. Low (afterward minister to China), and T. G. Phelps. These gentlemen, having been informed by the Secretary that he intended to make many changes, were invited one evening to his private office in the Treasury building, where they were entertained with a brief summary of Brown's report, after which Secretary Chase blandly informed the expectant congressmen that he had resolved to remove all of the leading officials and to supply their places with new men. He then read a list of the appointments as he had made them out, and waited with calm dignity to hear if the congressmen had anything to say. But as he had already announced his irrevocable decision in the matter, there was evidently nothing for them to say; and, having expressed themselves as resigned to the Secretary's will, they departed. It was reported that the three astonished congressmen uttered some strong language as they passed out of the Treasury building. A few days afterward, the California congressmen paid their respects to the President, and departed for New York on their way to San Francisco. There Mr. Phelps at once took a steamer homeward by way of Panama, and Messrs. Sargent and Low lingered for a day or two in the city.

While they were in New York, I was astonished one night by receiving from President Lincoln an urgent summons to come immediately to the White House. Upon my arriving there, Mr. Lincoln said that he had just learned that a number of removals and appointments in San Francisco had been de-

termined upon by Secretary Chase without consulting him or
the California congressmen; and that the three congressmen
had departed from Washington very angry and discomfited.
With some asperity of manner, he wanted to know if this was
true. I told him that it was true, and I recited the facts as they
had come to my knowledge from Messrs. Sargent, Low, and
Phelps. The President then angrily asked why I had not told
him this before. I replied that it was not my affair; that as
long as the congressmen had seen fit to conceal their feelings of
disappointment from the President when they bade him
good-by, it certainly was not my business to "tell tales out of
school." The President expressed his astonishment that he had
been kept in the dark about so grave a matter as the emptying
and filling of the most important Federal offices on the Pacific
Coast. Then he anxiously asked if there was any way by which
the California congressmen could be reached and brought
back; and when told that two of them were still in New York,
he produced a telegraph blank and insisted that I should at
once write a despatch to Messrs. Sargent and Low, and request
them to return to Washington and see the President. With that
careful attention to the smallest details which always characterized Lincoln, he enjoined upon me that I should send the
despatch and collect from him the charge therefor the next
time I came to the White House. The despatch was sent, the
two congressmen were recalled, and the slate which Secretary
Chase had so carefully prepared was eventually broken. Subsequently Mr. Lincoln informed me that Mr. Chase was "exceedingly hurt" by the President's interference with his plans. A
curious outcome of all this business was that Secretary Chase,
having been disappointed in his scheme for filling the office of
collector of the port of San Francisco, insisted that one of the
two congressmen who had returned to Washington should be
appointed in place of the person whom he (Chase) had previously selected for the post. The President suggested that all

three congressmen should get together in San Francisco, agree upon the list of appointments, and send it to him for ratification and approval. This, however, seemed impracticable; and when Messrs. Sargent and Low finally sailed for California, Mr. Low carried with him his commission as collector of the port.

Victor Smith, formerly a resident of Ohio, and a personal friend of Secretary Chase, was one of the disturbing elements that made the great Secretary's last days in the Treasury Department turbulent and unhappy. Victor Smith had been appointed by the Secretary to the place of collector of customs at Port Townsend, Washington Territory. Smith was a restless visionary, and in these later days would have been called a crank. While he was collector at Port Townsend, Smith succeeded in inducing the Government to move the custom-house from that point to another on Puget Sound. It was a foolish and harebrained scheme, and created a bitter feeling among business men. His new place was named Port Angelos. There the collector maintained himself for a time in a semi-barbaric proprietorship. It is related of him that he once invited the officers of the revenue cutter *Shubrick* to dine at his house; and the officers, considering that the collector of the port was a high functionary, arrayed themselves in full dress, with swords, gold lace, and other gorgeous insignia of their station, and went ashore in state to wait upon Collector Smith at his mansion, which was then in an unfinished condition. In due course of time the collector, assisted by his wife, brought out two carpenter's saw-horses, on which was placed a board covered with wrapping-paper. The repast, which was as simple as any ever partaken of by the hermits of olden time, was then set forth; and Smith, taking from his pockets three big apples, gave one to each of the three officers, with a small forked stick, remarking: "You'll have to roast your own apples."

This eccentric functionary once informed me that he had "so intertwined himself in the fibers of the government that his removal from office was an impossibility." Nevertheless, the outcry against Smith was so great that the President told Secretary Chase that the man must go. Every Federal officer, and nearly every prominent citizen in the Puget Sound collection district, had written letters or signed memorials protesting against the continuance of Smith in his office, and had demanded his removal and the return of the custom-house to the point from which it had been so needlessly carried away. The Secretary of the Treasury was obdurate; but finally, in May, 1863, the harassed President "took the bull by the horns," and resolved upon Smith's removal. The stream of expostulations, protests, and remonstrances that poured in upon him from the distracted region over which Victor Smith reigned had become intolerable; but, kind and considerate to the last, the President wrote to the Secretary (as we learn from the Nicolay-Hay history of Lincoln) to this effect:

My mind is made up to remove Victor Smith as collector of the customs at the Puget Sound district. Yet in doing this I do not decide that the charges against him are true; I only decide that the degree of dissatisfaction with him there is too great for him to be retained. But I believe he is your personal acquaintance and friend, and if you desire it I will try to find some other place for him.

When the Secretary received this note, he made out a commission for Victor Smith's successor, wrote his own resignation as Secretary of the Treasury, and sent both to the President. This was only one of several instances in which Chase manifested his disposition to retire from the public service in case his will was thwarted in any particular; but once more the President succeeded in placating the ruffled Secretary, who still remained at the head of the Treasury Department, notwithstanding the removal of the petty officer from his distant post on Puget Sound.

There is an interesting sequel to this story. One of the

most conspicuous opponents of Victor Smith was Dr. A. G.
Henry, surveyor-general of Washington Territory, an old friend
of the President, whose name has been mentioned [accompany-
ing the President on a trip to the Army] in a previous chapter
of these reminiscences. [Dr. Henry, a Springfield friend, together with Mrs. Lincoln, had suggested that Brooks replace
John Nicolay as the President's secretary.] He was the bearer
of a load of remonstrances that were finally influential in de-
termining the removal of Victor Smith. Dr. Henry and Smith
had long been on terms of enmity, and always declined to recognize each other when they passed by. On my return to
California after Lincoln's death, in 1865, Dr. Henry was a
fellow-passenger on the steamer from New York to Aspinwall.
Victor Smith had been in Washington on some one of his many
busy errands, and had departed for home on the steamer
Golden Rule, of the Nicaragua line, and in her had been
wrecked on Roncador Reef, since made famous by the catas-
trophe that deprived us of the historic *Kearsarge*. We found
the shipwrecked passengers at Panama waiting for transportation to San Francisco, and most of them embarked with us,
Smith among the number. This addition to our passenger-list
crowded the ship, and the newer arrivals were distributed among
those who had previously been allotted individual cabins. Soon
after we left our moorings in Panama Bay, Dr. Henry came to
me, in great agitation of mind, with the information that in
the new allotment Victor Smith had been given a berth in his
(Henry's) room. "I wouldn't dare to sleep in the same room
with that viper," said the doctor, excitedly. "He might get up
and kill me in the night. You know the purser; I wish you
would go to him and see if you cannot have Smith put in some
other man's room. I don't care who else is put into my room;
but Smith I will not have." Smiling at the good doctor's
vehemence, I started for the purser's office, but was intercepted
by Victor Smith, who said: "They have put me in the same

stateroom with that old devil, Dr. Henry. You know the purser; I wish you would use your influence with him and have me put in some other room. I wouldn't dare to sleep in the same room with that man." The necessary change was made, and Dr. Henry and Victor Smith were not obliged to recognize each other's existence on that ship at least.

But when they reached San Francisco later in the month (July, 1865), they both, with great reluctance, took passage on the steamer *Brother Jonathan,* bound for Portland, Oregon. There was no alternative except the slow transit by stage from Sacramento northward. The *Brother Jonathan* struck on a reef on this her last ill-fated voyage, and nearly all on board perished, among the lost being General George Wright, who, having survived the perils of war, was then on his way to take command of the Department of the Columbia. The waves also engulfed Dr. Henry and Victor Smith. In the supreme moment, when certain death yawned before these two determined enemies, did they clasp hands and forgive the past?

The tragical episode that marked the close of the career of Dr. Henry, Lincoln's good friend, may best be concluded here with a letter from Mrs. Lincoln in which touching reference is made to him and to her husband. I may as well explain that the "claims" referred to in Mrs. Lincoln's letter were certain shares of "wild-cat" stock, sent to her in her days of prosperity, and which the poor lady thought might be sold for a small sum. This is her letter:

CHICAGO, May 11, 1866.

NOAH BROOKS, ESQ., SAN FRANCISCO.

MY DEAR SIR: A few days since I received a very sad letter from Mrs. Henry, in which she vividly portrays her great desolation and dependence upon others for every earthly comfort. I am induced to enclose you the Nevada claims and also a petroleum claim, hoping that you may be able to secure a purchaser for them, in which case I will most cheerfully give Mrs. Henry some of the proceeds. I am aware that I am taxing your kindness very greatly, yet the remembrance of your great esteem for my beloved husband and Dr. Henry would excuse the intrusion upon you. I wish you were not so far removed from us—*true* friends, in these overwhelming days of affliction, I find to be very rare. I find myself clinging more tenderly to the memory of those who, if *not* so remote, would be more friendly.

I hope you will be able to visit Mrs. Henry the coming summer. I sometimes, in my wildness and grief, am tempted to believe that it is some *terrible, terrible* dream, and that my idolized husband will return to me. Poor Dr. Henry! he who wept so truly and freely with us in our great misfortune, how soon he was called to join the beloved one who had so recently "gone before"! In my own great sorrow, how often I have prayed for death to end my great misery!

My sons are well, and a great comfort to me. [I have another and *the right* Nevada claim—with "Mary," instead of "Frances," upon it, which I will send you, in the event—of your being able to dispose of it.] Robert and Taddie remember you very kindly. I hope you will write to us more frequently. I am well aware of the deep sympathy you feel for us, and the great affection and confidence my husband cherished for you draws you very near to us. With apologies for troubling you as I am now doing, I remain always sincerely your friend,   MARY LINCOLN.

[Additions to the letter, omitted by Brooks, are from the original in the possession of Francis Whiting Hatch, of Castine, Me.]

THE RESIGNATION OF CHASE

Lincoln was greatly exasperated by the Victor Smith incident; and when he had finally disposed of the matter, as he thought, he was much depressed by frequent repetitions of similar complications. From him and from one of the Senators who waited upon him after Chase's resignation I learned the facts of the last trial of the patience of the long-suffering Lincoln. The crisis which made it impossible for Mr. Chase to stay any longer in the Treasury Department was brought on, as everybody knows, by his determination to have his own way in making several important appointments in the city of New York. But, as we have seen, the trouble began long before, when Secretary Chase grew more and more determined to resent interference with any of the appointments in the Treasury Department. Whether his ambition to be President of the United States had anything to do with this hardening of his will in the matter of executive patronage, it is impossible to say; but from the time that his name was brought prominently before the public by Senator [Samuel C.] Pomeroy, of Kansas, and others, until his final exit from the Treasury Department, Mr. Chase was continually in hot water. His resignation, handed in when Victor Smith's removal was determined upon by the President, was written in May, 1863. His final resignation was tendered in June, 1864. It would appear that Mr. Chase believed that his great position in the United States Government was absolutely necessary to the welfare of the republic, and that he could not be permitted to leave it without inviting disaster; and his frequent threats of resignation were intended, apparently, to coerce the President into letting him have his own way in all matters of detail.

When the nomination of David Tod, of Ohio, went to the Senate in place of Salmon P. Chase, resigned, the Senators were struck dumb with amazement. In executive session the whole matter was at once referred to the Finance Committee, and in a few minutes Senators Fessenden, Conness, Sherman, Cowan, and Van Winkle were on their way to the White House. They had two questions to ask. One was, Why has Chase resigned, and is the act final? And the other was, Why has the name of David Tod been sent to the Senate? The President received the Senators with great affability, and there was a general and free

discussion of the situation, Senator Fessenden, chairman of the
Finance Committee, being the mouthpiece of the visiting states-
men. The President immediately disposed of the Tod branch
of the complication by reading a telegram from Governor Tod
declining the nomination. Then he gave the Senators a full
history of the original formation of the Cabinet in 1861, explaining why each man had been chosen, and expressing his
great confidence in Secretary Chase's abilities and integrity.
Then he followed with a detailed statement of the relations that
had existed between himself and the Secretary of the Treasury since the latter had taken office. He told the Senators all
the incidents concerning the many times that Chase had offered
his resignation, and he referred to the ill temper which the
Secretary had betrayed on those occasions. Then he took from a
pigeonhole all the correspondence between himself and the Secretary, showing numerous instances of the testiness of the
Secretary and the much-enduring patience of the President
during a period stretching over nearly all the years of the
administration down to that day.

Lincoln said that of course Mr. Chase had a full right to
indulge in his ambition to be President, and there was no
question as to his claim upon the gratitude of the American
people; but indiscreet friends of the Secretary had succeeded in
exciting a feeling disagreeable in itself, and embarrassing to
the President and to the Secretary. This had gone on, he said,
until they disliked to meet each other; and to him (Lincoln) the
relation had become unendurable, and he had accepted the
resignation of Mr. Chase as a finality. He told the committee
that he would not continue to be President with Mr. Chase in
the Cabinet; that if the Senate should insist upon it, they could
have his resignation, and take Mr. Hamlin for President. Of
one of the appointments which Secretary Chase had insisted
upon President Lincoln spoke with considerable feeling. This

appointment, which Chase had adhered to tenaciously, and which Lincoln said was discreditable to the Secretary, was one which the President insisted never would be made with his consent. He told the Senators that at a party where Mr. Chase's chosen appointee was present, this person was intoxicated, and kicked his hat in the air in the presence of ladies and gentlemen. Lincoln said he had told Chase that he would take any other nomination which he (Chase) would send him, but this man he could not and would not accept. Chase, notwithstanding Lincoln's statement concerning the man's habits and character, persisted in urging the nomination upon the President. This, Lincoln said, was "the last straw." As we know, Tod's declination of the nomination left the President free to send another name to the Senate, and the Finance Committee of that body was then for the first time enlightened as to the unfortunate relations which had so long existed between the Secretary of the Treasury and the President.

The way was now clear, and the next surprise to which the public was treated was the nomination and immediate confirmation of Senator William Pitt Fessenden as Secretary of the Treasury. It was a picturesque feature of this latter part of the business that Senator Fessenden was in the President's office conferring with him on the situation of affairs while his own nomination as successor to Chase was on its way to the Senate; and when Fessenden learned from the President that that nomination had actually been made, he went in hot haste to the Capitol, only to find that the appointment had been confirmed before he could enter his protest against it.

That evening I was at the White House, and Mr. Lincoln sent for me to come into the library, where I found him lying upon his back on a sofa, with his hands clasped over his chest, and looking weary beyond description. But he was in a comfortable frame of mind; and, after going over the incidents of this exciting episode, he said cheerfully, "When I finally struck the name of Fessenden as Governor Chase's successor, I felt as if the Lord hadn't forsaken me yet."

It is well known that the friends of Secretary Chase, and probably some of Lincoln's, insisted upon fomenting strife between these two illustrious men long after the Secretary had retired to private life and Lincoln's second nomination and election had eliminated the Presidential question, for a time at least, from all other relations which affected the two men. This mischievous influence was at work when, on the death of Roger B. Taney, the great office of Chief Justice of the United States became vacant, and Chase's name was immediately brought forward by his friends and admirers, who hoped to see him succeed to that post. Senator Sumner and other radical Republicans at once deluged Lincoln with letters and telegrams beseeching him to nominate Chase as Chief Justice. On the other hand, Lincoln was overwhelmed with protests from his own political and personal friends, who reminded him that Chase had not "behaved well" while Secretary of the Treasury, and had embarrassed the President with his inordinate ambition.

While the matter was pending, I had occasion to call on the President, and the rumors of Chase's appointment naturally came up for discussion. Mr. Lincoln had been, for him, very gay and cheery; but as soon as Chase and the chief-justiceship were mentioned, his visage lengthened, and with great seriousness he pointed to a pile of telegrams and letters on his table, and said: "I have been all day, and yesterday and the day before, besieged by messages from my friends all over the country, as if there were a determination to put up the bars between Governor Chase and myself." Then, after a pause, he added: "But I shall nominate him for Chief Justice, nevertheless." It was therefore with amusement that I learned from one of Chase's most ardent friends, about an hour later, that "Lincoln

was not great enough to nominate Secretary Chase as Chief
Justice"; and with inward satisfaction I bore in silence much
contumely and reproach from Chase's fast friends, from that
time until the country was delighted by the intelligence that
Chase's nomination had been sent to the Senate on December 6,
1864, in a message written by the President's own hand.

The political complications which immediately preceded
the Presidential nominations of 1864 were extremely distressing
to Lincoln. Washington was in a ferment, and to some degree,
although not to the extent that Washington politicians believed,
the country was responsive to the excitement which prevailed at
the national capital. It had become evident that Lincoln's
nomination was impending, although the friends of Mr. Chase
insisted that his renomination was unlikely, and that his reëlection was an absolute impossibility. At this later day, when the
political events of 1864 lie behind us like landmarks in a road
over which we have securely traveled, it is difficult to understand how any man of even moderate sagacity could have supposed, as not a few men did, that Lincoln had a very slight
chance of renomination and none at all of reëlection. It is difficult also to comprehend, even now, the motives that induced
so many honest and earnest Republicans at the seat of Government to be at great pains, as they were, to defeat what seemed
to be the popular will respecting Lincoln. It was urged by the
friends of Mr. Chase that no man should be elected to a second
term of the Presidency; and it was well known that Mr. Chase
himself made no secret of his strong belief in the saving grace
of the one-term principle. Many people were dissatisfied with
the alleged slowness of the Lincoln administration as regarded
both political and military operations. On the other hand, many
ardent Union men, in zealous advocacy of what they conceived
to be the conservative policy of the administration, went quite
as far on the other tack as the radicals did in the direction of a
more vigorous and aggressive policy on the part of the Presi-

dent and his cabinet. The eddying currents of political opinion surged about the Capitol while Congress was in session; and in both branches of that body the rival factions skirmished with each other, their real purpose being thinly veiled by a pretense of earnest devotion to the public business.

The Missouri imbroglio was a source of perpetual annoyance to the great body of public men who had no special interest in the unreasonable quarrel that raged in that State. Beginning with the brief and brilliant reign of General Frémont, and extending almost to the close of the war, the Unionist party in Missouri was divided into two hostile camps, radical and conservative. These never became friends and allies so long as the war endured, and political matters were consequently hopelessly mixed in Missouri. The quarrel was at its height during General Schofield's administration of military rule in the State, before the civil authority reasserted itself. Finally, when B. Gratz Brown and John B. Henderson came to the United States Senate as representatives respectively of the radical and the conservative wings of the Union party, there was for a while something like an armed truce. The Blair family, however, with a proclivity to mischief-making that was amazing, succeeded in fomenting the Missouri quarrel whenever it showed any indications of simmering down. Frank P. Blair, Jr., took his seat in the House of Representatives with the avowed determination of showing up, as he expressed it, the corruption which existed in the administration of the Treasury Department in Missouri. He represented the so-called conservative wing of his party, and he demanded the appointment of a committee to inquire into and report upon the alleged infraction by Treasury agents of the act of Congress regulating commercial intercourse with the States declared to be in insurrection. As a counterblast to this, some of the Missouri radicals brought charges against Blair in which it was alleged that he, as a commanding general in the Fifteenth Army Corps near Vicksburg in the summer of 1863, with his officers, had been engaged in a large speculation, in the course of which brandy, whisky, beer, wines, cigars, tobacco, and canned fruits had been bought in St. Louis, and smuggled through the military lines for the use of rebel officers on the other side of the military boundaries. The result of this charge against Blair was harmless. It was proved that a small order given by General Blair and his staff, the total cost of which would not have exceeded one hundred and fifty or one hundred and seventy-five dollars, had been fraudulently expanded by the agent to whom it was intrusted, so that it called for a variety of goods amounting to about nine thousand dollars in value. This disgraceful episode was only one of many which marked the long and stormy discussions dragged into the House day after day by the quarrelsome Missouri members; at the same time, Montgomery Blair in Maryland was pursuing Henry Winter Davis, a radical Republican, with the same relentlessness with which his brother Frank kept on the track of the Missouri radicals.

General Schofield, who had been Military Governor of Missouri during its reconstruction period, was nominated by the President for promotion to the rank of major-general in the volunteer Army. As this happened during the height of the Missouri excitement, Gratz Brown in the Senate, and his radical colleagues in the House, fell afoul of the nomination with rage and determination. Meanwhile, however, the War Department had attempted to quiet the disturbance by providing for Schofield at another point, and putting Rosecrans in his place. Although the changing of Schofield removed the immediate cause of the bitterness of the radical Missourians, opposition to his military promotion was still kept up, and Washington politics for weeks apparently consisted of nothing but the rumors and reports which circulated about General Schofield's nomination and his confirmation by the Senate.

The Blair family also came to the front conspicuously in

the fall of 1863, in a speech made at Rockville, Maryland, in October, by Montgomery Blair, then Postmaster-General. The speech, which was an elaborate defense of the alleged conservative policy of the President, was also a bitter arraignment of prominent members of the Cabinet, Senators, and Representatives. The speech was subsequently issued in pamphlet form, and created considerable stir in Washington, and among the President's real friends in Maryland. The title-page of the pamphlet edition of this speech gave the speaker considerable fictitious importance as "a member of Lincoln's Cabinet," and the speech was ingeniously worded so as to endue it with an appearance of having been sanctioned by the President in order to set himself right before the people as against the wicked aspersions of the more radical men in his party. Of course Lincoln eventually heard of this extraordinary oration, and a friend, calling on him one day, found him reading a little slip cut from a newspaper, from which he was endeavoring to get some idea of the then famous Rockville speech. The visitor offered to send the President a copy of the pamphlet as published by Blair; and, at his request, I took it to the President, who was greatly amused, as well as astonished, by the ingeniously worded title-page of that queer document.

Later on in that month, just after the Pennsylvania State elections, William D. Kelley and Colonel John W. Forney [publisher of the *Washington Daily Morning Chronicle* and the *Philadelphia Press*] called on the President with their congratulations, and Forney very plainly said to the President (Blair being then present) that his conservative friend, Governor [Andrew] Curtin, of Pennsylvania, desired the President to know that if the Rockville speech of Postmaster-General Blair had been made thirty days earlier, it would have lost the Union ticket in Pennsylvania twenty thousand votes. To Blair, Forney also expressed his astonishment that he, a Cabinet officer, should have had the hardihood to utter such sentiments in public just on the eve of important elections in other States. Blair responded that whatever Forney might think of the matter, he had only spoken his honest sentiments at Rockville. "Then," said the angry Forney, turning upon Blair, "why don't you leave the Cabinet, and not load down with your individual and peculiar sentiments the administration to which you belong?" The President sat by, a silent spectator of this singular and unexpected scene.

Colonel Forney gave me an account of this affair, and probably other newspaper correspondents had it from the same source. Among these, Whitelaw Reid [then the Washington correspondent of the *Cincinnati Gazette;* he signed his column "Agate"] published an account of the interview which was widely copied and commented upon. Thereupon the Washington correspondent of the *New York Herald,* on the authority of Postmaster-General Blair, denied that Colonel Forney had ever used to him, in the presence of Mr. Lincoln, the language attributed to him in the reports of that interview. I went to the President with the story as it was printed; and, having looked through the clipping, he said that he "guessed it was about correct." The incident is told here as a good example of the difficulties that Lincoln had with his own friends, and of the bitterness that divided some of them from each other. Nobody ever doubted Blair's devotion and loyalty to Lincoln; and certainly Forney never for a moment considered any man fit to take Lincoln's place, and heartily and enthusiastically supported his renomination. Yet these two men, Forney and Blair, could not meet on amicable terms.

In February, 1864, the long-vexed political complication came to a head in the appearance of the famous "secret circular" in which Senator Pomeroy, of Kansas, frankly proposed the nomination of Mr. Chase for the Presidency. This circular was marked "strictly private," and gave to Pomeroy, whose initals were S. C., the nickname of "Secret Circular Pomeroy."

At this late day it is hardly worth while to recall anything in
that document but its main propositions. These were that the
renomination of Lincoln was not only undesirable but impossible; that the honor of the nation and the cause of liberty and
union would suffer in consequence of his reëlection; that the
"one-term principle" was essential to the safety of republican
institutions; that Salmon P. Chase had more of the qualities
needed in a President at that critical time than any other man;
and that the discussion of Chase's availability had surprised
his warmest admirers by the development of his strength. It is
one of the curiosities of the time that this queer document,
which was in the hands of nearly every newspaper man and
politician in Washington, did not find its way into the public
prints until several days after its private circulation began.
Finally, on Washington's Birthday, its appearance in the *National Intelligencer* [Washington] greatly excited the quidnuncs [the gossips], although nearly everybody was already
familiar with its contents. It was not until March tenth, however, that Pomeroy took public notice of the commotion which
his fulmination had aroused. He was evidently pleased with his
sudden notoriety. But by that time it had become clearly
manifest that Mr. Chase could not possibly be nominated. The
Unionists of his own State had declared in favor of Lincoln;
and on the day after that declaration was made, Pomeroy
rose in his place in the Senate and attempted to justify his
foolish circular; a letter was then printed from Mr. Chase
withdrawing his name from the political canvass. Pomeroy,
who was an unctuous and sleek man, with a rosy countenance
and a suave manner, told the Senators that he was the author
of the now famous circular, but that some person whom he did
not name had appended to it the indorsement "strictly private,"
in order, as he said, to give it a wider circulation. He exulted in
the fact that he was chairman of a respectable association, with
widely ramifying branches all over the country, whose object

was to secure the election of "an efficient and radical candidate for the presidency in opposition to the time-serving policy of the day." He said that Mr. Chase "had been drafted into the service" of that organization; and that while he (Pomeroy) should not be considered as making war upon the present administration, he must insist that no executive could long sustain itself unless it had strong party affiliations to uphold it in Congress and in the country.

It was inevitable that the Missouri quarrel should be dragged into the discussion. Senator [Morton S.] Wilkinson, of Minnesota, who replied to Pomeroy, taunted him with gross inconsistency in putting himself forward as a champion of radicalism, while, at the same time, he was exerting himself in the Senate to secure the confirmation of General Schofield, whose supporters were the conservatives of the party. The incident naturally attracted interested attention in both houses of Congress; and while Wilkinson, who was by no means a keen debater, was tantalizing Pomeroy, members came flocking over from the other end of the Capitol, crowding the Senate-chamber to hear with amusement the parent of the now famous circular defend his action while he avowed its paternity. It was a desperate attempt to make the best of a failing cause. But it was of no avail. The tide of public opinion had set too strongly in the direction of Lincoln for any such feeble efforts as those of Pomeroy, Edmunds, Winchell, and their comrades to withstand the current any longer. That was a time of dramatic political sensations. The coincident appearance of Chase's letter, taking his name out of the list of possible Presidential candidates, and Senator Pomeroy's lame endeavor to give weight and reasonableness to the secret circular, were among the excitements of the day; but, although Mr. Chase's withdrawal, and the ignominious collapse of the scheme in whose interest the circular had been prepared, deprived the radical disorganizers of even the semblance of a leader and a head, it was not until the Union

Republican Convention of 1864 had renominated Lincoln that the restless and querulous opposition to his call to a second term was finally silenced. It is possible that this brief recital of the political events that preceded Lincoln's second election may suggest to politicians of this later day the ineffectiveness of merely factious tactics and schemes.

ENTER LIEUTENANT-GENERAL GRANT

It is interesting to call to mind some of the forces which made Grant the general-in-chief of the armies of the United States, and some of the incidents that attended the consummation of that historic work. It was by no means a grateful task for the congressmen of that time to lend a hand in creating the grade of lieutenant-general in the Army, although there was no question as to the man on whom the distinction should be conferred. I doubt very much if the bill to revive the grade of lieutenant-general would have then gone through Congress if it had not been for the general dissatisfaction with General Halleck, who was acting as general-in-chief with headquarters at Washington. This dissatisfaction was constantly increasing, and although the country at large did not seem to be keenly alive to Halleck's inadequacy to the situation, Washington, and especially the chambers of Congress, resounded with complaints of his sluggishness, his unwillingness to take reponsibilities, and his supposed incapacity to grasp the whole military situation. I doubt if the most outspoken and malignant Copperhead in Congress was so disliked, so railed against, and so reviled by the more radical members as this unfortunate general-in-chief. The belief that some new man, no matter who he might be, could vigorously prosecute the war and bring a speedy peace, if he were in Halleck's place, made possible the passage of the bill reviving the rank of lieutenant-general of the army. Oddly enough, men who complained that the President clung tenaciously to General Halleck as his military adviser never doubted for a moment that Mr. Lincoln was more than willing that the rank should be revived with the distinct understanding that Grant should be the wearer of the title, and by virtue thereof become at once the generalissimo of all the military forces of the United States.

That the President did cling to Halleck in spite of the very general popular disfavor with which the general was regarded is well known. When I ventured, one day, to say to the President that Halleck was disliked because many people supposed that he was too timid and hesitating in his military conduct, Mr. Lincoln's face at once wore a grave, almost severe expression, as he said that he was Halleck's friend because nobody else was. Other men had received from the President a somewhat similar impression; and whatever may have been thought of the very remote possibility that any other man than General Grant would be called to the head of the armies, congressmen who were clamorous for a more vigorous prosecution of the war were eagerly turning to the "lieutenant-general bill," as it was called, as the readiest way to be rid of General Halleck's alleged slowness.

This fact was brought out in the debate in the House when the measure was under consideration. With that free-and-easy frankness which so distinguished the House from the Senate, as it was then constituted, the Representatives did not hesitate to fling about a great many personalities while they discussed the expediency of reviving the grade of lieutenant-general. When the bill came up for its final passage on February 1, 1864, E. B. Washburne, who had the measure in charge, distinguished himself by the energy and impatience with which he fairly bulldozed the House into its immediate consideration. He ramped and roared, expostulated and threatened, until he wrought himself into a state of quivering excitement. Washburne had been from the very first an enthusiastic believer in Grant's great military genius, and this was not only his supreme effort to place on high the object of his love and idolatry, but, as he believed, to save the republic from years of wasteful war. It is entertaining now to recall the attitude of some of the conspicuous congressmen who opposed or supported the bill. Grant, it should be remembered, was at that time by no means the popular favorite that he very soon after became; although his wonderful series of successes in the Southwest had even then made him the cynosure of all eyes.

Garfield, of Ohio, who had fought under Grant, and was now a member of the House Military Committee, opposed the bill on the ground that the rank was not needed, and that the President and the War Department already had the power to detail any major-general to perform the functions with which a lieutenant-general would be intrusted. He said that if the proposed rank was to be conferred as a reward of merit, it would be better to wait until the war was over, and not seize upon an immature reputation as worthy of so great a reward. He said that if this rank had been created two years before, probably one of the several generals now shelved or retired would have been honored with it, and the country be thereby now mortified. Garfield was one of the first who frankly said in debate that General Grant would probably be nominated lieutenant-general if the bill became law; and he added that the country could not spare Grant from the great work he was doing in the West to transform him into "a bureau office in Washington." But, in view of the political influences that would be at work, he (Garfield) was not so sure that Grant would be the man after all.

Another member of the Military Committee—General [Addison] Farnsworth of Illinois—favored the bill because General Grant was "no carpet-knight," but would command the armies in person, "not in a richly furnished Brussels-carpeted chamber in Washington," after the manner of *some* commanders-in-chief. This hit at Halleck was greatly enjoyed by the galleries, and a general laugh rippled over the surface of the House. General Robert C. Schenck, who was chairman of the House Military Committee, supported the bill not because he believed General Grant was the man to fill it, but because he believed in the principle that a military man should be at the head of the Army and direct all operations in the field.

Washburne fretted and fumed when sundry members rose with amendments of various kinds; and there was every indication—the previous question not having been seconded—that the whole subject must go over for another day. "Thad" Stevens made a little speech in which he said, as Garfield had said, that he did not see the use of the proposed measure, because the President already had power to appoint a general-in-chief. He also objected to the bill because it restricted the President to the choice of a lieutenant-general from a small number of major-generals. "Why not allow military men of less note to have equal footing in the proposed race for the great prize? And why not even choose from citizens, some of whom are worth more than many major-generals, as military men? Saints are not canonized until after death," he said, "and the greatest of reputations is not secure until the possessor has rested from his labors." Stevens said he had been amused to hear some of the members speak as though it was certain that General Grant would be the honored recipient of the prize; but he was not so certain of that. Judging from the tenacity with which the President held on to Halleck, he thought the present general-in-chief might be the lucky man.

Washburne attempted to close the debate; he said he believed the war would not be ended until Grant was placed in supreme command. In reply to murmurs from the members he shouted: "I can't wait. I want this now. Grant must fight out this war, and he will never leave the field!" Washburne's patience fairly broke down when [Kellian] Whaley of West Virginia wanted to know if the conferring of this rank upon Grant would make that general ineligible for the presidency. Washburne bounced up, white with rage, and charged that the House was afraid to call for the previous question, as members would have to go upon the record in this matter; and he darkly hinted of another record to be made up thereafter which they could not dodge. To Boutwell of Massachusetts, who offered some opposition to the bill, Washburne retorted that New England was showing her sectional feeling in the matter because Grant was a Western man. Amid great heat and considerable excitement, the bill was finally passed by a vote of 86 to 41. Among the Republicans who voted against the bill were [J.M.] Ashley of Ohio, [George S.] Boutwell of Massachusetts, [John M.] Broomall of Pennsylvania, Henry Winter Davis, Garfield, G. W. Julian of Indiana, William D. Kelley of Pennsylvania, Thaddeus Stevens, and William B. Washburn of Massachusetts. The bill passed the Senate without much debate on February twenty-sixth, and three days later it was approved by the President.

If there was any doubt as to the popularity of Grant in Washington (and he was disposed to regard that city as a place of snares), the arrival of the newly-created lieutenant-general effectually dissipated it. He had been called to the capital, and arrived there late in the afternoon of March 8, 1864. He quietly went to Willard's Hotel to get his dinner. At that time he was a rather slightly built man, with stooping shoulders, mild blue eyes, and light-brown hair, with a reddish tinge in his bristling moustache. He had a shy but manly bearing, wore a shabby-looking military suit of clothes, and seemed distressed when he was recognized by the mob of diners. He had been discovered there taking his dinner just like ordinary mortals; and it was noised about that the hero of Belmont, Donnelson, and Vicksburg was in the room. A slight commotion presently spread from table to table; people got up and craned their necks in an anxious endeavor to see "the coming man." Then some enthusiastic admirer, mounting a chair, called for "three cheers for Lieutenant-General Grant." They were given with a will, amid a pounding on the tables which made everything dance. For a few minutes there was a scene of wild confusion, in the midst of which General Grant, looking very much astonished and perhaps annoyed, rose to his feet, awkwardly rubbed his moustache with his napkin, bowed, and resumed his seat and attempted to finish his dinner. The good sense of the cheering patriots prevailed, and the general was allowed to eat in peace. But as soon as he had finished his repast, and was on his way out of the dining-room, he was taken in hand by Representative [James K.] Moorhead of Pennsylvania, who acted as master of ceremonies, and introduced to the general the mob of admirers who now swooped down upon him. This was his first levee.

That evening, as it chanced, was the occasion of the usual weekly reception at the White House, and thither General Grant went by special invitation. Thither too went throngs of people when it was known that he would be on view with the President. So great was the crowd, and so wild the rush to get near the general, that he was obliged at last to mount a sofa, where he could be seen, and where he was secure, at least for a time, from the madness of the multitude. People were caught up and whirled in the torrent which swept through the great East Room. Ladies suffered dire disaster in the crush and confusion; their laces were torn and crinolines mashed; and many got upon sofas, chairs, and tables to be out of harm's way or to get a better view of the spectacle. It was the only real mob I ever saw in the White House. It was an indescribable scene of curiosity, joy, and pleasure. For once at least the President of the United States was not the chief figure in the picture. The little, scared-looking man who stood on a crimson-covered sofa was the idol of the hour. He remained on view for a short time; then he was quietly smuggled out by friendly hands, and next day departed from the city, which he then appeared to dread so much, to begin the last and mightiest chapter in his military career.

It is probable that Grant's early dislike and suspicion of

Washington and its alleged pernicious political influences were partly due to Sherman's positive belief that the national capital was a hot-bed of intrigue and chicane. I learned as much from the general's own lips long after the war, and after his two terms of the Presidency had given him other views of the city and its influence in public affairs. Sherman repeatedly warned Grant against what he considered its baleful moral miasma. During the summer succeeding his appointment as lieutenant-general, Grant did not come often to Washington, although his headquarters were for most of the time within a day's journey of the capital. Later in that year, armed with a letter of introduction from the President, I met him at City Point, while I was on a visit to the Army of the Potomac. [City Point, near the James River, is north of Petersburg, Va.]

At that time his headquarters were at City Point. On one side of his wall-tent stood the great commander's narrow bedstead; and a rude pine-table covered with maps and papers, two or three camp-chairs, a military chest, and a box or two, made up the furniture of the headquarters of Grant. The cares of the day were over when we paid our visit, and the general began an easy, offhand talk about politics and the then late elections, which he considered as being of immense importance because, as he said, the political legislation of Congress was now so closely allied to the prosecution of the war that every officer watched its course with the deepest anxiety. He spoke pleasantly of McClellan, was sorry for his personal mortification and defeat for the presidency, and said that he hoped that McClellan would see his way clear to accept the handsome salary that it was then reported had been offered him by the Illinois Central Railroad Company. Grant was evidently very well informed as to the antecedents and political record of nearly all of the congressmen, especially those from the West; and he spoke with evident pride of his own congressional district (Washburne's) in Illinois, which had lately given nine thousand majority for the Union ticket. Offering us cigars, he alluded jocularly to his national notoriety for smoking, and said that this had made him somewhat uncomfortable, as he did not want to be regarded as greatly addicted to any one personal habit, and that he had lately limited himself to four cigars a day. One of our party, who did not perhaps know that information as to the numerical force of an army was regarded as "contraband of war," innocently asked General Grant how many men he had in the Army of the Potomac, to which the general frankly responded, "Oh, a great many," an observation which closed inquiry in that direction.

Grant's famous expression, "I propose to fight it out on this line, if it takes all summer," was first made public in a little speech extorted from the President a few days after the final battle of the Wilderness. The general, in a letter to General Halleck dated May 11, 1864, had used the now historic phrase; and in the evening of the day on which that letter was received Washington had broken loose with a tremendous demonstration of joy over the recent victories achieved by the Army of the Potomac. There was something like delirium in the air. Everybody seemed to think that the war was coming to an end right away. Congress was in nominal session only, an adjournment being taken every three days, and the city was still filled with congressmen anxious "to be in at the death," as they fondly thought they soon would be.

About nine o'clock on the evening referred to a great crowd of cheering citizens surged around the White House, and the President came to the main door of the mansion, and stood bareheaded on the platform of the portico. He congratulated the people on the brighter prospects of the cause of the Union, and gave them the pith of General Grant's latest letter to Halleck. For a time it appeared as if most people thought that Grant would close the war and enter Richmond before the autumn leaves began to fall. Yet it was a full month after that day— on June 14 [1864]—that the President, regretfully viewing the unreasonable elation of friends of the Union, said to me: "I wish, when you write or speak to people, you would do all you can to correct the impression that the war in Virginia will end right off and victoriously. To me the most trying thing of all this war is that the people are too sanguine; they expect too much at once. I declare to you, sir, that we are to-day farther ahead than I thought, one year and a half ago, that we should be; and yet there are plenty of people who believe that the war is about to be substantially closed. As God is my judge, I shall be satisfied if we are over with the fight in Virginia within a year. I hope we shall be 'happily disappointed,' as the saying is; but I am afraid not—I am afraid not."

The solemn manner of the President, and the weightiness of his utterance, so impressed me that I drew toward me a sheet of paper and wrote down his words then and there. Then I read to him what I had written, in order that I might be sure that he was correctly reported. He suggested a verbal change, and I carried the paper away with me. At that time the art of interviewing had not been invented.

V

Two War-time Conventions

"CASTINE" was a more radical Republican than his President. He did not merely report objectively; few if any reporters did in those days of party-affiliated newspapers. He made no effort to suppress his feelings about Lincoln's renomination. Lincoln teased Brooks about the second place on the ticket, recognizing that Brooks was for another "New England man," Vice President Hamlin. Even in front of Brooks, Lincoln was careful not to express an opinion about the Vice-Presidency. The feeling among pro-Lincoln politicians was that a Border State man was needed. Brooks quotes Lincoln as saying, "Andy Johnson, I think, is a good man."

But the party splitters were at work in '64, as they had maneuvered against the Rail Splitter in '60. There were enough disgruntled generals around to choose from, some with only half their reputations shot away. In the Cabinet a candidate worked on his own behalf; but Mr. Chase had tripped himself by too flagrant politicking. The Republican wheel horses moved obliquely this time, for their candidate was a President who, to the public eye, watched the war more closely than the convention hall. On June 7, 1864, the Republicans met in Baltimore. The temporary chairman was Robert J. Breckinridge, Kentucky. "Does any man doubt," he asked, "that Abraham Lincoln shall be the nominee?" The delegates roared their approval. Henry J. Raymond of *The New York Times* served as chairman of the convention's platform committee. The roll call showed all votes for Lincoln, except 22 for Grant (the Missouri delegation); and later it was made unanimous.

When it came the Democrats' turn for convention, Brooks was told by Lincoln: "They must nominate a Peace Democrat on a war platform, or a War Democrat on a peace platform; and I personally can't say that I care much which they do." At the Cleveland convention of the Radical Democracy, General Frémont was nominated for President on a platform of a one-term Presidency, with reconstruction of the States to be left up to Congress —a strange convention united in its desire not to see Lincoln attain a second term. Frémont, for whom Lincoln had campaigned in '56, in accepting, declared that he did so to obviate Lincoln's second term.

The nomination of another general took place at Chicago, August 29, 1864. It was obvious that General McClellan, although a war leader and a war candidate, would get the nomination of the Democratic convention. "People wondered," said Brooks, "how the advocates of peace would arrange to square their war candidate on a peace platform." The results of the election itself proved that the Democratic contradictions were apparent, that the people wanted Lincoln again.

POLITICAL discussion in Washington during the months immediately preceding the second nomination of Lincoln was exceedingly animated. Although, as we afterward found, the country at large really thought of no name but Lincoln's, Washington politicians were all agog over a variety of compromises that would placate the ultra-radicals of the Republican party, and keep in line the conservatives. Frémont had been nominated at a hybrid convention in Cleveland, Ohio; and the enemies and unfriendly critics of the Lincoln administration were predicting all sorts of disasters, political and military, if the President were "forced upon the people." The commonest forecast of the situation made by these pessimists was that if the military movements of 1864 were successful, Grant would be the next

President; if they were unsuccessful, neither Grant nor Lincoln could be elected that year.

The Democrats, on the other hand, were irreconcilably divided. Although they were noticeably quiet during the weeks preceding the assembling of the Union Republican National Convention at Baltimore that summer, it was clear that the "Peace" and "War" factions of the party could not possibly be made to harmonize. The two hostile camps occasionally fired a shot at each other even in the infrequent sittings of Congress. S. S. Cox was one of the more talkative and vivacious representatives who led the War Democrats pledged to the cause of McClellan, and Fernando Wood was the acknowledged leader in Congress of the Peace faction, whose affections were fixed on Horatio Seymour.

The night before the meeting of the Baltimore Convention I had a long conversation with the President in regard to the probable action of that body. He requested me to come to him when I should return from Baltimore, and bring him the odd bits of political gossip that I might pick up in the convention, and which, as he said, would not get into the newspapers. I had hoped to see Mr. Hamlin renominated, and had anxiously given Mr. Lincoln many opportunities to say whether he preferred the renomination of the Vice-President; but he was craftily and rigidly non-committal, knowing, as he did, what was in my mind concerning Mr. Hamlin. He would refer to the matter only in the vaguest phrase, as, "Mr. Hamlin is a very good man," or, "You, being a New Englander, would naturally like to see Mr. Hamlin renominated; and you are quite right," and so on. By this time Lincoln's renomination was an absolute certainty, and he cheerfully conceded that point without any false modesty. But he could not be induced to express any opinion on the subject of the selection of a candidate for Vice-President. He did go so far as to say that he hoped that the convention would declare in favor of the constitutional amendment abolishing slavery as one of the articles of the party faith. But beyond that, nothing.

I may say here that when I returned from the convention I made a verbal report to the President, and entertained him with an account of some of its doings of which he had not previously heard; and he was then willing to admit that he would have been gratified if Mr. Hamlin could have been renominated. But he said: "Some of our folks [referring, as I believed, to Republican leaders] had expressed the opinion that it would be wise to take a War Democrat as candidate for Vice-President, and that, if possible, a Border State man should be the nominee." Mr. Lincoln appeared to have accepted the result, saying, "Andy Johnson, I think, is a good man." Nevertheless, I have always been confident that Lincoln, left to himself, would have chosen that the old ticket of 1860—Lincoln and Hamlin— should be placed in the field. It is reasonable to suppose that he had resolved to leave the convention entirely free in its choice of a candidate for the second place on the ticket.

The convention which assembled in Baltimore June 7, 1864, was not fortunate in its presiding officers. Ex-Governor E. D. Morgan of New York, as chairman of the National Committee, called the convention to order, but did not long remain in the chair, for which he had no marked aptitude. The temporary chairman was the Rev. R. J. Breckinridge, of Kentucky; he had a weak voice and an irresolute manner, and though he made a clear and logical speech on taking the chair, and was received with a whirlwind of the most boisterous applause, he was unable to make himself heard when the business of organization began, and the vast crowd that filled the Front Street Theater was unruly and restive under renewed delays. When the States were called upon to present the names of their delegates, Missouri appeared, as usual, with rival delegations. Another bone of contention was the claim of Tennessee, then in an inchoate condition, to be admitted to participation in the doings of the convention. Horace Maynard made a stirring speech in which he plaintively urged that "long-suffering and much-enduring Tennessee be admitted to this national council." The temper of the convention was readily manifest when the radical delegation from Missouri and the Tennessee petitioners were both admitted to seats in the convention. The cheering that greeted the consummation of these two acts was something tremendous. It was evident that the Missouri radicals, after all, had a strong hold upon the delegates who represented the loyal States in the Union. But it was noted with some degree of acrimony that when the claims of Tennessee came up for consideration, the Missourians, who had only just squeezed in, were solidly against allowing Tennessee that recognition which they had secured for themselves. It was perhaps this evidence of selfishness that induced the convention subsequently to admit also the conservative delegation from Missouri, thus giving both sides equal rights on the floor. As the persecuted State of Tennessee finally had permission to cast her fifteen votes in the convention, this was regarded as a marked indication of the preference of the convention for Andrew Johnson for Vice-President. New England, preferring Hamlin, had naturally voted against the admission of the Tennessee delegation. Later on it was seen that Missouri well-nigh prevented the final action of the convention from being unanimous. Of the other Southern States then in rebellion, South Carolina, Florida, Virginia, Louisiana, and Arkansas sent delegates to the convention; but as South Carolina, Florida, and Virginia had not taken any steps whatever toward reviving a State government, their delegates were not admitted; those of Louisiana and Arkansas, however, by a vote substantially identical with that which opened the door for Tennessee, obtained recognition in the convention.

The permanent chairman of the convention was Ex-Governor [William] Dennison of Ohio. He made a short speech, but he was not a vigorous or cool-headed presiding officer. Whenever a wave of excitement produced confusion in the convention, the chairman apparently lost his head, and showed inability to control the storm; and many a storm there was before the convention finished its business. But the most terrific contests were made when sundry well-meaning persons were almost ready to fly at one another's throats in their anxiety to have the honor of nominating Abraham Lincoln for the Presidency. As one sat on the platform, looking over the tempest-tossed assemblage, watching with amusement the frantic efforts of a score of men to climb over one another's heads, as it were, and snatch for themselves this inestimable privilege, one could not help thinking of the frequently repeated assertion of certain small politicians that Lincoln could not possibly be nominated by that convention. The most conspicuous claimants for the honor of naming Lincoln were Simon Cameron of Pennsylvania, Governor [William M.] Stone of Iowa, B. C. Cook of Illinois, and Thompson Campbell of California. The last-named gentleman, who had known Lincoln intimately during his young manhood in Springfield, Illinois, was especially desirious that he might be permitted to speak for Illinois, California, and his own native State—Kentucky. This had been virtually agreed upon, but before he could secure the floor, Simon Cameron got in ahead of him, and sent up to the clerk's desk a written resolution which he demanded should be read. When the clerk opened the paper and read its contents, it was found that the resolution demanded the renomination of Abraham Lincoln of Illinois and Hannibal Hamlin of Maine. No sooner had the clerk finished reading the resolution than a frightful clamor shook the hall. Almost every delegate was on his feet objecting or hurrahing, or in other ways making his emotions and his wishes known in stentorian tones. For a few minutes pandemonium reigned, and in the midst of it Cameron stood with his arms folded, grimly smiling, regarding with composure the storm that he had raised. After the turmoil had spent itself, Henry J. Raymond, of New York [chairman of the platform committee], in an incisive, clear-cut speech, ad-

vocated making nominations by a call of States. He urged that
as entire unanimity in the choice of the Presidential candidate
was expected, the moral effect would be better if no noisy accla-
mation were made, which would give slanderers an opportunity
to say that the nomination was rushed through by the overwhelming of all opposition, however small. Before the applause which
followed the adoption of Raymond's resolution had entirely
subsided, B. C. Cook of Illinois mounted a settee and cried:
"Illinois once more presents to the nation the name of Abraham Lincoln—God bless him!" Another roar of applause swept
through the theater, and Stone of Iowa succeeded in gaining his
point by seconding Cook's nomination; but Thompson Campbell
of California, who had been unfairly deprived of his coveted
privilege of making the nomination, leaped upon a settee and
addressed the chair. He was constantly interrupted with catcalls
and cries of "No speeches," "Get down," "Dry up," and "Call
the roll," etc. In the midst of the confusion, however, Campbell,
who was a tall, spare man with a saturnine visage and tremendous lung power, kept on speaking in dumb show, wildly ges-
ticulating, not a word of his speech being audible. Campbell
was evidently beside himself with rage and disappointment;
but those nearest him finally succeeded in coaxing him off his
perch, and he sat down sullen with anger.

That was a business convention, and when the roll-call began, Maine simply announced its sixteen votes for Abraham
Lincoln. New Hampshire, coming next, attempted to ring in
a little speech with its vote, but was summarily choked off with
cries of "No speeches," and the call proceeded in an orderly
manner, no delegation venturing to make any other announcement than that of its vote. The convention struck a snag when
Missouri was reached, and the chairman of the united delegations made a brief speech in which he said that the radical
delegation was under positive instructions to cast its 22 votes
for U. S. Grant; that he and his associates would support any

nominee of the convention, but they must obey orders from home. This caused a sensation, and growls of disapproval arose from all parts of the convention; for it was evident that this unfortunate complication might prevent a unanimous vote for Lincoln. The Missouri radical delegates, it should be understood, had been chosen many weeks before the nomination of Lincoln became inevitable. There never was any recall of the instructions given at a time when it was apparently among the possibilities that another than Lincoln might be the nominee of the National Convention. When the clerk of the convention announced the result of the roll-call, it was found that Abraham Lincoln had 507 votes and U. S. Grant 22 votes. Thereupon Mr. Hume, chairman of the Missouri delegation, immediately moved that the nomination be declared unanimous. This was done. Straightway the long-pent-up enthusiasm burst forth in a scene of the wildest confusion. Men hurrahed, embraced one another, threw up their hats, danced in the aisles or on the platform, jumped on the benches, waved flags, yelled, and committed every possible extravagance to demonstrate the exuberance of their joy. One of the most comical sights which I beheld was that of Horace Maynard and Henry J. Raymond alternately hugging each other and shaking hands, apparently unable to utter a word, so full of emotion were they. And when the big brass band burst out with "Hail, Columbia!" the racket was so intolerable that I involuntarily looked up to see if the roof of the theater were not lifted by the volume of sound. When quiet was restored, and other business was about to be resumed, the band again struck up "Yankee Doodle" in its liveliest manner, and another torrent of enthusiasm broke forth; and it was a long time before the excited and jubilant assemblage could be quieted down and order restored. In those days the mere sight of the American flag, or the sound of a national melody, would stir an assembly to fever-heat.

The chairman caused to be read a despatch addressed to

him by the Secretary of War, giving a favorable account of the military situation, and news of Hunter's victory in the Shenandoah Valley, all of which was received with applause. Thereupon the Rev. T. H. Pearne, of Oregon, read a despatch from his State announcing the result of the general election there on the previous day, which was a Union victory. The cheering again burst forth, and for a time it looked as though no other business but making announcements and "bursting into applause" would be done that day. But the convention finally got down to work, and when the Indiana delegates presented the name of Andrew Johnson for Vice-President, Stone, of Iowa, seconded the nomination, and Horace Maynard made a little speech in favor of the same. Simon Cameron nominated Hamlin without any speech; Kentucky presented General [Lovell H.] Rousseau; and Lyman Tremaine, in behalf of a portion of the New York delegation, presented the name of Daniel S. Dickinson. The popular demand for a War Democrat had induced some of the New Yorkers to present Dickinson's name; but it was well known that most of the New York delegates favored Hamlin, and their argument was that if Seward was to remain in the cabinet it could hardly be expected that a New Yorker would be made Vice-President. There was much buttonholing and wire-pulling while the vote was being taken, and before it was officially announced: but of the 520 votes cast Andrew Johnson had 202, Hannibal Hamlin 150, Daniel S. Dickinson 109, Benjamin F. Butler 28, and 31 votes were scattering; so there was no choice. As Johnson was considerably in the lead of all other candidates, his nomination was made certain by Kentucky, which, having paid its compliments to General Rousseau, threw its 22 votes for Andrew Johnson, with much *empressement* on the part of the spokesman of the delegation. Oregon, having given its five votes to Schuyler Colfax, followed the lead of Kentucky. Then Pennsylvania, amid the greatest excitement of that episode of the convention, threw a solid vote of 52 for the

Tennesseean, and Andrew Johnson was declared the nominee of the convention, applause, cheering, and much enthusiasm greeting the final announcement.

The next evening, when I called on the President at home, I was astonished by his jokingly rallying me on my failure to send him word of his nomination. It appeared that nobody had apparently thought it worth while to telegraph him the result of the balloting for the Presidential nominee of the convention. Probably each one of the many men who would have been glad to be the sender of pleasant tidings to the President had thought that some other man would surely anticipate him by a telegram of congratulation. In the confusion that reigned in the convention nobody went to the wires that were led into the building but the alert newspaper men, who thought only of their own business.

It turned out that the President, having business at the War Department, met Major Eckert, superintendent of the military bureau of telegraphs, who congratulated him on his nomination. "What! Am I renominated?" asked the surprised chief. When assured that this had been done, Mr. Lincoln expressed his gratification, and asked Major Eckert if he would kindly send word over to the White House when the name of the candidate for Vice-President should have been agreed upon. Lincoln, later on, was informed by Major Eckert that Johnson had been nominated, and (as the President himself subsequently told me) made an exclamation that emphatically indicated his disappointment thereat. Major Eckert afterward confirmed this statement with a hearty laugh.

While we were talking over some of the curious details of the convention (Lincoln being especially sorry for his friend Thompson Campbell's disappointment), a band came to the White House, and a messenger brought up the information that the members of the Ohio delegation to the Baltimore Convention desired to pay their respects to the President, whereupon he

went down to the door, hat in hand, and when the cheering and
music had subsided, spoke as follows:

GENTLEMEN: I am very much obliged to you for this com-
pliment. I have just been saying, and as I have just said it, I will
repeat it: The hardest of all speeches which I have to make is an
answer to a serenade. I never know what to say on such occasions.
I suppose that you have done me this kindness in connection with
the action of the Baltimore Convention which has recently taken
place, with which, of course, I am very well satisfied. [Laughter
and applause.] What we want still more than Baltimore Conventions or presidential elections is success under General Grant. [Cries
of "Good!" and applause.] I propose that you constantly bear in
mind that the support you owe to the brave officers and soldiers in
the field is of the very first importance, and we should bend all our
energies to that point. Now, without detaining you any longer, I
propose that you help me to close up what I am now saying with
three rousing cheers for General Grant and the officers and soldiers
under his command.

The President's request was acceded to, and three rousing
cheers were given, Lincoln himself leading off, and waving his
hat as enthusiastically as anybody else.

During the afternoon of the same day, the committee appointed by the convention to wait upon the President and notify
him of his nomination was received in the East Room of the
White House, and Ex-Governor Dennison of Ohio, president of
the convention, made a very good little speech, and presented
Lincoln with an engrossed copy of the resolutions adopted by the
convention. The President appeared to be deeply affected by
the address, and with considerable emotion and solemnity accepted the nomination in a short speech, in which he referred
to pending propositions of amnesty, and to such an amendment
to the Constitution as became a fitting and natural conclusion
to the final success of the Union cause. His last words, referring

to the amendment to the Constitution abolishing slavery, were: "Now, the unconditional Union men, North and South, perceive its importance and embrace it. In the joint names of Liberty and Union, let us labor to give it legal form and practical effect."

CONTENTION OVER RECONSTRUCTION PLANS

Yet, within a month from that happy and jubilant time, everything was once more in confusion in Washington, and the political skies were again darkened by clouds returning after the rain. Between the notable events of the nomination of Lincoln at Baltimore and of McClellan at Chicago, there intervened the publication [in the *New York Tribune,* August 5, 1864] of what is known in history as the Wade-Davis manifesto [which reprimanded Lincoln for "encroachments of the Executive on the authority of Congress"]. This incident in the long struggle over Southern reconstruction—a struggle that extended into the administration of Andrew Johnson—was almost inevitable when it is considered that the radicals in Congress were greatly dissatisfied with the outlines of the reconstruction policy of President Lincoln, as these appeared in his message of the previous year (1863). The pivotal point in the discussion then going on was, Are the States lately in rebellion in the Union or out of the Union? The Republican party was divided on this question, a portion contending that the so-called acts of secession were inoperative in every respect; while others, in theory and practice, appeared to assume that those States had been outside of the Union, and had been conquered and brought back. On such refinements of reasoning a dangerous schism was opened in the party that was expected to support Lincoln in that canvass.

Senator Sumner was one of those who received the President's message of 1863 with undisguised impatience, and who subsequently found fault with his reconstruction speech made in answer to a serenade at the end of the war. Although it has been said that Mr. Sumner was not displeased with that message, it is certain that he expressed himself to his friends with some warmth, descanting on the President's omission to say whether the rebel States were in or out of the Union. While the message was being read, Sumner listened attentively until he saw its drift, and then he apparently withdrew his attention from the reading, and in a boyish and petulant manner slammed his books and documents about his desk and upon the floor, and generally exhibited his ill-temper to an astonished and admiring gallery. Later on in that session a bill was introduced in the House by Henry Winter Davis in which were embodied the notions of the radical Republicans. In brief, Mr. Lincoln's policy was to build up a civil government in each State as soon as military resistance should disappear; and, under the authority of military governors to be appointed by him, to develop the nucleus of an orderly government, whose powers and authority should be submitted to Congress for recognition. The scheme of Henry Winter Davis and his friends was to provide for the appointment of a provisional governor (a civil officer) in each of the States lately in rebellion, under whose authority a majority of the white male citizens of the State should elect delegates to a convention to reëstablish a State government. The new constitution which should be adopted by such a convention was to provide three things—exclusion of military and civil officers of the Confederacy, the abolition of slavery, and the total repudiation of all rebel debts.

This bill was in direct opposition to the well-known plans and opinions of Lincoln, and could not be made to square with his plan of reconstruction, the details of which were already well understood. Nevertheless, the measure did not awaken much opposition among the Unionist members of Congress, and was opposed by the Democrats only on general principles. Singularly enough, although Henry Winter Davis had been steadily hostile to every policy favored by Lincoln, nobody seemed to think that this extraordinary scheme would be disapproved by the President, or that the friends of the administration ought to be shy of any proposition which came from a man who was constantly bristling with hostility to Lincoln's political ideas. Davis was a singularly alert and singularly violent politician. In his speeches advocating the passage of his bill he imputed low motives to the President, and treated his scheme of reconstruction, outlined in the amnesty proclamation and the message of December, 1863, with frank contempt. This was in exact accord with the rash and egotistical course which Davis pursued in regard to any man or any measure that did not receive his full approbation. For example, Assistant-Secretary Fox of the Navy Department had in some way incurred Davis's enmity, and in one of his diatribes against the alleged inefficiency of the Navy, Davis disposed of the fight between the *Monitor* and the *Merrimac* as follows: "The *Monitor* accidentally came into Hampton Roads as the *Merrimac* was trying to destroy, as it had already destroyed, some of our vessels. The collision took place; neither fleet was destroyed; neither vessel was sunk; neither party was whipped, as the boys say; and the country ran wild over two guns in a cheese-box having done anything." Extravagances like this injured the reputation of Davis for statesmanship, and should have put the friends of Lincoln on their guard when Davis formulated his policy for the reconstruction of the Southern States. Lincoln was unwilling to lay down a hard-and-fast rule to be applied to each State as it should be brought once more into Federal relations with the other States of the Union. Davis's plan contemplated restricting the President to one iron-bound scheme applicable to each and all of the States. His bill, after much speech-making on both sides of the House, went over to the Senate in the summer of 1864. It was almost immediately passed, but with some amendments; was sent back to the House; and was ready for the signature of the President just before Congress adjourned on July fourth of that year.

The last days of a congressional session are characterized by confusion which would turn the head of any one unused to this fantastic turmoil; and the end of that particular session was unusually noisy and chaotic. Many bills of importance were pitchforked into shape at the last moment, and were tossed between the Senate and the House even to the latest hour of the session. Both branches of Congress had agreed to adjourn at twelve o'clock on July fourth; but the Senate, which was inextricably mixed up with important and unfinished business, importuned the House to extend the session ten minutes. This was done three times, so that the final hour of adjournment did not arrive until half-past twelve o'clock on that day. Great interest was felt in an important bill to amend the Pacific Railroad Act. This bill virtually increased the compensation of the railroad builders, and in other ways enhanced their interests. It was finally dragged through, but two other measures of more importance failed. One of these was Washburne's Whisky Tax Bill, and another was a bill to establish a commission for the purpose of ascertaining the public financial resources, and the best means of levying judicious taxation on the same. It was noticeable, however, that notwithstanding the fact that many bills of national import failed to get through, there was no failure of a bill which gave every member of the Thirty-ninth Congress a complete set of the *Congressional Globe* from the beginning of its publication until the close of that Congress.

Ten minutes before the hour of adjournment had arrived, pages darted to and fro with messages and bills, and engrossing clerks rushed madly about with sheets of parchment for the signatures of Speaker and clerk. Cabinet ministers were numerous on the floor of the House, and lobbyists in the general disorder slipped in through the doors and buttonholed members, while the mill of legislation slowly ground out its last grist. The President was signing bills in the room set apart for his use in the Senate wing of the Capitol, being attended from time to time during the morning by members of his cabinet. As the hands of the clock drew near the fateful hour of adjournment, it was suddenly whispered about the House that the President had so far failed to sign the Wade-Davis Reconstruction Bill. Men held their breath at this unexpected turn of affairs, and asked, "Will he send in a veto message, or will he pocket it?" It was, of course, too late to think of a veto message, and the general opinion of those who believed that the bill would not receive his sanction was that he would give it a pocket veto. Now for the first time men who had not seriously opposed the passage of the reconstruction bill began to wish that it had never gone to the President; but all was uncertainty, and although it was the supreme moment, the reading clerk was droning forth in occasional fragments the Declaration of Independence, which somebody had demanded should be read. Most of the members and Senators appeared to forget their petty jobs and schemes in the all-absorbing question, What will the President do with the reconstruction bill? Finally messages from the Senate and from the President informed the House that no further communications were to be expected from them, and Speaker Colfax, in a few pleasant words, dismissed the members to their homes, and declared the session ended. In the disorder which followed, Davis standing at his desk, pale with wrath, his bushy hair tousled, and wildly brandishing his arms, denounced the President in good set terms. It was known at last that the bill had failed to receive the President's signature. Congress had adjourned, leaving the great scheme of Wade, Davis, and their co-laborers a mass of ruins.

This event, in the minds of those who were in at the death of that session, looms up more conspicuously in the history of that July 4, 1864, than any other that had lately occurred in Washington. I certainly was astonished to hear the bitter denunciations heaped upon the head of President Lincoln by some of the radical Senators and Representatives. Pomeroy, of Kansas, was of course exceedingly wrathful and sarcastic; and he went around saying, "I told you so." The Missourians were unexpectedly quiet, and Senator Gratz Brown, who had all along taken a somewhat conservative view of the matter, expressed himself as being well satisfied with the ultimate fate of the bill. Among those whom I heard express great disappointment and sharp disapproval of the President's "pocket veto" was Representative Garfield. But these malcontents soon poured out of the doors of the Capitol on all sides, leaving the gilded and decorated halls to loneliness and dusky splendor. They betook their complaints, their congratulations, their hopes and fears, to their own homes, and the first session of the Thirty-eighth Congress ended in a curious condition of unrest and dissatisfaction.

Political matters were lost sight of when, very soon after the adjournment of Congress, the capital was threatened by Early on his famous raid [General Early led his raiders down the Shenandoah Valley; arrived before Washington's fortifications on July eleventh; escaped across the Upper Potomac into Virginia two days later]; but the excitement of that brief beleaguering having passed away, the publication of a letter signed by Senator Wade and Representative Davis criticizing the President with severity, again created a lively condition of things in national politics. The letter appeared on August fifth. It is needless to recall the points of that now historic document. Its appearance created something like a panic in the ranks of the President's supporters. It was the work of two members of his own party. It was at first said that it was written by James A. Garfield, and on the strength of that report his renomination for Congress was subsequently in danger. Garfield, however, although he frankly acknowledged that he was in sympathy with the signers of the manifesto, flatly declared that he had nothing to do with its production. It was generally understood that Henry Winter Davis was the author of the document, and it certainly bore evidence of his well-known skill in the art of putting things. Upon President Lincoln this letter, which was addressed to "the supporters of the Government," had a most depressing effect. Four days after Congress adjourned he had issued a proclamation, and had embodied in that document a copy of the Wade-Davis bill as it passed Congress, and had given his reasons for withholding from it his approval. This proclamation had been generally received with every sign of popular satisfaction, and the Wade-Davis manifesto, coming as it did afterward like a thunderbolt out of a clear sky, threw politicians of every stamp into the wildest confusion. The address imputed to the President the meanest of motives, and insinuated very broadly that his policy of reconstruction was the natural outcome of his intense desire to be reëlected. It was this unjust suggestion that cut Lincoln to the heart. A day or two after the Wade-Davis manifesto appeared, Lincoln, in conversation with me, said: "To be wounded in the house of one's friends is perhaps the most grievous affliction that can befall a man. I have tried my best to meet the wishes of this man [Davis], and to do my whole duty by the country." Later on in the same conversation, while lamenting with sincere grief the implacable hostility which Henry Winter Davis had manifested, he said that Davis's pride of opinion led him to say and do things of which he (Lincoln) was certain in his own private judgment his (Davis's) conscience could not approve. When I said that it sometimes seemed as though Davis was mad, Lincoln replied, "I have heard that there was insanity in his family; perhaps we might allow the plea in this case." It was this attack upon him, apparently so needless and so unprofitable, and so well calculated to disturb the harmony of the Union party, that grieved the President more than the framing and the passage of the bill; but commenting in his own shrewd way on that bill, Lincoln said that he had somewhere read of a robber tyrant who had built an iron bedstead on which he compelled his victims to lie. If the captive was too short to fill the bedstead, he was stretched by main force until he was long enough; and if he was too long, he was chopped off to fit the bedstead. This, Lincoln thought, was the sort of reconstruction which the Wade-Davis plan contemplated. If any State coming back into Federal relations did not fit the Wade-Davis bedstead, so much the worse for the State. Lincoln's habitual diffidence in quoting erudite or classic sayings usually induced him to refer to such stories in this vague way; and although he probably knew very well who Procustes was, he slurred over the illustration as something of which he had remotely heard.

As a matter of record, I may as well say here that at the next and last session of that Congress—the Thirty-eighth—Davis reintroduced his pet measure; and after it had been amended considerably, it was finally tabled February 21, 1865, in spite of the fiery speech which its distinguished author made in its favor. Although the bill passed both branches of Congress without serious opposition in the first instance, public opinion had so far changed under Lincoln's guiding hand, eight months later, that it was finally killed by a vote of 91 to 64, which laid it on the table.

THE DARK DAYS OF 1864

In the memory of men who lived in Washington during the months of July and August, 1864, those days will appear to be the darkest of the many dark days through which passed the friends and lovers of the Federal Union. The earlier years of the war, it is true, had been full of grief, despondency, and even agony; but the darkness that settled upon us in the summer of 1864 was the more difficult to be endured because of its unexpectedness. The hopes so buoyantly entertained by our people when Grant opened his campaign in Virginia had been dashed. No joyful tidings came from the Army now; a deadly calm prevailed where had so lately resounded the shouts of victory.

In every department of the Government there was a manifest feeling of discouragement. In the field of national politics confusion reigned.

When Congress adjourned on July fourth, with the Wade-Davis Reconstruction Bill left unsigned, the turmoil inside of the Union Republican party was something terrific; and when, a month later, the Wade-Davis manifesto appeared, the consternation of the Republican leaders was very great. Early's invasion of Maryland and dash upon Washington, which caused a good deal of panic in the country generally, occurred about the middle of July. Right on the heels of this event came the President's call for five hundred thousand men, which was issued July eighteenth, and then the placing of another great loan, which dropped upon the people about the same time. Nor was the military situation any more cheerful. The awful fighting in the Wilderness and at Cold Harbor had fairly startled the country by the enormous loss of life sustained by the Army of the Potomac, apparently without any corresponding gain of position. The failure of the Petersburg mine, July thirtieth, was another addition to the burden carried in the hearts of patriotic Americans. [A mine had been set under the Confederate lines which, at first, killed over 275 of the enemy, but the crater became a death pit for charging Union soldiers.] Chase's resignation of the secretaryship of the Treasury, and the muddle which Horace Greeley had succeeded in creating by his futile mission to the rebel emissaries at Niagara Falls [he had been used as a dupe by the Confederates, who wished Lincoln's defeat in November '64], had so worried the people that nobody appeared to know what was in the air—a compromise in the interest of peace, or a more vigorous prosecution of the war.

The raid of Early, which occurred in July, 1864, gave us our only serious scare in the national capital, although many alarms were sounded during the war and after the first terrors of the civil insurrection had died away. That incursion of the

dashing rebel hosts was evidently twofold in its purpose, forage
and plunder in Maryland and Pennsylvania being part of the
scheme, while the more important and highly desired purpose
was to seize upon Washington, then left comparatively defense-
less so far as troops were concerned. The news of the approach
of Early was brought to the city (whatever may have been the
information lodged in the War Department) by the panic-
stricken people from Rockville, Silver Spring, Tennallytown,
and other Maryland villages. These people came flocking into
Washington by the Seventh Street road, flying in wild disorder,
and bringing their household goods with them. In a general way
we understood that the city was cut off at the north and east,
and that the famine of market-stuff, New York newspapers,
and other necessaries of life, was due to the cutting of railway
lines leading northward. For two or three days we had no mail,
no telegraphic messages, and no railway travel. Our only communication with the outer world was by steamer from Georgetown, D. C., to New York. Washington was in a ferment; men
were marching to and fro; able-bodied citizens were swept up
and put into the District militia; and squads of department
clerks were set to drilling in the parks. It was an odd sight to
see men who had been thus impressed into the public service,
dressed in linen coats or in partial uniform, being put through
the manual of arms by an impromptu captain, who in turn was
coached by his orderly sergeant (a messenger employed in the
War Department). These sons of Mars were all under command
of Brigadier-general [Peter] Bacon, a worthy grocer of Washington, who was the militia commander of the District of Columbia. The city was also garrisoned by one hundred men, Veteran
Reserves as they were called (or Invalid Corps), with a few dismounted cavalry. The actual garrison of the city, available for
duty and including the Veteran Reserves, one-hundred-day-men,
District militia, and other odds and ends of fighting material,
numbered less than ten thousand effective, and these were mostly

raw men. These weak and unorganized forces were thrown into the fortifications, and Washington stood agape while we listened to the sound of the rebel cannon less than ten miles away. General Halleck was then living on Georgetown Heights, where the blue-coated Invalids mounted guard over his residence, and the bugles nightly blew "tattoo" and "taps." Ill-natured people were ready to suggest that the rebels might be guilty of petty larceny should they rapidly march down Rock Creek and seize upon Halleck, who for various reasons was bitterly unpopular in Washington. The President and his family were at their summer residence, the Soldiers' Home, on the outskirts of Washington, about half-way between the outer line of fortifications at Fort Stevens and the city; but on Sunday night [July 10, 1864], Secretary Stanton, finding that the enemy was within striking distance of that point, sent out a carriage with positive orders that the President should return to the White House. Lincoln, very much irritated, and against his will, came back to town. He was subsequently greatly discomposed and annoyed when he found that the Assistant Secretary of the Navy, Captain G. V. Fox, had kept under orders a small Navy vessel in the Potomac for the President's escape in case the rebel column should succeed in piercing the line of fortifications. The wildest estimates of the force of the invaders were made, and flying rumors were to the effect that Early, Ewell, Imboden, and Breckinridge were in command of some forty thousand men. As a matter of fact, there were, according to the records, not many more than twelve thousand men. There was a vast amount of hurrying to and fro between the War Department, the White House, and the exterior lines of defense, and the telegraph wire was constantly worked to its fullest capacity. There were not a few domestic rebels in Washington who looked on this commotion with undisguised glee.

In Georgetown one nest of secessionists was rudely broken in upon by the provost guard, who discovered a half-finished

Confederate flag in the house. The men were marched over to the guardhouse, and the unfinished colors, probably intended to be presented to Early, were promptly confiscated. This was not the only flag made to be presented to the rebels when they should effect their triumphal entry into Washington. But early on Monday morning part of the Sixth Corps of the Army of the Potomac landed at Washington, having come from the James River in swift transports; another division (James B. Ricketts's) was already in Maryland. The thirteen thousand men landing in Washington were commanded by General Horatio G. Wright. About noon the Nineteenth Corps, under Command of General W. H. Emory, arrived from the Gulf of Mexico by way of Fort Monroe, and Washington breathed more freely.

General Alexander McD. McCook was in command of the troops and fortifications; and General Augur, who at that time was commander of the Department of Washington, had under him all the available men of the District of Columbia, including a considerable number of drafted men from Camp Convalescent at Alexandria. Colonel Wisewell, military governor of the city, had orders to detail all of the able-bodied men in the hospitals; and before the night of Monday, thirty-two hundred fighting men from those institutions, officered, provisioned, and armed, were on their way to the front. "Contraband" Negroes and refugees were also pressed into the service, and at twelve o'clock on the night of July 11 it was estimated that there were within the fortifications of Washington sixty thousand men, armed and equipped for fight. Clearly, the time for a successful assault by the rebel column had passed. But if the invasion of Maryland was designed to create a diversion from Grant's Army, then in front of Richmond, that end was successful; and while a great force of effective men was kept at bay within the defenses of Washington, the bulk of Early's army was busy sweeping up all available plunder, and sending it southward across the Potomac.

It was popularly believed in the North at that time that President Lincoln was greatly disturbed by the imminence of the danger of the capture of Washington; but I learned from his own lips that his chief anxiety was that the invading forces might not be permitted to get away. Speaking of their escape, afterward, he said that General Halleck's manifest desire to avoid taking any responsibility without the immediate sanction of General Grant was the main reason why the rebels, having threatened Washington and sacked the peaceful farms and villages of Maryland, got off scatheless.

If Lincoln was the meddlesome marplot in military affairs which some have represented him to be, he would have peremptorily ordered a sortie of the Union forces, then numerously massed inside the defenses of Washington; but although he was "agonized" (as he said) over the evident failure of all attempts at pursuit, he kept his hands off.

Grant's distance from the scene, Halleck's disinclination to take the responsibility of pursuit, and Lincoln's firm refusal to decide any military question of detail, resulted in the safe departure of Early and his forces. It may as well be said that throughout the long and weary months of the war which followed this panic in Washington, Lincoln frequently referred to the escape of Early as one of the distressing features of his experience in the city of Washington. He went out to Fort Stevens during the skirmish in front of that fortification on July twelfth, and repeatedly exposed himself in the coolest manner to the fire of the rebel sharp-shooters. He had once said to me that he lacked physical courage, although he had a fair share of the moral quality of that virtue; but his calm unconsciousness of danger while the bullets were flying thick and fast about him was ample proof that he would not have dropped his musket and run, as he believed he certainly would, at the first sign of physical danger.

The scene of the desultory fighting in front of Washington

was novel and striking to a party of us (civilians) who surveyed
the field immediately after the rebels had fled. We saw the last
glimpse of the dust which the skedaddling pickets left behind
them as they rode off in the direction of Edwards's Ferry. We
found traces of rebel occupation five or six miles from Washington, where houses had been held by the invaders, the rightful
owners thereof having incontinently fled at the approach of the
enemy. Horses had been picketed in the orchards; fences were
torn down and used for firewood, and books, letters, and women's
wearing-apparel were scattered about the grounds, showing that
the raiders had made the best use of their time in looting the
houses where they had been quartered. In one comfortable family mansion, now in a sad state of wreck, we found such a disorder as might have reigned if a wild Western cyclone had swept
through the building. Furniture was smashed, crockery broken,
and even a handsome piano was split up in the very wantonness
of destruction. Obscene drawings covered the walls, and one
inscription, scrawled with charcoal over the place where the
piano had stood, read, "Fifty thousand Virginian homes have
been devastated in like manner." The houses were littered with
the tattered remnants of butternut-colored uniforms, as if the
invaders had effected that fair exchange which in time of war
is no robbery; and a picturesque disorder reigned in my lady's
chamber, as well as in kitchen and pantry of homes suddenly
vacated at the approach of the rebel soldiery.

It should be said that the panic in Washington, although
tolerably severe among the more uninformed of the residents,
was by no means so utter as people at a distance from the national capital generally supposed; and in Government circles
there was no fear entertained after the first dash had been in-
effectively made by Early's troops. In the country at large,
however, the effect of this demonstration was somewhat depressing. The capital had been threatened; the President's safety
had been imperiled; only a miracle had saved treasures, records,

and archives from the fate that overtook them when Cockburn seized the city during the War of 1812. These were some of the highly colored pictures presented to the people of the United States by alarmists and prophets of disaster during the week of the raid and thereafter. But there was no such frantic panic in Washington.

MCCLELLAN'S NOMINATION AT CHICAGO

At such a time as this the men who were determined on a declaration of "peace at any price" met in Chicago to nominate a candidate for the presidency. The Democratic convention of that year had first been called to meet on July fourth; but the doings of the Cleveland convention, which had nominated Frémont, and those of the Baltimore convention, at which Lincoln had been nominated, probably induced the Democratic managers to postpone the assembling of their convention until a later date—August 29, 1864. By this time it was pretty well settled that McClellan, although a war leader and a war candidate, would be the nominee of the Democratic convention; and people wondered how the advocates of peace would arrange to square their war candidate on a peace platform. A few days before the meeting of the Democratic convention, just prior to my leaving Washington for Chicago, the President said to me: "They must nominate a Peace Democrat on a war platform, or a War Democrat on a peace platform; and I personally can't say that I care much which they do."

About this time, as we now learn from Nicolay and Hay's *History of Lincoln* [the ten-volume work came out in 1890 from the Century Company], the President wrote, sealed, and put aside the following memorandum, which was dated August 23, 1864: "This morning, as for some days past, it seems exceedingly probable that this administration will not be reëlected. Then it will be my duty to so coöperate with the President elect as to save the Union between the election and the inauguration; as he will have secured his election on such ground that he cannot possibly save it afterward." [Lincoln asked his Cabinet to sign the sealed envelope.] On the evening of August twenty-fourth I called on the President to say good-by, as I intended to leave for Chicago the following day; and although Lincoln had already put himself on record as more than doubtful of his own reëlection, he said: "Good-by. Don't be discouraged; I don't believe that God has forsaken us yet." Possibly the good President desired to inspire those whom he met with something of the confidence which he did not himself feel. But, at any rate, he did regard with great interest the doings of the Democrats who were about to nominate their candidate and build their platform. Knowing that I would not return to Washington until a week or two after the convention had adjourned, he asked me to write two or three letters, as the convention should unfold its plans, giving him "some of the political gossip that would not find its way into the newspapers." These letters, of course, I wrote according to his request; and it is a curious illustration of his care for all papers coming into his hands that they were found after his death in his carefully preserved and voluminous private correspondence.

Although the train on which I traveled westward was burdened with many distinguished and jubilant Democratic leaders, it was notable that the most conspicuous person was Congressman Harris of Maryland, who had been censured by the House for so-called treasonable language. It was known that he was on the train, and whenever we stopped—and that was pretty often—the Butternuts yelled vociferously for him. I made his acquaintance, and found him a very companionable person; he frankly said that he found himself much more popu-lar in the West than in Maryland. It had been bruited abroad that McClellan was on our train, and at Plymouth, Indiana, there was a great call for "Little Mac." A Union colonel, going home on furlough, was readily passed off as the redoubtable general by some of the fun-loving Democrats, who were determined that their Indiana compatriots should not be disappointed. The colonel made a very ingenious little speech in the character of McClellan, and was received with tremendous cheers.

When we got to Chicago, and the convention began to assemble in the great wigwam near the lake shore, Vallandigham, Alexander Long, and Representative Harris were the "stars" of the occasion. Calls for them were made at every possible opportunity, and it was easy to see that these eminent Peace Democrats were more popular than any other of the delegates to the convention. It was a noisy assemblage, and it was also a Peace Democratic convention. While Alexander Long was reading a set of resolutions, which he proposed to have the convention adopt, asking for a suspension of the draft until after the election, "Sunset" Cox interfered with a motion to have all resolutions referred, without reading or debate, to the proper committee; whereupon he was roundly hissed, and the spectators, who to the number of thousands filled the pit of the great building, yelled, "Get down, you War Democrat!" much to his discomfiture. The crowd of on-lookers in the pit was so great that many of them climbed up and roosted on a fence which separated them from the delegates, and their weight soon broke down this slender barrier, creating the greatest confusion. Frantic ushers and policemen attempted to preserve order; now and then a train crashing by on the Lake Shore tracks close at hand added to the racket, and filled the huge building with smoke and cinders.

Horatio Seymour, then Governor of New York, was the president of the Chicago convention; and it must be said that he made a much better presiding officer than ex-Governor Dennison had proved himself in the chair of the Republican convention at Baltimore. Seymour was tall, fine-looking, of an imposing figure, with a good though colorless face, bright, dark eyes, a high, commanding forehead, dark-reddish hair, and slightly bald. He had a clear, ringing voice, with a slight imperfection in his speech, and he was in the main an attractive and effective speaker, and a capital presiding officer. His opening address, which was very calm and cool, was not well received by the crowd, who evidently wanted something more heartfiring, and who incessantly shouted, "Vallandigham! Vallandigham!" But the distinguished exile, though he was not far away, was discreet enough to remain out of sight until his time came. His name was presented by the State of Ohio for membership of the committee on platform, and it was well known that the most important plank in that structure—that which related to the prosecution of the war—was his. One of the conspicuous figures in that convention was James Guthrie of Kentucky, a tall, huge-limbed, white-haired man about seventy years old, with a florid complexion, a clear and well-modulated voice, and the general appearance of a well-fed, well-groomed Kentucky gentleman of the old school. Another was Samuel J. Tilden of New York, who took an active part in the business of building the platform, and who surprised all to whom he was a stranger by his agile movements, his fresh, smooth, almost boyish face, and his generally alert manner. When the platform finally came before the convention, late in the afternoon of the second day, the resolution which was greeted with the most vociferous applause was that with which Vallandigham's hand had been busy. This was the famous clause which explicitly declared that "after four years of failure to restore the Union by the experiment of war, during which, under the pretense of a military necessity, or war power higher than the Constitution, the Constitution itself has been disregarded in every part, . . . the public welfare demands that immediate efforts be made for a cessation of hostilities with a view to an ultimate convention of the States, or other peaceable means to the end that at the earliest practicable moment peace may be restored on the basis of the Federal union of the States." This was the peace platform which Lincoln had expected. The war candidate, of course, was soon to be forthcoming. The faces of some of the delegates when the platform was read and adopted were a study. S. S. Cox clasped his hands in his lap and dropped his head, a picture of despair. August Belmont, who was the chairman of the National Committee that year, also looked profoundly sad. But Vallandigham and Alexander Long rubbed their hands with unrestrained glee, and as soon as his famous resolution was adopted the former was surrounded by congratulating friends. It was clear that the returned exile was the hero of the occasion.

When the presidential nominations were finally before the convention, Harris of Maryland took the floor, and attempted to make a speech against McClellan. Although the chairman at first ruled him to be out of order, he went on shrieking and vociferating, denouncing McClellan for his so-called arbitrary arrests in Maryland, and saying that he had initiated tyranny and oppression before Lincoln had. The house rose at Harris as one man, cheering and encouraging him to go on. Promising to speak in order, he went up to the platform, and proceeded with his vituperation and abuse. He insisted that Lincoln had found an assassin of State rights in George B. McClellan, and shrieked, "Will you vote for such a man? I never will!" At this point several War Democrats objected to his proceeding, because, as they very properly said, if he would not promise to support the nominee of the convention, he was not fit to be a member of that body, much less to make a speech to it. He was accordingly ruled out and disappeared from the platform; and as he went back to his seat a New York delegate rose and called him a "traitor." Harris promptly struck his defamer, and for a time there was a scene of general uproar and riotous confusion.

The Maryland delegates as a rule were opposed to McClellan on account of his so-called arbitrary arrests in their State earlier in the war. General [George] Morgan, an Ohio delegate, attempted a defense of McClellan's conduct in Maryland, and said that McClellan would have been a traitor if he had not acted as he did, boldly and promptly, in arresting the conspirators in the Maryland legislature. At this there was a wrathful outburst from the Maryland delegation, who contradicted the Ohioan, and compelled him to diverge from that branch of the discussion.

Alexander Long was another irreconcilable delegate who insisted that freedom of speech had been denied him in this Democratic convention, and who, when indulgently allowed to speak, went on to say that McClellan was "the worst and weakest man" who could be nominated at that time; he begged that the convention would nominate Seymour of New York, or Vallandigham, or anybody but "this weak tool of Lincoln's." Speeches like these from both wings of the jarring Democracy wore out the patience of the delegates and the spectators, and the second day closed without a nomination.

Chicago was wild that night with brass bands and cheering Democrats, who visited the different hotels, and insisted upon speeches from prominent delegates. In front of the Sherman House there was a vociferous demand for Dean Richmond, who, tall, corpulent, big-nosed, austere and arbitrary in his manner, and looming up with his high white hat and blue-tailed coat, was stalking about the lobbies of the hotel, while his friend Peter Cagger, "three sheets in the wind," was impersonating Richmond at an upper window, and making a speech which convulsed the crowd with laughter.

Although McClellan was the inevitable nominee of the convention, he did not receive the honor until one formal ballot had been taken. The first ballot gave him 150 votes; Thomas H. Seymour of Connecticut had 43 votes, and Horatio Seymour of New York received 7. There were 2 scattering votes cast. The roll call had been finished, but the balloting was practically settled by the action of Missouri, which, having previously voted solidly for Thomas H. Seymour, now divided its strength, and cast 7 votes for McClellan, and 4 for Thomas H. Seymour, amid great cheering. There was then a great landslide of votes for McClellan, until all but the most uncompromising of the Peace Democrats had gone over to the inevitable nominee. Long, Vallandigham, and others held out until the last; and after all changes were made, the final vote was announced thus: McClellan, 202½; Thomas H. Seymour, 23½. Instantly the pent-up feelings of the crowd broke forth in the most rapturous manner: cheers, yells, music, and screams indescribable rent the air, and outside the wigwam a park of cannon volleyed a salute in honor of the nominee. The long agony was over, and men threw up their hats, and behaved as much like bedlamites as men usually do under such circumstances. When order was restored, Vallandigham, who until then had not spoken, mounted the rostrum, and moved that the nomination be made unanimous. It is impossible to describe the tremendous applause which greeted the appearance of the Ohio "martyr," who had only lately returned through Canada from his exile. His appearance on the platform, bland, smiling, and rosy, was the signal for a teriffic outburst before he could open his mouth; and when his little speech was done, another whirlwind of applause greeted his magnanimous motion in favor of a war candidate.

Some of the speeches that followed were full of venom and denunciation. Charles A. Wickliffe, who was commonly known in Washington as "Old Kentucky," offered a resolution to the effect that his State expected that the first act of the new Democratic administration would be "to open the prison doors, and let the oppressed go free." Wickliffe had previously raised a laugh in the convention by nominating ex-President Pierce in an amusing and wandering speech. Later on, after the nomination of vice-president, Wickliffe again distinguished himself by adjuring the convention to refrain from an adjournment *sine die.* He insisted that he and his colleagues in the West were "of the opinion that circumstances may occur between now and March fourth next which will make it proper for the Democracy of the country to meet in convention again." Although the real motive for this proposed action was not apparent to anybody, so far as I could learn by talking with the delegates afterward, Wickliffe's suggestion was received with a shout of boisterous applause. Mystery characterized many of the proceedings of the convention, and the mysteriousness of this proposition appeared to be significant to the delegates. It was taken as a warning that the managers of the party expected something extraordinary to happen, and were determined to be ready for any emergency that might arise; so the convention accordingly adopted a resolution to "remain as organized, subject to be called at any time and place that the Executive National Committee shall designate." It is a matter of history, however, that the convention never was called together again, and the reason for this cautious anchor to windward has never been disclosed.

George H. Pendleton was nominated for vice-president without much difficulty, although there were several other candidates in the field. Indiana had proposed the name of her favorite son, "The Tall Sycamore of the Wabash," D. W. Voorhees; Pennsylvania had nominated George W. Cass; Vermont, James Guthrie of Kentucky; Illinois, Judge John D. Caton; Delaware, Lazarus W. Powell of Kentucky; Missouri, John S. Phelps of that State; and Iowa, Augustus Cæsar Dodge, once minister to Spain. It was the large vote of New York which finally made Pendleton's nomination inevitable. This State had withheld its vote until it was obvious that its sudden dropping would decide the contest; then it was ponderously thrown to Pendleton, and the contest was virtually over. Pendleton was present as a delegate from Ohio, and, mounting the platform, made a pleasant speech. The convention broke up in the most admirable disorder, and that night the city of Chicago seemed drunk with political excitement. Although many of the leaders had left by afternoon trains, the marching mobs halted under the windows of all the principal hotels, and demanded speeches until midnight fell, and something like silence reigned in the city.

It was during the last days of August that the convention declared that the war was a failure, and that peace must be sought in a convention of Federals and Confederates. On September third Washington received from Sherman the good news of the fall of Atlanta, and President Lincoln issued an order in which the national thanks were given to General Sherman and the officers and soldiers of his command before Atlanta "for the distinguished ability, courage, and perseverance displayed in the campaign in Georgia, which, under divine favor, has resulted in the capture of Atlanta." And at the same time Grant, at City Point, telegraphed to Sherman: "In honor of your great victory I have ordered a salute to be fired with shotted guns from every battery bearing upon the enemy. The salute will be fired within an hour, amid great rejoicing." The tide had turned. The Democratic campaign in 1864 began under very different auspices from those which had attended the assembling of the convention which nominated a war candidate on a peace platform. The dark days were over.

CHASE ON THE SUPREME BENCH

Another historic event which marked the wonderful transition in political affairs in this republic was the inauguration of Salmon P. Chase as Chief Justice of the United States. It was a curious coincidence that his immediate predecessor, Roger B. Taney, was, like himself, an ex-secretary of the Treasury. Students of American political history will recollect that Taney was appointed Secretary of the Treasury by Andrew Jackson in his fierce and vindictive prosecution of a war against the United

States Bank. William J. Duane, as Secretary of the Treasury, had refused to become the willing tool of Jackson in that contest; and Taney, who promised to do the bidding of "Old Hickory," was appointed in his place, and did the work required of him. Subsequently, when the office of Chief Justice became vacant, Taney was promoted to that exalted station; and it surely is no violence to the memory of either of these two famous men to say that the chief-justiceship was Taney's reward for his services in removing the government deposits from the United States Bank, as Andrew Jackson had decreed.

Many years had passed since that time, and the incidents of Taney's earlier career had been well-nigh forgotten when he once more made his name conspicuous by the infamous Dred Scott decision, which was to the effect that the Negro has no rights that the white man is bound to respect, although these were not the exact terms of the dictum then given. Lincoln himself thus summarized the opinion of the United States Supreme Court, as enunciated by the Chief Justice: "The Constitution of the United States forbids Congress to deprive a man of his property without due process of law. The right of property in slaves is distinctly and expressly affirmed in that Constitution: therefore, if Congress shall undertake to say that a man's slave is no longer his slave when he crosses a certain line into a Territory, that is depriving him of his property without due process of law." Now, in the fullness of time, Taney had passed away, and another Secretary of the Treasury, of high character, distinguished alike for his services to the cause of human freedom and to the American nation, received the noblest honor in the gift of the national executive. It was unfortunate that some of the new Chief Justice's overzealous and indiscreet friends gleefully claimed that President Lincoln was coerced into making that appointment, and scornfully insisted that it was a popular choice forced upon the President by men who controlled confirmations in the Senate. It was lamentable that when Lincoln willingly paid a noble honor to one who had been his competitor for the presidential nomination, he could not have at least the poor satisfaction of knowing that the purity of his motives and the fixity of his intention were appreciated by those who made Chase and Chase's ambitions the excuse for conspiring against the good name of Lincoln. As a matter of history, it should be recorded that Lincoln never intended to appoint any other man than Chase to the Chief Justiceship, and never for one moment had he entertained the name of any other person. It was a peculiar trait of Lincoln that, in order to preclude all possibility of doubt in his own mind concerning the expediency of any contemplated act, he would state to those with whom he came in contact many doubts and objections not his own, but those of others, for the express purpose of being confirmed and fixed in his own judgment. For example, when a Chicago ministerial delegation visited Lincoln, and urged upon him the expediency of issuing an emancipation proclamation, it was this mental habit that induced him to argue with his visitors as though his mind were not already made up, and as if he were really uncertain as to his course in regard to that great measure. When those Chicago clergymen read the emancipation proclamation, for the coming of which Lincoln had given them no hope, they must have been amazed by what they perhaps thought was an evidence of Lincoln's secretiveness. And, as a matter of truth, it may be said that when Sumner and others importuned President Lincoln to nominate Chase to the Chief Justiceship, and he replied in a doubtful manner, he had really made up his mind to nominate Chase.

A curious complication arose over the appointment of Chase, which made his public inauguration a matter of doubt for a week or two. The form of procedure prescribed in such a case requires that the letters patent of a justice of the Supreme Court shall pass through the hands of the Attorney-General of the United States. At that time Mr. James Speed had been

appointed Attorney-General in place of Mr. Edward Bates, resigned. The Senate judiciary committee held up the nomination
several days, not because they hesitated at confirming Speed,
but, as one of that committee said, "to convey a mild insinuation
to the President that they did not know who James Speed of
Kentucky was." Meanwhile the documents necessary to complete the induction of Mr. Chase into his new office could not
be issued. Bates was out, and Speed was not in. Five times
people who frequented the Capitol filled the limits of the Supreme Court room, in the expectation that they would see the
inauguration of the Chief Justice, and five times were they
disappointed; for the Senate boggled over the confirmation of
the functionary whose signature was all that was needed to
enable the new Chief Justice to put on his official robes. Finally,
however, on December 15, 1864, for the sixth time the crowd
assembled, and all was ready. The noble room of the Supreme
Court was overflowing with an immense throng of dignitaries
of various degrees, ladies, congressmen, foreign ministers, and
others who wished to view the simple but impressive ceremony
of swearing in the chief judicial officer of the republic. The
rush was very great, and a rippling tide of humanity, chiefly
women, overflowed into the sacred precincts of the bar, where
sat ponderous Tom Ewing, white-headed Reverdy Johnson,
Secretary Seward, and other distinguished lawyers. There were
Senator Sprague, with his wife, Mrs. Kate Chase Sprague, and
her sister, gorgeously dressed; Nathaniel P. Banks, erect and
martial-looking; gray-headed Ben Wade; and other personages
whose names are famous. Just in the rear of the Supreme
Bench, on the right, the elegant form of Charles Sumner leaned
against one of the marble columns in a fine and studied pose;
his handsome features plainly showed his inward glow of gratification. The soft stir of the chamber was broken by the voice
of the usher, who announced in a loud official tone, "The Honorable Justices of the Supreme Court of the United States";

whereupon through the side entrance behind the bench entered the gowned justices, headed by Justice Wayne, the senior member of the bench, arm in arm with the newly appointed Chief Justice. The justices advanced to their several chairs, and bowed to the left and to the right; and the bar, remaining standing, collectively bowed in return. Then the new Chief Justice came forward to his chair, and Justice [James M.] Wayne handed him a paper containing the oath, which Mr. Chase opened, and read in a clear but tremulous voice, as follows: "I, Salmon P. Chase, do solemnly swear that I will, as Chief Justice of the Supreme Court of the United States, administer equal and exact justice to the poor and to the rich, in accordance with the Constitution and the laws of the United States, to the best of my ability." Then, laying down the paper, he lifted his right hand, looked upward to the beautiful dome of the court-room, and with deep feeling added, "So help me God." A breathless hush pervaded the chamber, and the Chief Justice of the United States took his seat. Then the clerk, with a good deal of tremor in his voice, read aloud the letters patent of the Chief Justice; the simple ceremony was over, and the routine business of the court began.

As the crowd decorously moved out of the room I came face to face with "Bluff Ben Wade." My eyes met his, which were actually suffused with tears; and with great grimness, but with much fervor, he said, "Lord, now lettest thou thy servant depart in peace, for mine eyes have seen thy salvation."

A few days after the appointment of Chief Justice Chase the President was visited by the members of the Electoral College of Maryland, who, in the course of the interview, expressed their satisfaction with the act of the President in elevating Mr. Chase to the Supreme Bench. In reply the President said that he trusted that the appointment would be for the best. The country, he added, needed some assurances on two points of great national importance; and there was an assurance that could be better given by the character and well-known opinions of the appointee than by any verbal pledges. By the appointment of Mr. Chase all holders of United States securities in America and Europe felt assured that the financial policy of the Government would be upheld by its highest judicial tribunal. In sustaining that policy, Judge Chase would be only sustaining himself, for he was the author of it. The other point to which Lincoln referred was that relating to the constitutionality of the emancipation policy of the Government. He said that other distinguished gentlemen had been named as competent to undertake the great trust now borne by Judge Chase; but these did not bear the same relations to those important issues that Chase did, although they were doubtless equally sound. When we reflect that the financial policy of the Government, so far as it was involved in the legal-tender law, was subsequently disapproved by the distinguished author of it, we may well wonder what Lincoln would have thought if he had lived to read the Chief Justice's decision thereupon.

VI

The Death of Slavery

MUCH nonsense has been written about Lincoln's position on slavery and the events leading up to the Emancipation Proclamation and constitutional amendment against slavery or involuntary servitude. Historical lint-pickers have found quotations here and there to "prove" that Lincoln was indifferent to the status of the Negro. These fail to take into account the lifetime record of the man, especially the moral man, whose position for equality of Negro rights never wavered.

Here, Brooks describes the Congressional maneuvering and reasoning which preceded passage of the Thirteenth Amendment. Here are the behind-the-scenes views of Congress and the excitement in the galleries whenever the amendment was discussed. On a more intimate level, Brooks tells of the heat engendered in Washington by the segregated streetcars—"colored persons may ride in this car"—in the midst of war, and a final spirit of Abolition.

The background of Lincoln's position on the constitutional amendment reached deep into his life. When he was twenty-eight years of age and a Representative in the Illinois General Assembly, resolutions were passed by a strongly pro-Southern legislature saying that "the right of property in slaves is sacred to the slave-holding States by the Federal Constitution, and that they cannot be deprived of that right without their consent." Only two legislators dissented—"Dan Stone and A. Lincoln, Representatives from the County of Sangamon." They said: "We believe that the institution of slavery is founded on both injustice and bad policy; but that

178

the promulgation of abolition doctrines tends rather to increase than to abate its evils." Thus Lincoln, as far back as 1837, speaking out qualifiedly against slavery.

In the White House, events moved swiftly toward emancipation. Abolitionists hammered away; American and European newspapers and attitudes were a factor; and, from a military standpoint, the slaves could be a source of manpower, disabling the South, fortifying the North. Lincoln sent a special message to Congress on March 6, 1862, calling for a resolution "that the United States ought to coöperate with any State which may adopt gradual abolishment of slavery, giving to such state pecuniary aid, to be used by such state in its discretion, to compensate for the inconveniences public and private, produced by such change of system." He hoped that such a resolution would "lead to important practical results." Those results in Congress—a strongly divided legislature, with many splinter groups—are described here.

AS late as June, 1862, although slavery had been abolished in the District of Columbia, the infamous Fugitive-Slave laws still remained on the statute-books. In that month a fugitive-slave case came up in Washington, and John Dean, a prominent lawyer, counsel for a fugitive from labor, was indicted for aiding and assisting in the escape of his client, one Andrew Hall, alleged to have been owned by a Virginia gentleman, who still clung to his property. Andrew, while waiting for the action of the court in his case, enlisted in one of the colored regiments then being raised in Washington, and thus settled his status for himself. The indictment of the attorney in the case was based upon his alleged offense committed in a "scrapping match" which took place when the fugitive had been discharged from a first arrest, and was about to be again taken into custody. The alleged owner of the alleged fugitive was on hand when the man was discharged, and was about to take him into custody until an arresting officer could arrive with papers for his further detention. In the little riot which followed, Mr. Dean, the attorney for the Negro, interfered and beat off the men who were engaged in the attempt to detain Andrew by force of arms while waiting for the papers. The punishment for Dean's offense, or alleged offense, would have been six months imprisonment, or one thousand dollars fine, under the Fugitive-Slave Law of 1850. The case dragged on from term to term, and was finally dropped out of sight; but Andrew's enlistment in the United States service of course had made him a free man, so far as any obligation to an alleged owner of human flesh and blood was concerned. So far as I know, this was the last case under the fugitive-slave laws of which the United States courts took any cognizance. The affair created intense excitement in Washington, more especially in both Houses of Congress, which were then in session.

SLAVERY IN THE DISTRICT OF COLUMBIA

It will be remembered that when Lincoln served his single term in Congress he introduced a bill (January [10], 1849) for the gradual abolition of slavery in the District of Columbia. It failed to pass. In December, 1861, Senator Wilson, of Massachusetts, introduced bills in the Senate providing for the immediate emancipation of all slaves in the District of Columbia, and the payment to loyal owners of an average sum of three hundred dollars per head, and providing for the appointment of a Board of Commissioners to assess the amounts to be paid to each slave owner, and appropriating one million dollars for that purpose. Singularly enough, this measure was at first opposed by a considerable number of Democratic Senators whose loyalty to the Union was not for a moment questioned. Senator Willey of West Virginia, for example, opposed the bill in a speech in which he insisted that the policy of the Union party had noth-

ing whatever to do with the abolition of slavery or with its
maintenance; that the slavery question was one entirely outside
of all measures for the preservation of the Union. The debate
ran on several days, and during that time a great many decent-
looking and intelligent-appearing colored men thronged to the
Senate to hear what the speakers had to say on the general
question. Garrett Davis said he was astonished at the impudence
of these colored people, who were concerned to know whether
they were to be property or free men; and in a particularly
vituperative speech, one afternoon, he called attention to the
predominance of black people in the galleries, and said: "A
few days ago, I saw several Negroes thronging the open door
of the Senate and listening to the debate on this subject. I
suppose in a few months they will be crowding white ladies out
of the galleries!" Senator Davis's opinion was that the liberation of the slaves in the rebellious States would be of no avail,
because as soon as the States should be reorganized as an in-
tegral part of the Union, "the white inhabitants of those States
would reduce the slaves again to a state of bondage or would
expel them from their borders and hunt them like wild animals."
But notwithstanding the opposition of such men as the erratic
Kentuckian, the Wilson bill finally passed the Senate by 29
votes to 6.

Thaddeus Stevens had charge of the bill when it came up
in the House early in the following April. It was opposed in
the House by the same class of politicians that had fought it in
the Senate. Even so liberal a Democrat as John J. Crittenden
spoke and voted against the bill, and Wickliffe of Kentucky
said: "I hope the friends of this bill will not so far outrage the
laws of the District as to authorize slaves or free Negroes to be
witnesses in any case before the courts." Vallandigham also
opposed the measure with great vehemence, and declared that
there were not ten men in the next preceding Congress who
would have voted for the abolition of slavery in the District of

Columbia. But the bill passed the House by a vote of 92 to 38. This famous act was finally approved by the President, and became a law on April 16, 1862, and great was the jubilation, not only throughout the District, but all over the loyal States. The city of Washington was the scene of a remarkable parade, alleged to be made up of free Negroes, but as a matter of fact it was not until months after that that freedom was attained in the District.

One morning in the latter part of January, 1863, while passing through the Treasury Department, I noticed a large crowd of persons gathered in a corridor and waiting their turn to enter Room No. 18. My curiosity was satisfied when I found that the Commissioners appointed by Congress, attended by their clerk and the cashier of the Sub-Treasury, were paying for the emancipated slaves of the District. Think of it! As the claimants walked up one after another and gave their names, the Commissioners' clerk looked up the number of the claim and the Sub-Treasury cashier produced a check which bore the same number. Thereupon the claimant signed a receipt, received his check, and went to General [Francis] Spinner, United States Treasurer, where he signed another receipt, and the check, being duly countersigned, was payable at the Sub-Treasury. About three hundred persons were then in line waiting their turn for payment. Three or four days were required to settle all the claims of the ex-slaveholders, and when the accounts were eventually balanced it was found that the total amount of money paid for slaves purchased in the District of Columbia by act of Congress was considerably within the sum appropriated— one million dollars. It should be said that some of the more radical Republican members of Congress opposed the abolition bill on the ground that it was wicked to pay for slaves, thus recognizing the right of property in human beings. Their attitude was like that of the Prohibitionists of the present day, who would refuse licenses to liquor-dealers on a somewhat similar principle. But compensated emancipation was at that time considered by most sensible people as the easiest and most practicable solution of the great impending difficulty—the abolition of slavery.

COMPENSATED EMANCIPATION

Maryland was one of the first States to take advantage of the so-called compensated emancipation scheme. Henry Winter Davis, notwithstanding his wrong-headed and self-willed course, was a consistent and ardent supporter of all measures that had for their purpose the abolition of slavery and a vigorous prosecution of the war. He supported Lincoln with a very bad grace in 1864, saying that he gave him his vote for the reason that the worst man whom the Union party could put up was far better than the best man the Democrats could nominate. As a stump speaker Henry Winter Davis was brilliant, effective, and widely popular; and his services in the emancipation movement in Maryland were above all value. The emancipation party carried that State in 1863, electing a majority of the legislature; and in January, 1864, a resolution was adopted by the legislature declaring that the true interests of Maryland demanded that the policy of emancipation should be immediately inaugurated. That legislature called for a convention to amend the constitution of the State and provide for emancipation. Henry Winter Davis, and other friends of the good cause, took the field with such vigor that a popular majority of twelve thousand was thrown in favor of the convention; and of the ninety-six delegates chosen, sixty-one were in favor of emancipation. The new constitution was finally submitted to a vote of the people and adopted in October, 1864, and on the nineteenth day of that month a great crowd of Marylanders went on to Washington to congratulate the President upon the final entrance of Maryland into the column of free States. It was a beautiful, bright day, and with music, banners, and cheers the loyal Marylanders made the welkin ring with their jubilation. The President came out in answer to their calls and made a little speech, in which he congratulated his visitors, their State and the nation, upon the great event. He said that he regretted that emancipation had not come two years sooner, because he thought that, if it had, it would have saved the nation more money than would have met all the private losses incident to emancipation under the present order of things. Later on in the day he said in private conversation: "I would rather have Maryland upon that issue than have a State twice its size upon the Presidential issue. It cleans up a piece of ground." Any one who has ever had anything to do with cleaning up a piece of ground, digging out the roots and stumps, as Lincoln had, can appreciate the homely simile applied to Maryland, where slavery had at last been rooted out.

AMENDING THE CONSTITUTION

But of course the great act in the war drama was the final passage of the amendment to the Constitution abolishing slavery throughout the length and breadth of the Republic. This amendment first passed [38 to 6] the Senate, April 8, 1864. The proposition was debated with much earnestness, but without much heat. Among the Democrats who voted for it were Senators from Maryland, Missouri, West Virginia, Oregon, and California. There were only six votes cast against the measure. These were from Garrett Davis of Kentucky, Thomas A. Hendricks of Indiana, [James A.] McDougall of California, [Lazarus] Powell of Kentucky, and [George R.] Riddle and [Willard] Saulsbury of Delaware. There was a faint rumble of applause when the result of the voting was announced, but no such demonstration as was made when the House finally passed the bill, nearly a year later—on January 31, 1865. In the earlier

months of the same Congress, in 1864, the measure had failed
to receive the two thirds vote of the House necessary for its
passage; and Representative Ashley, of Ohio, who had then
changed his vote in order that he might move a reconsideration,
gave notice that he would call up the constitutional amendment
on January 6, 1865. The debate ran on fitfully for the remainder
of that month, and whenever it was noised abroad that the
constitutional amendment to abolish slavery would come up in
the House, the galleries were thronged to overflowing, and the
speeches were listened to with great intentness. But to the very
last day it was feared that the necessary two thirds vote could
not be obtained. Although West Virginia, Missouri, Arkansas,
Maryland, and Louisiana had by that time accepted the situation, and had adopted measures looking to the immediate
emancipation of slaves, there were not a few men in the House
of Representatives who opposed the constitutional amendment.
William S. Holman and George H. Pendleton, from the Northern States, were among those who voted against it. It should be
recalled that the House on the previous occasion, when it failed
to pass, June 15, 1864, gave the amendment 95 ayes to 66 noes,
a two-thirds vote being necessary; and when the measure came
up for final passage on January 31, [1865], anxiety and expectation sat on every countenance. But on the floor of the House,
where the friends of liberty and freedom were circulating tally-
lists which they had prepared for their own private information,
there was a general air of cheerfulness and confidence. The
galleries, corridors, and lobbies were crowded to the doors, and
the reporters' gallery was invaded by a mob of well-dressed
women, who for a time usurped the place of the newspaper men ;
and these, considering the importance of the proceedings and the
gravity of the impending event, surrendered their seats with
good grace. On the floor of the House were Chief Justice Chase
and the Associate Justices Swayne, Miller, Nelson, and Field,
Secretary Fessenden, Postmaster-General Dennison, senators

by the dozen, the electoral messengers from Oregon, Nevada, and California, ex-Postmaster-General Montgomery Blair, and hosts of other prominent persons.

When the hour for taking the vote approached, Archibald McAllister, a Pennsylvania Peace Democrat, astonished everybody by sending up to the clerk's desk a note in which he said that as all peace negotiations and missions had failed, he was satisfied that nothing short of their independence would satisfy the Southern Confederates, and he therefore determined to cast his vote against the corner-stone of the Southern Confederacy— slavery. Several other Democrats and Border State men, who had heretofore withheld their support of the constitutional amendment, also came in with brief explanations of the vote which they now proposed to cast in the affirmative. The supreme moment finally arrived, Speaker Colfax's ringing voice demanded of the House "Shall the Joint Resolution pass?" The roll-call proceeded, and as the clerk's call went slowly down the list, knots of members gathered around their fellows who were keeping tally; and a group of Copperheads hung around Pendleton, looking gloomy, black, and sour. Occasionally, when a member whose opposition to the amendment had been notable voted "aye," a clatter of applause, irrepressible and spontaneous, swept through the House. When the name of John Ganson, a New York Peace Democrat, gave back an echo of "aye," much to the surprise of everybody, there was a great burst of enthusiasm; for this marked the safety of the amendment. On the final vote there were one hundred and nineteen in the affirmative, fifty-six in the negative, and eight absentees.

When the roll-call was concluded, Speaker Colfax exercised his prerogative and asked the clerk to call his name, whereupon his voice rang out with an "aye." Then, the record being made up, the Speaker, his voice trembling, said: "On the passage of the Joint Resolution to amend the Constitution of the United States the ayes have 119, the noes 56. The constitutional

majority of two thirds having voted in the affirmative, the Joint
Resolution has passed." For a moment there was a pause of
utter silence, as if the voices of the dense mass of spectators
were choked by strong emotion. Then there was an explosion,
a storm of cheers, the like of which probably no Congress of the
United States ever heard before. Strong men embraced each
other with tears. The galleries and aisles were bristling with
standing, cheering crowds. The air was stirred with a cloud
of women's handkerchiefs waving and floating; hands were
shaking; men threw their arms about each other's necks, and
cheer after cheer, and burst after burst followed. Full ten
minutes elapsed before silence returned sufficient to enable
Ebon C. Ingersoll, of Illinois, to move an adjournment "in
honor of the sublime and immortal event," upon which B. C.
Harris, the deeply censured Marylander, shaking with wrath,
arose and demanded the ayes and noes on the motion. This little
artifice to procure delay did not amount to much, for, as the
roll call began, members answered to their names and passed
out, most of the defeated Copperheads taking their hats and
stealing away before their names were reached. As the roll call
went on amidst great confusion (for there was no longer any
pretense of maintaining order), the air was rent by the thunder
of a great salute fired on Capitol Hill, to notify all who heard
that slavery was no more.

Every Republican member of the House voted for the final
passage of the amendment: not one of them was absent when
the vote was taken. Of the 119 members who finally voted for
the amendment, 10 were Democrats; their votes were necessary
to secure the constitutional two thirds. These men were James
E. English, of Connecticut; Anson Herrick, William Radford,
Homer A. Nelson, John B. Steele, and John Ganson, of New
York; A. H. Coffroth and Archibald McAllister, of Pennsylvania; Wells A. Hutchins, of Ohio; and Augustus C. Baldwin,
of Michigan. There were 8 Democrats absent when the vote was

taken; these were Jesse Lazear, of Pennsylvania; John F. McKinney and Francis C. LeBlond, of Ohio; Daniel W. Voorhees and James F. McDowell, of Indiana; George Middleton and A. J. Rogers, of New Jersey; and Daniel Marcy, of New Hampshire. It is fair to assume that these absentees were not unwilling that the amendment abolishing slavery should prevail, but were not willing to give it their active support.

At that time there were seven Territories represented by delegates in Congress. These were Colorado, Utah, Nebraska, Arizona, Dakota, Idaho, and New Mexico. The delegates of these Territories, not having the right to vote on any measure in the House of Representatives, were granted leave to enter upon the Journal of the House a paper in which they expressed their deep interest in the proposition to amend the Federal Constitution, forever abolishing slavery, and declared their unqualified approbation of the same.

The Joint Resolution to amend the Constitution, and thus provide for the perpetual abolition of slavery, being an accomplished fact so far as the action of Congress was concerned, the consent of the States was now necessary. It will be remembered that in the so-called Wade-Davis bill provision had been made for the abolition of slavery by requiring that each reconstructed State, as it took its place in returning to the Union, should adopt a constitution forever prohibiting slavery within its borders. This feature of the measure commended it to all friends of human freedom. Very many who did not pause to consider the effect of what Mr. Lincoln called "this bed of Procrustes" were taken by the proposition that slavery would be abolished, provided the measure should receive the favorable action of the reconstructed States; and in their manifesto the authors of the bill laid great stress upon that clause of their elaborate scheme; and they asked, with fine sarcasm, how President Lincoln could possibly expect slavery could be abolished

when the House had already refused the necessary two thirds
vote required by the Constitution. At that time, it will be remembered, the House had taken its first and undecisive action
on the bill, in June, 1864. Now that the amendment, however,
having safely passed the ordeal of both branches of Congress,
was to go to the States for ratification, the final act giving
vitality to the amendment was merely a matter of time. Two
States, Rhode Island and Michigan, led the column, their legis-
latures having ratified the amendment February 2, 1865; but it
was not until after Lincoln's death that the necessary three
fourths of the thirty-six States of the Union had ratified the
amendment so that it became valid as a part of the Constitution
[33 out of 36 states ratified]. Official proclamation of that consummation was finally made by Secretary Seward, then in
Johnson's cabinet, December 18, 1865.

Before the adoption of the Thirteenth Amendment, slavery
was possible within the limits of any State, at the will of a
majority of the voters of such State; or, slavery could be
abolished in any State in like manner. Now, slavery was forever prohibited within the United States by the authority of the
nation. And as the amended Constitution declared that "Congress shall have power to enforce this article by appropriate
legislation," the power of the States to meddle with the question of slavery was forever taken away. In September, 1859,
Lincoln compressed into a single brief sentence the gist of the
Dred Scott decision thus: "The Constitution of the United
States forbids Congress to deprive a man of his property without due process of law. The right of property in slaves is distinctly affirmed in the Constitution: therefore, if Congress shall
undertake to say that a man's slave is no longer his when he
crosses a certain line into a Territory, that is depriving him
of his property without due process of law." The Thirteenth
Amendment, proposed by Congress and adopted by the States,

drew the fangs of the monster which Taney, and those who believed with him, had insisted was sleeping in the Constitution —the right of property in slaves.

One of the curiosities of the time was the anxiety of every member who voted for the amendment, and many others who were not members of Congress, to procure officially enrolled copies of the historic act as it had passed both branches of Congress. It became one of the industries of the clerks of the House and Senate to engross on a sheet of parchment the few brief and pregnant sentences of the amendment, and procure thereto the autograph signatures of the Senators and Representatives who voted for it, and also the autographs of the President and Secretary of the Senate, the Speaker and Clerk of the House of Representatives, the President of the United States, and the Secretary of State. So far as I know, hundreds of such parchments, bearing the signatures of these now historic personages, were in existence when Congress adjourned in March, 1865. It has always been the custom for pages and others about the House and Senate to procure the autographs of members. These, arranged in albums, have finally come to be regarded as an article of commerce; but the signing of the names of the Senators and Representatives, and other high officials responsible for the enactment of the Thirteenth Amendment, was certainly done with more cheerfulness than any similar exercise of that semi-public function. As a matter of fact, the signature of the President was not necessary to give effect to the action of Congress in passing the amendment. Inadvertently, however, the Joint Resolution was laid before the President on the day of its passage by the House, and he signed it in due course of business. Subsequently, however, the Senate, at the instance of Senator Lyman Trumbull, who was a gifted hair-splitter, adopted a resolution that such approval by the President was unnecessary to give effect to the action of Congress; and it was then declared that the negative of the President applied only to the

ordinary cases of legislation, and that he had nothing to do with
the proposition or the adoption of amendments to the Constitution. Nevertheless, the attaching of the President's signature
to the Thirteenth Amendment did establish for him a precedent
which thereafter required him to sign his name to the hundreds
of facsimiles of the document which set forth the momentous
fact that Congress had on the thirty-first day of January, 1865,
formally abolished slavery throughout the United States; and
he was deeply gratified that his name was officially connected
with that act.

"COLORED PERSONS MAY RIDE IN THIS CAR."

Another sign of the times (though far less important in its
way) that showed that the world still moves, and slavery is an
anachronism, was the gradual emancipation of the colored
people of the District of Columbia from the ban under which
they had always lived. The introduction of street railways into
the national capital was in itself an innovation. The fine old
aristocrats of the *ancien régime* looked upon these vehicles with
great disfavor. They soon discovered that the "c'yar box," as
they called the street-car, would not come up to the sidewalk at
the wave of a parasol or the beckoning of a hand, as had been the
servile habit of the omnibuses, formerly the principal means
of public conveyance in Washington streets. And it was a long
time before these dignified sticklers for old manners and customs
permitted themselves to enter the queer "Yankee contrivance"
so lately introduced. Negroes had been permitted in ancient
times to ride on the roof of the omnibus, and when the street-
cars began their slow progress on Pennsylvania Avenue, colored
people were graciously allowed to face the dust, or the snow,
sleet, and rain of the variable climate, in company with the
driver on the front platform; but when the abolition of slavery
in the District became inevitable, and free Negroes from the

disordered States adjacent began to flock into Washington, these narrow accommodations were soon found insufficient. Under no pretext whatever was a colored person, however well dressed, however cleanly, permitted inside of one of the "c'yar boxes" sacred to the Caucasian race. Protests against their exclusion found their way into the newspapers, and the street-car company, in deference to a popular demand of increasing loudness, added one or two antique cars, which bore upon the roof in big letters this concession: "Colored Persons May Ride In This Car." The poor outcasts who had been denied the luxury of a seat, although they paid their full fare just as cheerfully as white people, now had an opportunity of riding inside of a car once in an hour; and occasionally a white person of bitter prejudices would stray ignorantly into one of the vehicles conceded to the colored race, and would indignantly demand of the conductor the expulsion of every person but himself, much to his own subsequent discomfiture. Before the introduction of the so-called "colored cars" I saw a handsomely dressed and lady-like woman sent out on the front platform by a conductor, whose practised eye detected Ethiopian traces in her white face and straight hair, although a person less expert in ethnology could not possibly have discerned them. When the lady had made her exit, which she did with a quick blush mantling her beautiful face, the conductor angrily said that it was just as likely as not that of a dark evening the woman had ridden back and forth in the cars and "nobody had known nothin' of it." When somebody asked, "Well, what of that?" the amazed Caucasian conductor was incapable of reply.

As the street-car company was a creature of Congress, and Congress was at that time busily engaged in considering how all traces of slavery should be eradicated, petitions began to flow in, and indignant lovers of freedom occasionally raised a racket in the Senate or House over the long-continued proscription of the colored people. Finally the crisis came when Dr.

A. T. Augusta, a colored surgeon, of the Seventh United States Colored Troops, dressed in the full uniform of a major, was expelled from a street-car under peculiarly exasperating circumstances. He was on his way to a court-martial, where he was an important witness, and, being compelled to get out into the rain and slush of a February day, was a long time delayed in reaching the court. He had been told by the conductor that he could ride on the front platform, where the rain was driving in sheets, but he explained that unless he could ride in the car, he would not ride at all. He was therefore compelled to walk a long distance in mud and rain, and when he reached the court he addressed to the Judge-Advocate a communication, giving the reason of his failure to report when ordered. In due course of time this incident came before the Senate, and a resolution was passed inquiring into the right of the street-car company to set up a rule by which colored people were excluded from any of their vehicles. The company very soon found that their charter contemplated no such discrimination against any person, and after a while the concessionary sign on the tops of the few "colored cars" disappeared, and this invidious distinction was heard of no more. If there was any real invasion of the rights of white people which unpleasantly affected the superior race at that time, it was never made manifest; but it is singular that such men as [Charles R.] Buckalew of Pennsylvania, [Thomas] Hendricks of Indiana, [James] Nesmith of Oregon, [William] Richardson of Illinois, and a few other Northern men with fixed principles of hostility to the "unbleached Americans," persistently opposed the resolution to inquire into the facts concerning the exclusion of colored people from the street-cars.

VII

Lincoln's Reëlection

"AMONG the memories of a lifetime," Brooks said, concerning his presence at the Second Inaugural, "doubtless there are none more fondly cherished by those who were so fortunate as to stand near Lincoln at that historic moment than the recollection of the beautiful solemnity, the tender sympathy, of these inspired utterances, and the rapt silence of the multitudes. There were many cheers and many tears as this noble address was concluded."

In the time between election and inaugural, there were forebodings and moments of military triumph. Lincoln recollected, and told Brooks of, the "illusion" he had seen of himself in a swinging glass. Mrs. Lincoln saw this as a sign that her husband would be elected to a second term but would not live it through. Brooks discussed the story with Mrs. Lincoln, who expressed surprise that Mr. Lincoln was willing to say anything about it to someone beside herself. The Brooks story was confirmed later by John Hay, Lincoln's secretary.

The peace overtures by the Confederates occupied Washington's attention early in January, 1865. The Peace Democrats were emboldened in the Capitol. On the steamer *River Queen* at Hampton Roads, the President and Secretary of State Seward had talked with three Confederate commissioners. The Senate and House in February insisted on knowing what was going on. Brooks relates how the President's message was seen and heard from the reporters' gallery.

The inaugural on March 4, 1865 (for a second term to expire

in 1869), was a day in Washington when cannon boomed and crowds cheered. Victory was in the wind. But the South saw the event differently. The *Daily Express,* Petersburg, Va., said that "not one of his predecessors ever stood up in that Eastern portico [of the Capitol] with hands red with the slaughter of his fellow-beings." The Virginia paper called it a great day in "Yankeedom" for "Emperor Abraham's coronation." Bennett's *New York Herald,* which had finally come out for Lincoln after being among his severest critics, now found him "the unquestioned master of the situation in reference to American affairs, at home and abroad." The *National Intelligencer,* of Washington, D. C., found the religious tone of the Inaugural conspicuous, and declared that the final paragraph—"With malice toward none, with charity for all, with firmness in the right as God gives us to see the right, let us strive on to finish the work we are in; to bind up the nation's wounds; to care for him who shall have borne the battle, and for his widow and his orphans; to do all which may achieve and cherish a just and a lasting peace among ourselves and with all nations" —deserved to be printed in gold.

The day had begun in darkness and rain. Later, to Noah Brooks, Lincoln had said: "Did you notice that sunburst? It made my heart jump."

THE day of the presidential election in November, 1864, was dark and rainy. About noon I called on President Lincoln, and to my surprise found him entirely alone, as if by common consent everybody had avoided the White House. It was "Cabinet day," and at the meeting, which had been held earlier, only two members of the Cabinet were present. Stanton was at his home, sick with chills and fever; Seward, Usher, and Dennison had returned to their own States to vote; and Fessenden was closeted with New York financiers in conference over ways and means to place a new loan. So Secretary Welles and Attorney-General Bates were left to "run the machine," and very little time had been occupied by them in their session with the President. Lincoln took no pains to conceal his anxious interest in the result of the election then going on all over the country, and said: "I am just enough of a politician to know that there was not much doubt about the result of the Baltimore convention; but about this thing I am very far from being certain. I wish I were certain." I spent nearly all the afternoon with the President, who apparently found it difficult to put his mind on any of the routine work of his office, and entreated me to stay with him. In the course of the afternoon he told an amusing story about a pet turkey of his boy "Tad." It appears that Jack, the turkey, whose life had been spared the year before at Tad's earnest request, had mingled with the "Bucktail" soldiers from Pennsylvania, quartered in the grounds on the river front of the White House. The soldiers were voting under the direction of a commission sent on from their State, as was the custom in several States of the Union, and Tad, bursting into his father's office, had besought the President to come to the window and see the soldiers who were "voting for Lincoln and Johnson." Noticing the turkey regarding the proceedings with evident interest, Lincoln asked the lad what business the turkey had stalking about the polls in that way. "Does he vote?" "No," was the quick reply of the boy; "he is not of age." The good President dearly loved the boy, and for days thereafter he took pride in relating this anecdote illustrative of Tad's quick-wittedness.

Late in the evening I returned to the White House, and found that the only returns then received were from Indiana, which showed that a gain of 1500 had been made in Indianapolis for the Republican ticket. Later on we went over to the War Department, and there heard good news from Baltimore, that city having sent in a majority of more than 10,000. Other reports soon came in, but not very rapidly, as a rain-storm had interfered with the transmission of news over the telegraph wires. There was a long lull about ten o'clock in the evening, during which the President amused the little company in the War Office with entertaining reminiscences and anecdotes naturally suggested by the political intelligence that dropped in from time to time. For instance, when New Jersey broke the calm by announcing a gain of one congressman for the Union, but with a fair prospect of the State going for McClellan, Lincoln had an amusing story to tell about that particular congressman, Dr. Newell, who had long been a family friend of the Lincolns. A despatch from New York City, claiming the State by 10,000, was received by the chief magistrate with much incredulity; and when Greeley telegraphed that the State would probably give 4000 majority for Lincoln, he said that that was much more reasonable than the absurd statement of a bigger majority. By midnight Pennsylvania, the New England States, Maryland, Ohio, Indiana, Michigan, and Wisconsin were tolerably certain for Lincoln; but the President was greatly disappointed that neither Illinois nor Iowa was heard from. The wires continued to work badly on account of the long storm, and it was not until two days later that satisfactory returns were had from Illinois or from any of the States beyond the Mississippi.

About midnight of the day of the election it was certain that Lincoln had been reëlected, and the few gentlemen left in the office congratulated him very warmly on the result. Lincoln took the matter very calmly, showing not the least elation or excitement, but said that he would admit that he was glad to be relieved of all suspense, and that he was grateful that the verdict of the people was likely to be so full, clear, and unmistakable that there could be no dispute. About two o'clock in the morning a messenger came over from the White House with the news that a crowd of Pennsylvanians were serenading his empty chamber, whereupon he went home; and, in answer to repeated calls, he made a happy little speech full of good feeling and cheerfulness. He wound up his remarks by saying, "If I know my heart, my gratitude is free from any taint of personal triumph. I do not impugn the motives of any one opposed to me. It is no pleasure to me to triumph over any one, but I give thanks to the Almighty for this evidence of the people's resolution to stand by free government and the rights of humanity."

Next day, in private conversation, he said: "Being only mortal, after all, I should have been a little mortified if I had been beaten in this canvass before the people; but the sting would have been more than compensated by the thought that the people had notified me that my official responsibilities were soon to be lifted off my back." Dr. A. G. Henry of Washington Territory, whose name has frequently been mentioned in these papers as an old friend of the President, had been promised that he should receive a despatch from Mr. Lincoln when the result of the Presidential election of that year should be definitely ascertained. Accordingly, on this day, which was November ninth, President Lincoln dictated a despatch, the terms of which were as follows: "With returns and States of which we are confident, the reëlection of the President is considered certain, while it is not certain that McClellan has carried any State, though the chances are that he has carried New Jersey and Kentucky." When I had written the despatch at the President's dictation, I passed it to him for his signature; but he declined to "blow his own horn," as he expressed it, and said: "You sign the message, and I will send it." A day or two later, when Delaware, whose vote had been uncertain, declared for McClellan, Lincoln sent a second despatch in order to give his friend on the far-off Pacific Coast a clear and exact idea of what had happened, explaining that he took it for granted that Dr. Henry would hear all the news, but might think it odd that the President should leave him without clearing up the situation thus left somewhat undecided in the uncertainties of the election returns.

On the day mentioned, Lincoln narrated an incident the

particulars of which I wrote out and printed directly after. These are his own words, as nearly as they could then be recalled: "It was just after my election in 1860, when the news had been coming in thick and fast all day and there had been a great 'hurrah, boys,' so that I was well tired out, and went home to rest, throwing myself down on a lounge in my chamber. Opposite where I lay was a bureau with a swinging glass upon it" (and here he got up and placed furniture to illustrate the position), "and looking in that glass I saw myself reflected nearly at full length; but my face, I noticed, had *two* separate and distinct images, the tip of the nose of one being about three inches from the tip of the other. I was a little bothered, perhaps startled, and got up and looked in the glass, but the illusion vanished. On lying down again, I saw it a second time, plainer, if possible, than before; and then I noticed that one of the faces was a little paler—say five shades—than the other. I got up, and the thing melted away, and I went off, and in the excitement of the hour forgot all about it—nearly, but not quite, for the thing would once in a while come up, and give me a little pang as if something uncomfortable had happened. When I went home again that night I told my wife about it, and a few days afterward I made the experiment again, when" (with a laugh), "sure enough! the thing came again; but I never succeeded in bringing the ghost back after that, though I once tried very industriously to show it to my wife, who was somewhat worried about it. She thought it was a 'sign' that I was to be elected to a second term of office, and that the paleness of one of the faces was an omen that I should not see life through the last term." This is a very remarkable story—a coincidence, we may say, to which some significance was given by the cruel death of the President soon after the beginning of his second term. I told Mrs. Lincoln the story, and asked her if she remembered its details. She expressed surprise that Mr. Lincoln was willing to say anything about it, as he had up to that time refrained from mentioning the incident to anybody; and as she was firm in her belief that the optical illusion (which it certainly was) was a warning, I never again referred to the subject to either the President or his wife. Subsequently, Lincoln's version of the story was confirmed by Private Secretary John Hay, who, however, was of the opinion that the illusion had been seen on the day of Lincoln's first nomination, and not, as I have said, on the day of his first election. Commenting on the result of the election of the day before, Lincoln said, with great solemnity: "I should be the veriest shallow and self-conceited blockhead upon the footstool, if in my discharge of the duties that are put upon me in this place, I should hope to get along without the wisdom that comes from God, and not from men."

On the night of November tenth an impromptu procession, gay with banners and resplendent with lanterns and transparencies, marched up to the White House, and a vast crowd surged around the main entrance, filling the entire space within the grounds as far as the eye could reach from the house. Martial music, the cheers of people, and the roar of cannon, shook the sky. Tad, who was flying around from window to window arranging a small illumination on his own private account, was delighted and excited by the occasional shivering of the large panes of glass by the concussion of the air produced when the cannon in the driveway went off with tremendous noise. The President wrote out his little speech, and his appearance at "the historic window" over the doorway in the portico was the signal for the maddest cheers from the crowd, and it was many minutes before the deafening racket permitted him to speak. The same procession marched around to the houses of some of the members of the cabinet, among others to that of Secretary Seward, who had returned from his visit to New York.

The Secretary of State was in an exceedingly jocose frame of mind, and after congratulating the crowd on the result of the election, made a funny speech substantially as follows: "I advise you to go and see Mr. Fessenden, for if he gets discouraged we shall all come to grief; also be good enough to poke up Mr. Stanton; he needs poking up, for he has been seriously sick, I hear, for several days past. You cannot do better also than to call upon my excellent friend Gideon Welles, and ask him if he cannot make the blockade off Wilmington more stringent, so that I shall not need to have so much trouble with my foreign relations." To say that the crowd was delighted with this comical little speech is faintly to describe the frame of mind in which the Secretary's jocose remarks were received.

THE PRESIDENT'S SHREWDNESS AT HAMPTON ROADS

Great was the excitement in Washington when, at the close of the next January (1865), it was noised abroad that negotiations looking for peace were to be opened between the Federal administration and the rebel president. Francis P. Blair, Sr., had returned from the second of his fruitless missions to Richmond, bringing to the President the information that Jefferson Davis was "ready to enter into conference with a view to secure peace to the two countries." The general tenor of Blair's verbal account of what he saw and heard in Richmond, more than anything else, perhaps, encouraged Mr. Lincoln in the belief that peace might be obtained by negotiation, and the Union be restored upon terms which would be acceptable to the country. I say "perhaps," because there is probably no living man who knew exactly what was Mr. Lincoln's opinion concerning the possibility of securing terms of peace at that time on any basis that would be acceptable to himself and to the whole country. But in any case we may be sure that he determined to exhaust all the means within his reach to satisfy the country whether peace with honor could or could not be obtained by negotiation. My own belief then (which was strengthened by one or two conversations with Mr. Lincoln) was that after the failure of the

Niagara Falls conference [involving the meddlesome Horace
Greeley] in July, 1864, he had no faith whatever in any proposition pretending to look in the direction of peace which might
come from the Confederate authorities.

But when it was found that not only had Secretary Seward
gone to Hampton Roads to meet the so-called rebel commissioners, Stephens, Campbell, and Hunter, but that the President of the United States had actually followed him, the per-
turbation in Washington was something which cannot be readily
described. The Peace Democrats went about the corridors of the
hotels and the Capitol, saying that Lincoln had at last come to
their way of thinking, and had gone to Hampton Roads to open
peace negotiations. The radicals were in a fury of rage. They
bitterly complained that the President was about to give up the
political fruits which had been already gathered from the long
and exhausting military struggle. It was asserted that the policy
of confiscation and emancipation was to be abandoned, and that
as a further concession to the "returning prodigal," the abolition
of slavery by the action of States that had not yet voted was to
be blocked then and there. There were, however, not a few
moderate, and I may say conservative, Republicans whose faith
in the sagacity and patriotism of Abraham Lincoln still remained unshaken; but these were in a minority, and it was
apparently with feeble hope that they admonished radical Republicans and Copperhead Democrats to wait until Lincoln had
returned from Hampton Roads and was ready to tell his story.
Among the bitterest to denounce the course of Lincoln was Thaddeus Stevens, who, a few days before, had said in his place in
the House of Representatives that if the country were to vote
over again for President of the United States, Benjamin F.
Butler, and not Abraham Lincoln, would be their choice. Others
of the same uncompromising and unreasonable stripe actually
hinted at impeachment and trial. Colonel John W. Forney un-
wittingly added fuel to the flames by publishing in the *Wash-*

ington Chronicle a series of editorial articles ablaze with all the clap-trap of double leads and typographical device, in which it was sought to prepare the public mind for the sacrifice of something vaguely dreadful and dreadfully vague. These articles counseled popular acquiescence in the repeal of the confiscation law and other kindred measures as a condition of peace, and were telegraphed all over the country, and indorsed by thoughtless men as the outgivings of President Lincoln. They were read by astonished and indignant thousands, were flouted and scouted by the followers of Wade and Davis, and they filled with alarm and dejection the minds of multitudes of readers not conversant with the facts. It must be remembered that the war upon President Lincoln for his alleged slowness in regard to the slavery question having no longer that excuse for being, the ultra-radicals had flown to Negro suffrage and a more vigorous system of retaliation upon rebel prisoners as convenient weapons in a new aggressiveness; and when it was confidently stated that Lincoln had gone to Hampton Roads because he feared that Seward would not make his terms "liberal enough," the excitement in and around the Capitol rose to fever heat.

When the President and the Secretary of State returned to Washington after their conference on board the steamer *River Queen* at Hampton Roads, the tenseness of political feeling in Congress was slightly relaxed. The radicals grudgingly admitted that Lincoln and Seward had not yet compromised away the substantial fruits of four years of war and legislation. But with common consent everybody agreed that the President must at once enlighten Congress as to the doings of himself and Secretary Seward and the rebel commissioners at Hampton Roads. On February eighth culminated a long and acrimonious quarrel which had been brewing in the Senate between some of the conservative and radical members of that body. Sumner introduced a resolution calling on the President for information concerning the Hampton Roads conference. To this Senator

[James R.] Doolittle of Wisconsin objected. He urged that such a request, at such a time, was an indirect censure of the President, and would be construed as a senatorial demand for him to give an account of himself. Mr. Doolittle was somewhat anxious to be regarded as the special champion of Lincoln and his administration. Sumner made a thrust at Doolittle, saying that the Wisconsin senator had made that speech before in the Senate, and that he [Sumner] would caution him not to "jump before he got to the stile." Irritated by this and other gibes at his alleged super-serviceableness, Doolittle replied that he classed Senator Powell of Kentucky and Senator Wade of Ohio together; for although, as he said, they were acting from different motives, they were attempting a common aim. Both, he said, were opposed to the readmission of the States lately in rebellion where the Federal authority had been partially restored— Louisiana at that time being the bone of contention. Senator Wade soon got the floor, and replied to Doolittle's speech with great bitterness, losing his temper, and referring to Doolittle's position as "poor, mean, miserable, and demagogical." He frankly said that he bore the Senator from Wisconsin "no malice and very little good will," and he added that the President was certainly in a bad way if he was reduced to having "such a poor prop" as Doolittle. Senator Wade exhibited great violence of temper, and Doolittle did not appear to advantage in his attempt to parry the violent blows of the angry senator from Ohio. The upshot of this painful business was that the resolution calling on the President for information concerning the Hampton Roads conference was adopted.

On the same day the House, without much ado, passed a resolution of similar import; but it was not until two days later (February tenth) that the message and accompanying documents came in. Meanwhile, before the President's return from Fort Monroe, Fernando Wood made in the House an extraordinary speech, which in the opinion of some people was designed to injure Lincoln with his own party by its fulsome praises of the President's patriotic action in going to Hampton Roads to participate in the now historic conference with the rebel commissioners. Among other things, Wood said: "If it be true that the President of the United States and the Secretary of State have gone personally to meet ambassadors, or representatives, or commissioners, as you may please to call them, from Richmond, I think that instead of this proceeding being obnoxious to the censure which I have heard bestowed upon it, they but follow the precedent of Washington and Hamilton, who in a similar emergency went (the one President and the other Secretary of the Treasury) to treat with rebels who were engaged in the whisky insurrection in Pennsylvania in 1796. If, therefore, it be true that the President of the United States has made an honest effort to stop this shedding of blood, this exhaustion of the energies of our great country; if it be true that, realizing his responsibility to his country and his God, he has thus risen superior to partisanship and the unfortunate influences that have surrounded him, I say all thanks to him, and God speed him in the work of mercy and justice and right." Even at this late day one can imagine the effect of remarks like these falling from the lips of one of the most notorious of the Northern Copperheads, eulogistic of the chief magistrate, who, as Wood would have had us believe, had taken a tedious journey to a point near the rebel lines in order to reopen those peace negotiations which the Democratic National Convention of the previous summer had declared necessary. On the same day, however, Wood offered a resolution declaring as the sense of the House that it was the duty of the President to proffer and accept only such negotiations as should imply the continued integrity and indissolubility of the Federal government.

The House, as seen from the reporters' gallery, when the President's message and accompanying documents relating to the Hampton Roads conference came in, was a curious and interesting study. There had been a call of the House on the previous evening, and a great number of absentees were now summarily brought up at the bar to make such excuses as they could for their non-appearance at the previous session. These proceedings were going on when the message from the President was announced. Instantly, by unanimous consent, all other business was suspended, and the communication from the President was ordered to be read. The reading began in absolute silence. Looking over the hall, one might say that the hundreds seated or standing within the limits of the great room had been suddenly turned to stone. The auditors who strained their attention were not merely interested to know what was the story to be unfolded: they were apparently fascinated by the importance and mysteriousness of the possible outcome of this extraordinary incident. It is no exaggeration to say that for a little space at least no man so much as stirred his hand. Even the hurrying pages, who usually bustled about the aisles waiting upon the members, were struck silent and motionless. The preliminary paragraphs of the message recited the facts relating to F. P. Blair, Sr.'s, two journeys to Richmond, and, without the slightest appearance of argument, cleared the way for the departure of Secretary Seward to meet the commissioners at Fort Monroe. Then came the three indispensable terms given in the instructions to the Secretary, on which alone could any conference looking to peace be held. These were:

1. The restoration of the national authority throughout all the States.

2. No receding, by the Executive of the United States, on the slavery question, from the position assumed thereon in the late annual message to Congress and in preceding documents.

3. No cessation of hostilities short of an end of the war and the disbanding of all forces hostile to the government.

When the clerk read the words at the close of the instructions to Seward, "You will not assume to definitely consummate anything," there ran a ripple of mirth throughout the great assembly of congressmen; and the tenseness with which men had listened to the reading was for the first time relaxed, although there had been a subdued rumble of applause when the clerk read in the instructions to Mr. Blair that the President would be always ready to receive any agent whom Davis, or other influential person, should send to him with a view of securing peace to the people of "our one common country." As the reading of the message and documents went on, the change which took place in the moral atmosphere of the hall of the House was obvious. The appearance of grave intentness passed away, and members smilingly exchanged glances as they began to appreciate Lincoln's sagacious plan for unmasking the craftiness of the rebel leaders; or they laughed gleefully at the occasional hard hits with which the wise President demolished the pretensions of those whose fine-spun logic he had so ruthlessly swept aside in the now famous interview. Of course the details of that interview were not then spread before the country, but enough was given in the documents submitted by the President to Congress to show the subtle wisdom with which his mission had been conducted and concluded. When the reading was over, and the name of the writer at the end of the communication was read by the clerk with a certain grandiloquence, there was an instant and irrepressible storm of applause, begun by the members on the floor, and taken up by the people in the gallery. It was instantaneous, involuntary, and irrepressible, and the Speaker only perfunctorily attempted to quell it. It was like a burst of refreshing rain after a long and heartbreaking drought.

In the midst of the great inspiration of satisfaction which followed the conclusion of the reading of the message, Representative James Brooks, of New York, made a partisan speech in which he expressed his regret that negotiations with "the separate States" had not been opened by the President; and from this he went on to the usual phrases of "effusion of blood," "fratricidal strife," and "enormous debt," and endeavored to break the force of the President's communication, which for a time at least had made every Unionist in that House a friend of every other, regardless of the titles of "conservative" and "radical" which had heretofore divided them. Thaddeus Stevens, who had been among the most acrid of Lincoln's critics during the period of doubt which intervened while the true intent and purpose of the visit to Hampton Roads were not understood, replied to Brooks briefly and pungently, and paid a high tribute to the sagacity, wisdom, and patriotism of President Lincoln. S. S. Cox was another speaker who praised the President. He said that the chief magistrate deserved the thanks of the country for his noble course in disregarding "mere politicians," and in looking over their heads to the people for indorsement and approval.

In a few days all of the material details of the Hampton Roads conference were spread before the country. The President's reply to the Senate's call for information chiefly consisted of a despatch prepared at the State Department for transmission to Mr. [Charles F.] Adams, the United States minister to England, in which the whole story was told with some degree of detail. Those censorious critics of Lincoln's policy who had pretended to believe that the President's visit to Fort Monroe was prompted by his desire to second Secretary Seward's eagerness and to stimulate his desire for peaceable negotiations, were greatly chagrined when they ascertained that it was General Grant, the idol of the hour, who had influenced Lincoln to take that step. Grant had confidentially written to the Secretary of War expressing his regret that the Confederate commissioners would return home "without any expression from any one in authority." While he recognized the difficulty of receiving the commissioners, he feared the "bad influence" which their failure to get an authoritative reply would have on the minds of the people, probably South as well as North. It was Grant's message, in which he deplored the failure of the commissioners to see the President, that had impelled Lincoln to go to Fort Monroe. Although General Grant recognized the difficulties in the way of receiving the commissioners, and probably had no faith in any substantial gain to be secured thereby, he did say that he was sorry that the errand of the three men would be bootless. He regarded only the moral effect of the mission on both sides of the lines.

Lincoln was in his grave before all the facts relating to this remarkable conference were made public by those who participated in it; and when those details did come out, the heroic attitude of Abraham Lincoln, as he sturdily stood up for all the results of the long contest which had then been secured in the interest of the Federal Union and the rights of man, was defined with exceeding clearness. The wisdom and sagacity with which he conducted the delicate business then in hand were acknowledged by friend and foe alike, when the session of the House broke up after his remarkable communication had been read to it; and, years later, those who had heard that message read recalled with a thrill of pride the exposition of shrewdness contained in the document. But among the various incidents of the conference the world will probably longest remember that recorded by Alexander H. Stephens, one of the three commissioners, who, afterward writing of the event, said that Mr. Hunter made a long reply to the President's refusal to recognize another government inside of that of which he alone was President by receiving ambassadors to treat for peace. "Mr. Hunter," says Stephens, "referred to the correspondence between King Charles I. and his parliament as a trustworthy precedent of a constitutional ruler treating with rebels. Mr. Lincoln's face then wore that indescribable expression which generally preceded his hardest hits, and he remarked: 'Upon questions of history I must refer you to Mr. Seward, for he is posted in such things, and I do not pretend to be bright. My only distinct recollection of the matter is that Charles lost his head.' That settled Mr. Hunter for a while."

LINCOLN'S SECOND INAUGURATION

The day of Lincoln's second inauguration, March 4, 1865, was as somber and drizzly as the November day of his second election. When the hour of noon arrived, great crowds of men and women streamed around the Capitol building in most wretched plight. The mud in the city of Washington on that day certainly excelled all the other varieties I have ever seen before or since, and the greatest test of feminine heroism—the spoiling of their clothes—redounded amply to the credit of the women who were so bedraggled and drenched on that memorable day. The only entrance to the Senate wing, where the preliminary ceremonies were held, was by the main or eastern portico, the other entrances being used only by privileged persons. From the reporters' gallery one could see that the senators were all massed on one side of their chamber, the other side being left for the members of the House and the few notables who should come in later. When the doors of the gallery were opened, and the crowd of women had finally been admitted, the sight was a beautiful one. Senator Foote of Vermont was in the chair, and was greatly discomfited to find that the fair ladies in the gallery had not the slightest idea that they were invading a session of the Senate. They chattered and clattered like zephyrs among the reeds of a water-side. The presiding officer in vain tapped with his ivory mallet. The gay people in the galleries talked on just as though there was no Senate in session in the United States; but when the attention of the fair mob was diverted by the arrival of eminent personages, something like a calm prevailed, and there was a silent gazing. There was Hooker, handsome, rosy, and gorgeous in full uniform; "the dear old Admiral," as the women used to call Farragut; Mrs. Lincoln in the diplomatic gallery, attended by gallant Senator Anthony; a gorgeous array of foreign ministers in full court costume; and a considerable group of military and naval officers, brilliant in gold lace and epaulets. There was a buzz when the justices of the Supreme Court came in, attired in their robes of office, Chief Justice Chase looking very young and also very queer, carrying a "stove-pipe" hat and wearing his long black silk gown. The foreign ministers occupied seats at the right of the chair behind the Supreme Court justices; and behind these were the members of the House. The members of the cabinet had front seats at the left of the chair, Seward at the head, followed by Stanton, Welles, Speed, and Dennison. Usher was detained by illness, and Fessenden occupied his old seat in the Senate. Lincoln sat in the middle of the front row.

All eyes were turned to the main entrance, where, precisely on the stroke of twelve, appeared Andrew Johnson, Vice-President elect, arm in arm with Hannibal Hamlin, whose term of office was now expiring. They took seats together on the dais of the presiding officer, and Hamlin made a brief and sensible speech, and Andrew Johnson, whose face was extraordinarily red, was presented to take the oath. It is needless to say here that the unfortunate gentleman, who had been very ill, was not altogether sober at this most important moment of his life. In order to strengthen himself for the physical and mental ordeal through which he was about to pass, he had taken a stiff drink of whisky in the room of the Vice-President, and the warmth of the Senate chamber, with possibly other physical conditions, had sent the fiery liquor to his brain. He was evidently intoxicated. As he went on with his speech, he turned upon the cabinet officers and addressed them as "Mr. Stanton," "Mr. Seward," etc., without the official handles to their names. Forgetting Mr. Welles's name, he said, "and you, too, Mr. ———," then, leaning over to Colonel Forney, he said, "What is the name of the Secretary of the Navy?" and then continued as though nothing had happened. Once in a while, from the reporters' gallery, I could observe Hamlin nudging Johnson from behind, reminding him that the hour for the inauguration ceremony had passed. The speaker kept on, although President Lincoln sat before him, patiently waiting for his extraordinary harangue to be over.

The study of the faces below was interesting. Seward was as bland and serene as a summer day; Stanton appeared to be petrified; Welles's face was usually void of any expression; Speed sat with his eyes closed; Dennison was red and white by turns. Among the Union Senators, Henry Wilson's face was flushed; Sumner wore a saturnine and sarcastic smile; and most of the others turned and twisted in their Senatorial chairs as if in long-drawn agony. Of the Supreme Bench, Judge Nelson only was apparently moved, his lower jaw being dropped clean down in blank horror. Chase was marble, adamant, granite in immobility until Johnson turned his back upon the Senate to take the oath, when he exchanged glances with Nelson, who then closed up his mouth. When Johnson had repeated inaudibly the oath of office, his hand upon the Book, he turned and took the Bible in his hand, and, facing the audience, said, with a loud, theatrical voice and gesture, "I kiss this Book in the face of my nation of the United States."

This painful incident being over, Colonel Forney, the Secretary of the Senate, read the proclamation of the President convoking an extra session, and called the names of the members elect. Thereupon the newly chosen Senators were sworn in, and the procession for the inauguration platform, which had been built on the east front of the Capitol, was formed. There was a sea of heads in the great plaza in front of the Capitol, as far as the eye could reach, and breaking in waves along its outer edges among the budding foliage of the grounds beyond. When the President and the procession of notables appeared, a tremendous shout, prolonged and loud, arose from the surging ocean of humanity around the Capitol building. Then the sergeant-at-arms of the Senate, the historic Brown, arose and bowed, with his shining black hat in hand, in dumb-show before the crowd, which thereupon became still, and Abraham Lincoln, rising tall and gaunt among the groups about him, stepped forward and read his inaugural address, which was printed in two broad columns upon a single page of large paper. As he advanced from his seat, a roar of applause shook the air, and, again and again repeated, finally died far away on the outer fringe of the throng, like a sweeping wave upon the shore. Just at that moment the sun, which had been obscured all day, burst forth in its unclouded meridian splendor, and flooded the spectacle with glory and with light. Every heart beat quicker at the unexpected omen, and doubtless not a few mentally prayed that so might the darkness which had obscured the past four years be now dissipated by the sun of prosperity,

> Till danger's troubled night depart,
> And the star of peace return.

The inaugural address was received in most profound silence. Every word was clear and audible as the ringing and somewhat shrill tones of Lincoln's voice sounded over the vast concourse. There was applause, however, at the words, "both parties deprecated war, but one of them would *make* war rather than let the nation survive, and the other would *accept* war rather than let it perish"; and the cheer that followed these words lasted long enough to make a considerable pause before he added sententiously, "and the war came." There were occasional spurts of applause, too, at other points along this wonderful address. Looking down into the faces of the people, illuminated by the bright rays of the sun, one could see moist eyes and even tearful cheeks as the good President pronounced these noble words: "With malice toward none, with charity for all, with firmness in the right as God gives us to see the right, let us strive on to finish the work we are in; to bind up the nation's wounds; to care for him who shall have borne the battle, and for his widow and his orphans; to do all which may achieve and cherish a just and a lasting peace among ourselves and with all nations." Among the memories of a lifetime, doubtless there are none more fondly cherished by those who were so fortunate as to stand near Lincoln at that historic moment than the recollection of the beautiful solemnity, the tender sympathy, of these inspired utterances, and the rapt silence of the multitudes.

There were many cheers and many tears as this noble address was concluded. Silence being restored, the President turned toward Chief Justice Chase, who, with his right hand uplifted, directed the Bible to be brought forward by the clerk of the Supreme Court. Then Lincoln, laying his right hand upon the open page, repeated the oath of office administered to him by the Chief Justice, after which, solemnly saying, "So help me God," he bent forward and reverently kissed the Book, then rose up inaugurated President of the United States for four years from March 4, 1865. A salvo of artillery boomed upon the air, cheer upon cheer rang out, and then, after turning, and bowing to the assembled hosts, the President retired into the Capitol, and, emerging by a basement entrance, took his carriage and was escorted back to the White House by a great procession.

The Book was probably opened at a venture by a clerk. Chief Justice Chase noted the place where Lincoln's lips touched the page, and he afterward marked the spot with a pencil. The Book so marked was given by the Chief Justice to Mrs. Lincoln. The President had pressed his lips on the twenty-seventh and twenty-eighth verses of the fifth chapter of the Book of Isaiah, where were these words:

None shall be weary nor stumble among them; none shall slumber nor sleep; neither shall the girdle of their loins be loosed, nor the latchet of their shoes be broken:

Whose arrows are sharp, and all their bows bent, their horses' hoofs shall be counted like flint, their wheels like a whirlwind.

There was the usual reception at the White House that evening, and, later on, the traditional inauguration ball, at which the President and his wife, most of the members of the cabinet, General Hooker, Admiral Farragut, and other great people were present. The ball was held in the great Hall of Patents in the Interior Department building, and was a very handsome affair; but its beauty was marred by an extraordinary rush of hungry people, who fairly mobbed the supper-tables, and enacted a scene of confusion whose wildness was similar to some of the antics of the Paris Commune.

But chiefly memorable in the mind of those who saw that second inauguration must still remain the tall, pathetic, melancholy figure of the man who, then inducted into office in the midst of the glad acclaim of thousands of people, and illumined by the deceptive brilliance of a March sunburst, was already standing in the shadow of death.

VIII

The End of Lincoln's Career

AT eight fifteen on the morning of April 3, 1865, Richmond fell.
The next day Lincoln visited the capital of the Confederacy. To
the Negroes who saw him there, Lincoln said, "Don't kneel to me.
You must kneel to God only, and thank Him for the liberty you
will hereafter enjoy." Washington was wild with celebrations when
Lincoln returned. Inevitably the crowds would wind up at the
White House, walking arm in arm, singing, bands playing (including
"Dixie," which Lincoln had declared war contraband, just as in
World War II "Lili Marlene" had been captured from the German
Afrika Korps). Lincoln would come to the window to acknowl-
edge the cheers; his son Tad waved a captured Rebel flag.

Brooks played a small part in Lincoln's last formal speech to
the people of the capital city. On April eleventh, the President appeared at a window of the Executive Mansion while thousands
of people "with bands, banners, and loud huzzahs" filled the semi-
circular avenue before him. The crowd had come spontaneously
—but Lincoln's speech was prepared. Brooks was with the President that night, and noticed a roll of manuscript in his hand. The
President explained that this was to prevent criticism of his offhand remarks, such as an expression he had once used, "The
rebels turned tail and ran." Now Lincoln came to the window.
Brooks says: "From a point of concealment behind the window
drapery I held a light while he read, dropping the pages of his
written speech one by one upon the floor as he finished them."
The President had begun to read his speech holding a candle in

his left hand and the manuscript in his right, but found difficulty doing so. "He made a comical motion with his left foot and elbow, which I construed to mean that I should hold his candle for him, which I did." The speech itself was serious—a paper which tried to formulate a generous reconstruction policy. It urged that everyone join in doing all the acts necessary to restore the proper practical relations between the seceded States and the Union, without legally deciding that these States had ever left in the first place.

A few days later, Brooks recalls that he had filled an appointment by calling on the President at the White House. The President told Brooks that he had had a notion of sending for him to go to the theater that evening. . . .

IN the latter part of the month of March, 1865, Washington saw many signs of a collapse of the rebellion. The Confederate army appeared to be thoroughly demoralized, and deserters, who arrived constantly in large numbers, reported that men from Alabama, Georgia, Florida, and the Carolinas could not be expected to have any heart in a fight which then seemed only for the defense of Virginia, while their own States were occupied by the armies of the Union. During the month of March more than three thousand deserters were received at Washington, and great numbers were quartered at Fort Monroe, Annapolis, and other points nearer the lines, where they were put to work in the quartermaster's department or in the naval service. One curiosity of the times was a Confederate regimental band which had deserted in a body with its instruments, and was allowed to march through the streets of the national capital playing Union airs. This was one of the oddest signs of the final breakup. People recalled a story, told by Hooker, how, when the Union army scaled and occupied Lookout Mountain, a rebel sentry on duty on the crest of one of the most difficult precipices saw our men rise up in solid masses over steps which had been thought inaccessible, and was so surprised that he forgot to run, but stood with feet rooted to the spot, watching the Union force climbing up, and streaming past him, and driving the enemy far to the rear, until he was left alone, a statue of amazement. Recovering himself at last, he threw down his musket, stripped off his rebel-gray jacket, stood on them both, and, looking far off to the sunny South, stretched out as a map below him, said, "How are you, Southern Confederacy?"

But, notwithstanding such indications of a collapse of the rebellion, at this very time many Northern Union newspapers, led by Horace Greeley and others of his stamp, were demanding that appeals should be made to the Southern people "to stop the flow of blood and the waste of treasure," and that some message should be sent to the Southerners "so terse that it will surely be circulated, and so lucid that it cannot be misconstrued or perverted," by way of an invitation to cease firing. Curiously enough, the nearer the time came for a final surrender, the more fervid was the demand for negotiation and appeal from the unreasonable radicals in the ranks of Northern Unionists. But all this was soon to end; and while a small party was asking, "Why not negotiate?" the downfall came.

The Army of Grant had been enveloping Petersburg on March twenty-eighth and twenty-ninth, and about ten o'clock on the morning of April third word was received in Washington from President Lincoln at City Point that that city had been evacuated, and that our Army was pushing into it, sweeping around it, and pursuing the flying squadrons of Lee. At a quarter to eleven in that forenoon came a despatch to the War Department from General Weitzel, dated at Richmond, announcing the fall of the Confederate capital. It was not many minutes before the news spread like wildfire through Washington, and the intelligence, at first doubted, was speedily made certain by the circulation of thousands of newspaper "extras" containing the news in bulletins issued from the War Department. In a moment of time the city was ablaze with excitement the like of which was never seen before; and everybody who had a piece of bunting spread it to the breeze; from one end of Pennsylvania Avenue to the other the air seemed to burn with the bright hues of the flag. The sky was shaken by a grand salute of eight hundred guns, fired by order of the Secretary of War—three hundred for Petersburg and five hundred for Richmond. Almost by magic the streets were crowded with hosts of people, talking, laughing, hurrahing, and shouting in the fullness of their joy. Men embraced one another, "treated" one another, made up old quarrels, renewed old friendships, marched through the streets arm in arm, singing and chatting in that happy sort of abandon which characterizes our people when under the influence of a great and universal happiness. The atmosphere was full of the intoxication of joy. The departments of the Government and many stores and private offices were closed for the day, and hosts of hard-worked clerks had their full share of the general holiday. Bands of music, apparently without any special direction or formal call, paraded the streets, and boomed and blared from every public place, until the air was resonant with the expression of the popular jubilation in all the national airs, not forgetting "Dixie," which, it will be remembered, President Lincoln afterward declared to be among the spoils of war.

The American habit of speech-making was never before so conspicuously exemplified. Wherever any man was found who could make a speech, or who thought he could make a speech, there a speech was made; and a great many men who had never before made one found themselves thrust upon a crowd of enthusiastic sovereigns who demanded of them something by way of jubilant oratory. One of the best of those offhand addresses extorted by the enthusiastic crowds was that of Secretary Stanton, who was called upon at the War Department by an eager multitude clamorous for more details and for a speech. The great War Secretary, for once in his life so overcome by emotion that he could not speak continuously, said this:

Friends and fellow-citizens: In this great hour of triumph my heart, as well as yours, is penetrated with gratitude to Almighty God for his deliverance of the nation. Our thanks are due to the President, to the Army and Navy, to the great commanders by sea and land, to the gallant officers and men who have periled their lives upon the battle-field, and drenched the soil with their blood. Henceforth all commiseration and aid should be given to the wounded, the maimed, and the suffering, who bear the marks of their great sacrifices in the mighty struggle. Let us humbly offer up our thanks to divine Providence for his care over us, and beseech him to guide and govern us in our duties hereafter, as he has carried us forward to victory; to teach us how to be humble in the midst of triumph, how to be just in the hour of victory, and to help us secure the foundations of this republic, soaked as they have been in blood, so that it shall live for ever and ever. Let us not forget the laboring millions in other lands, who in this struggle have given us their sympathies, their aid, and their prayers; and let us bid them rejoice with us in our great triumph. Then, having done this, let us trust the future to him who will guide us as heretofore, according to his own good will.

Nearly every line of this address was punctuated with applause.

The Secretary then read Grant's despatch, announcing the capture of Richmond, and the fact that the city was on fire, upon which the Secretary asked the crowd what they would reply to Grant. Some cried, "Let her burn!" others, "Burn it! burn it!" but one voice shouted, "Hold Richmond for the Northern mudsills!" which sally was received with considerable laughter. Mr. Stanton introduced to the crowd Willie Kettles, a bright-faced Vermont boy about fourteen years old, an operator in the telegraph room of the War Office, who had been the lucky recipient of the important despatch announcing the cap-

ture of Richmond. Of course the crowded wanted a speech
from the lad, who discreetly held his tongue, and bowed with
modesty. Secretary Seward, who happened to be at the War
Department to hear the news, was espied and called out, and he
made a little address in which he said that he had always been
in favor of a change in the cabinet, particularly in the War
Department, and that recent events proved that he was right.
"Why," said he, "I started to go to 'the front' the other day,
and when I got to City Point they told me it was at Hatcher's
Run, and when I got there I was told it was not there but somewhere else, and when I get back I am told by the Secretary that
it is at Petersburg; but before I can realize that, I am told
again that it is at Richmond, and west of that. Now I leave you
to judge what I ought to think of such a Secretary of War as
this." The crowds continually circulated through the city, and
from a building near the War Department, Senator Nye of
Nevada and Preston King of New York spoke, and at Willard's
Hotel General Butler, Green Clay Smith of Kentucky, and
Vice-President Johnson responded to the eager and uproarious
demand. The day of jubilee did not end with the day, but rejoicing and cheering were prolonged far into the night. Many
illuminated their houses, and bands were still playing, and
leading men and public officials were serenaded all over the city.
There are always hosts of people who drown their joys effectually in the flowing bowl, and Washington on April third was
full of them. Thousands besieged the drinking-saloons, cham-
pagne popped everywhere, and a more liquorish crowd was never
seen in Washington than on that night. Many and many a man
of years of habitual sobriety seemed to think it a patriotic duty
to "get full" on that eventful night, and not only so, but to
advertise the fact of fullness as widely as possible. I saw one
big, sedate Vermonter, chief of an executive bureau, standing
on the corner of F and Fourteenth streets, with owlish gravity
giving away fifty-cent "shin-plasters" (fractional currency) to

every colored person who came past him, brokenly saying with each gift, "Babylon has fallen!"

On the night of April fourth, in pursuance of a recommendation by the Secretary of State, the city was generally illuminated. All the public buildings and a great proportion of private residences and business houses were alight with fireworks and illuminations of every description. The War Department was gorgeously decorated with a mass of flags, the windows were filled with lights, and a huge transparency of patriotic devices crowned the portico. The same was true of the Navy Department, the Winder building (occupied by the Government), the White House, and the State and Treasury buildings. Secretary Seward was the author of a much-admired motto over the portico of the State Department, which read: "At home Union is order, and Union is peace. Abroad Union is strength, and strength is peace." Over another entrance of the building was: "Peace and good will to all nations, but no entangling alliances and no foreign intervention." The Treasury had over its chief entrance a huge transparency which was a tolerable imitation of a ten-dollar interest-bearing United States note, with a mammoth facsimile of Treasurer Spinner's signature in all its unique ugliness. The Treasury motto was: "U.S. Greenbacks and U.S. Grant. Grant gives the greenbacks a metallic ring."

With that wonderful adaptability which is characteristic of the American people, Richmond was no sooner in our hands than all the machinery of war, transportation, and subsistence began to tend thither, and orders were at once carried out to rebuild railroads, equip steamboat lines, and put up piers and bridges, so that in a few days Washington was in regular communication with Richmond, and that city was used as a base of supplies against whatever of rebellion might be left in arms. The Orange and Alexandria route to Richmond was reëstablished, although for the time being the line of transportation was from Washington via Aquia Creek and Fredericksburg. Steamers were despatched from Washington to Richmond with hospital supplies, and a United States mail agent took possession of the Richmond post-office; and while Washington was celebrating the downfall of the rebel capital, the general post-office received its first regular mail from the captured city. Governor [Francis H.] Pierpoint, who, as Senator Sumner said, had been carrying the State government of loyal Virginia in his trousers-pocket for several years, announced that the peripatetic ark of the government finally rested in its proper seat; and so the "Common Council of Alexandria," as Sumner had styled the "loyal" legislature of Virginia, was once more holding sittings in Richmond.

But greater things were yet to come. Most people were sleeping soundly in their beds when, at daylight on the rainy morning of April 10, 1865, a great boom startled the misty air of Washington, shaking the very earth, and breaking the windows of houses about Lafayette Square, and moving the inhabitants of that aristocratic locality to say once more that they would be glad when Union victories were done with, or should be celebrated elsewhere. Boom! boom! went the guns, until five hundred were fired. A few people got up in the chill twilight of the morning, and raced about in the mud to learn what the good news might be, while others formed a procession and resumed their parades,—no dampness, no fatigue, being sufficient to depress their ardor. But many placidly lay abed, well knowing that only one military event could cause all this mighty pother in the air of Washington; and if their nap in the gray dawn was disturbed with dreams of guns and of terms of armies surrendered to Grant by Lee, they awoke later to read of these in the daily papers; for this was Secretary Stanton's way of telling the people that the Army of Northern Virginia had at last laid down its arms, and that peace had come again.

But the great news had really reached Washington the

night before (Palm Sunday), and a few newspaper men and others of late habits, who were up through the darkness and the dampness of those memorable hours, had sent the glad tidings all over the Union from Maine to California, and had then unbent themselves in a private and exclusive jollification. When the capital was broad awake, and had taken in the full value of the news, the fever-heat that had fired the city on the day after the fall of Richmond did not return. Popular feeling had culminated then, and after that great event there was nothing that could surprise us, not even if "Jeff" Davis himself had come to Washington to surrender. The streets were shockingly muddy, but were all alive with people singing and cheering, carrying flags, and saluting everybody, hungering and thirsting for speeches. General Butler was called out, among others, and he made a speech full of surprising liberality and generosity toward the enemy. The departments gave another holiday to their clerks; so did many business firms; and the Treasury employees assembled in the great corridor of their building and sang "Old Hundredth" with thrilling, even tear-compelling effect. Then they marched in a body across the grounds to the White House, where the President was at breakfast, and serenaded him with "The Star-Spangled Banner."

As the forenoon wore on, an impromptu procession came up from the Navy Yard, dragging six boat-howitzers, which were fired through the streets as they rolled on. This crowd, reinforced by the hurrahing legions along the route, speedily swelled to enormous proportions, and filled the whole area in front of the White House, where guns were fired and bands played while the multitude waited for a speech. The young hope of the house of Lincoln—Tad—made his appearance at the well-known window from which the President always spoke, and was received with great shouts of applause, whereupon he waved a captured rebel flag, to the uproarious delight of the sovereign people below. When Lincoln came to the window shortly after, the scene before him was one of the wildest confusion. It seemed impossible for men adequately to express their feelings. They fairly yelled with delight, threw up their hats again and again, or threw up one another's hats, and screamed like mad. From the windows of the White House the surface of that crowd looked like an agitated sea of hats, faces, and arms. Quiet being restored, the President briefly congratulated the people on the occasion which called out such unrestrained enthusiasm, and said that, as arrangements were being made for a more formal celebration, he would defer his remarks until that occasion; "for," said he, "I shall have nothing to say then if it is all dribbled out of me now." He said that as the good old tune of "Dixie" had been captured on the ninth of April, he had submitted the question of its ownership to the Attorney-General, who had decided that that tune was now our lawful property; and he asked that the band should play it, which was done with a will, "Yankee Doodle" following. Then the President proposed three cheers for General Grant and the officers and men under him, then three cheers for the navy, all of which were given heartily, the President leading off, waving his hand; and the laughing, joyous crowd dispersed.

The special celebration to which Lincoln referred was that of the eleventh of April, when, in answer to the customary serenade, the President made a long and formal speech. All of the Government buildings were again illuminated, and the people, almost with unanimity, followed the example. The night was misty, and the exhibition was a splendid one. The reflection of the illuminated dome of the Capitol on the moist air above was remarked as being especially fine; it was seen many miles away. Arlington House, across the river, the old home of Lee, was brilliantly lighted, and rockets and colored lights blazed on the lawn, where ex-slaves by the thousand sang "The Year of Jubilee."

The notable feature of the evening, of course, was the President's speech, delivered to an immense throng of people, who, with bands, banners, and loud huzzahs, poured into the semi-circular avenue in front of the Executive Mansion. After repeated calls, loud and enthusiastic, the President appeared at the window, which was a signal for a great outburst. There was something terrible in the enthusiasm with which the beloved Chief Magistrate was received. Cheers upon cheers, wave after wave of applause, rolled up, the President patiently standing quiet until it was all over. The speech was longer than most people had expected, and of a different character. It was chiefly devoted to a discussion of the policy of reconstruction which had been outlined by him in previous public documents. It began with the words, now classic, "We meet this evening, not in sorrow, but in gladness of heart. The evacuation of Petersburg and Richmond, and the surrender of the principal insurgent army, give hope of a righteous and speedy peace, whose joyous expression cannot be restrained. In the midst of this, however, he from whom all blessings flow must not be forgotten. A call for a national thanksgiving is being prepared, and will be duly promulgated. Nor must those whose harder part gave us the cause of rejoicing be overlooked. Their honors must not be parceled out with others. I myself was near the front, and had the high pleasure of transmitting much of the good news to you, but no part of the honor for plan or execution is mine. To General Grant, his skillful officers and brave men, all belongs. The gallant navy stood ready, but was not in reach to take active part."

While the crowd was assembling in front of the house, and before the President went up-stairs to the window from which he was to speak, I was with him, and noticed that his speech was written out, and that he carried a roll of manuscript in his hand. He explained that this was a precaution to prevent a repetition of the criticisms which had sometimes been made by fastidious persons upon his offhand addresses. Senator Sumner, it

may be remembered, had objected to the President's using on a
former occasion the expression, "The rebels turned tail and
ran," as being undignified from the lips of the President of the
United States. Lincoln recalled that criticism with a placid
smile. From a point of concealment behind the window drapery
I held a light while he read, dropping the pages of his written
speech one by one upon the floor as he finished them. Little Tad,
who found the crowd no longer responsive to his antics, had
now sought the chief point of attraction, and scrambled around
on the floor, importuning his father to give him "another," as
he collected the sheets of paper fluttering from the President's
hand. Outside was a vast sea of faces, illuminated by the lights
that burned in the festal array of the White House, and stretching far out into the misty darkness. It was a silent, intent, and
perhaps surprised, multitude. Within stood the tall, gaunt figure
of the President, deeply thoughtful, intent upon the elucidation
of the generous policy which should be pursued toward the
South. That this was not the sort of speech which the multitude
had expected is tolerably certain. In the hour of his triumph as
the patriotic chief magistrate of a great people, Lincoln appeared to think only of the great problem then pressing upon
the Government—a problem which would demand the highest
statesmanship, the greatest wisdom, and the firmest generosity.

I have said that some of Lincoln's more fastidious critics
had objected to certain of his offhand phrases, which readily took
with the multitude, and which more graphically conveyed his
meaning than those commonly used by the scholars. Against
advice, he had, in a formal message to Congress, adhered to the
use of the phrase "sugar-coated pill." He argued that the time
would probably never come when the American people would
not understand what a sugar-coated pill was; and on this historic
occasion he used another favorite figure of his when he said,
"Concede that the new government of Louisiana is only to what
it should be as the egg is to the fowl, we shall sooner have the

fowl by hatching the egg than smashing it." But it turned out
that Senator Sumner, for one, was no better pleased with this
metaphor than he had been with others on previous occasions;
for in a letter to Dr. Lieber of Philadelphia, next day, he wrote:
"The President's speech, and other things, augur confusion
and uncertainty in the future, with hot controversy. Alas!
alas!" And still later in that year Sumner said: "The eggs of
crocodiles can produce only crocodiles, and it is not easy to see
how eggs laid by military power can be hatched into an American State."

Years have passed since then [from Brooks's vantage point
in the 1890's], and the grave has long since closed over the
President and the senators who opposed his policy and his judgment. Posterity has vindicated the wisdom of Lincoln, and has
dealt charitably with the errors of those who in their day lacked
that charity which is now entreated of mankind for them.
That they meant well, that they were patriotic, that they were
sincere, no man can doubt; but as we turn our thoughts backward to that April night when the great President made his last
public speech to a silent and wondering crowd, we may well
regard his figure with veneration and reverence, aware now, if
we were not then, that he builded better than they knew. In the
general jubilation of that hour, however, there was very little
criticism of the President's last public speech. It was felt, perhaps, that the man who had brought us safe through the great
trial of our strength and patience, himself strong and patient,
might well be trusted with the adjustment of terms of reunion.
Reunion was then the foremost thought in the minds of men.
Slavery was dead, peace had returned, and henceforth the grateful task of reuniting the long-estranged brotherhood of the
States was ours. Is it any wonder that men fairly cried with
joy when the certainty of this happy consummation rose in their
minds?

But even while we stood under the light of a new day, joyful as a people, triumphant as citizens, there was preparing for us a portentous and inconceivable disaster.

THE GREAT TRAGEDY

The afternoon and evening of April 14, 1865, were cold, raw, and gusty. Dark clouds enveloped the capital, and the air was chilly with occasional showers. Late in the afternoon I filled an appointment by calling on the President at the White House, and was told by him that he "had had a notion" of sending for me to go to the theater that evening with him and Mrs. Lincoln; but he added that Mrs. Lincoln had already made up a party to take the place of General and Mrs. Grant, who had somewhat unexpectedly left the city for Burlington, New Jersey. The party was originally planned for the purpose of taking General and Mrs. Grant to see "Our American Cousin" at Ford's Theater, and when Grant had decided to leave Washington, he (the President) had "felt inclined to give up the whole thing"; but as it had been announced in the morning papers that this distinguished party would go to the theater that night, Mrs. Lincoln had rather insisted that they ought to go, in order that the expectant public should not be wholly disappointed. On my way home I met Schuyler Colfax, who was about leaving for California, and who tarried with me on the sidewalk a little while, talking about the trip, and the people whom I knew in San Francisco and Sacramento and whom he wished to meet. Mr. Lincoln had often talked with me about the possibilities of his eventually taking up his residence in California after his term of office should be over. He thought, he said, that that country would afford better opportunities for his two boys than any of the older States; and when he heard that Colfax was going to California, he was greatly interested in his trip, and said that he hoped that Colfax would bring him back a good report of what his keen and practised observation would note in the country which he (Colfax) was about to see for the first time.

The evening being inclement, I stayed within doors to nurse a violent cold with which I was afflicted; and my room-mate McA—— and I whiled away the time chatting and playing cards. About half-past ten our attention was attracted to the frequent galloping of cavalry, or the mounted patrol, past the house which we occupied on New York Avenue, near the State Department building. [Brooks lived at three different places in Washington.] After a while quiet was restored, and we retired to our sleeping-room in the rear part of the house. As I turned down the gas, I said to my room-mate: "Will, I have guessed the cause of the clatter outside to-night. You know Wade Hampton has disappeared with his cavalry somewhere in the mountains of Virginia. Now, my theory of the racket is that he has raided Washington, and has pounced down upon the President, and has attempted to carry him off." Of course this was said jocosely and without the slightest thought that the President was in any way in danger; and my friend, in a similar spirit, banteringly replied, "What good will that do the rebs unless they carry off Andy Johnson also?" The next morning I was awakened in the early dawn by a loud and hurried knocking on my chamber door, and the voice of Mr. Gardner, the landlord, crying, "Wake, wake, Mr. Brooks! I have dreadful news." I slipped out, turned the key of the door, and Mr. Gardner came in, pale, trembling, and woebegone, like him who "drew Priam's curtain at the dead of night," and told his awful story. At the time it was believed that the President, Mr. Seward, Vice-President Johnson, and other members of the Government, had been killed; and this was the burden of the tale that was told to us. I sank back into my bed, cold and shivering with horror, and for a time it seemed as though the end of all things had come. I was aroused by the loud weeping of my comrade, who had not left his bed in another part of the room.

When we had sufficiently collected ourselves to dress and go out of doors in the bleak and cheerless April morning, we found in the streets an extraordinary spectacle. They were suddenly crowded with people—men, women, and children thronging the pavements and darkening the thoroughfares. It seemed as if everybody was in tears. Pale faces, streaming eyes, with now and again an angry, frowning countenance, were on every side. Men and women who were strangers accosted one another with distressed looks and tearful inquiries for the welfare of the President and Mr. Seward's family. The President still lived, but at half-past seven o'clock in the morning the tolling of bells announced to the lamenting people that he had ceased to breathe. His great and loving heart was still. The last official bulletin from the War Department stated that he died at twenty-two minutes past seven o'clock on the morning of April 15.

Instantly flags were raised at half-mast all over the city, the bells tolled solemnly, and with incredible swiftness Washington went into deep, universal mourning. All shops, Government departments, and private offices were closed, and everywhere, on the most pretentious residences and on the humblest hovels, were the black badges of grief. Nature seemed to sympathize in the general lamentation, and tears of rain fell from the moist and somber sky. The wind sighed mournfully through streets crowded with sad-faced people, and broad folds of funeral drapery flapped heavily in the wind over the decorations of the day before. Wandering aimlessly up F street toward Ford's Theater, we met a tragical procession. It was headed by a group of army officers walking bareheaded, and behind them, carried tenderly by a company of soldiers, was the bier of the dead President, covered with the flag of the Union, and accompanied by an escort of soldiers who had been on duty at the house where Lincoln died. As the little cortège passed down the street to the White House, every head was uncovered, and the profound silence which prevailed was broken only by sobs and by the sound of the measured tread of those who bore the martyred President back to the home which he had so lately quitted full of life, hope, and cheer.

On the night of the seventeenth the remains of Lincoln were laid in the casket prepared for their reception, and were taken from the large guest-chamber of the house to the famous East Room, where so many brilliant receptions and so many important public events had been witnessed; and there they lay in state until the day of the funeral (April nineteenth). The great room was draped with crape and black cloth, relieved only here and there by white flowers and green leaves. The catafalque upon which the casket lay was about fifteen feet high, and consisted of an elevated platform resting on a dais and covered with a domed canopy of black cloth which was supported by four pillars, and was lined beneath with fluted white silk. In those days the custom of sending "floral tributes" on funereal occasions was not common, but the funeral of Lincoln was remarkable for the unusual abundance and beauty of the devices in flowers that were sent by individuals and public bodies. From the time the body had been made ready for burial until the last services in the house, it was watched night and day by a guard of honor, the members of which were one major-general, one brigadier-general, two field officers, and four line officers of the Army and four of the Navy. Before the public were admitted to view the face of the dead, the scene in the darkened room—a sort of *chapelle ardente*—was most impressive. At the head and foot and on each side of the casket of their dead chief stood the motionless figures of his armed warriors.

When the funeral exercises took place, the floor of the East Room had been transformed into something like an amphitheater by the erection of an inclined platform, broken into steps, and filling all but the entrance side of the apartment and the area about the catafalque. This platform was covered with black cloth, and upon it stood the various persons designated as participants in the ceremonies, no seats being provided. In the northwest corner were the pall-bearers—Senators Lafayette S. Foster of Connecticut, E. D. Morgan of New York, Reverdy Johnson of Maryland, Richard Yates of Illinois, Benjamin F. Wade of Ohio, and John Conness of California; Representatives Henry L. Dawes of Massachusetts, A. H. Coffroth of Pennsylvania, Green Clay Smith of Kentucky, Schuyler Colfax of Indiana, E. B. Washburne of Illinois, and H. G. Worthington of Nevada; Lieutenant-General Grant, Major-General Halleck, and Brevet Brigadier-General Nichols; Vice-Admiral Farragut, Rear-Admiral Shubrick, and Colonel Zeilin, of the Marine Corps; civilians O. H. Browning, George Ashmun, Thomas Corwin, and Simon Cameron. The New York Chamber of Commerce was represented by its officers, and the New York Associated Merchants by Simeon Draper, Moses Grinnell, John Jacob Astor, Jonathan Sturges, and Hiram Walbridge. Next to them, at the extreme southern end of the room, were the governors of the States; and on the east side of the coffin, which lay north and south, and opposite the main entrance of the East Room, stood Andrew Johnson, President of the United States. He was supported on each side by his faithful friend Preston King and ex-Vice-President Hamlin. Behind these were Chief Justice Chase and his associates on the Supreme Bench, and near them were the members of the Cabinet and their wives, all of whom were in deep mourning. On the right of the Cabinet officers, at the northern end of the room, were the diplomatic corps, whose brilliant court costumes gleamed in strange contrast with the somber monotony of the rest of the spectacle. The members of the Senate and House of Representatives were disposed about the room and adjoining apartments, and at the foot of the catafalque was a little semi-circle of chairs for the family and friends. Robert T. Lincoln, son of the President, was the only one of the family present, Mrs. Lincoln being unable to leave her room, where she remained with Tad. General Grant, separated from the others, stood alone at the head of the cata- falque, and during the solemn services was often moved to tears. The officiating clergymen were the Rev. Dr. Gurley, pastor of the President, who preached the funeral sermon; the Rev. Dr. Hall, of the Epiphany Episcopal Church; the Rev. Dr. Gray, who was then chaplain of the Senate; and Bishop Simpson, who was an intimate friend of Lincoln. [Bishop Matthew Simpson of the Methodist Episcopal Church visited Lincoln in the White House.] A singular omission, whether intentional or not I do not know, was that no music of any sort was mingled with the exercises.

The sight of the funeral pageant will probably never be forgotten by those who saw it. Long before the services in the White House were over, the streets were blocked by crowds of people thronging to see the procession, which moved from the house precisely at two o'clock, amid the tolling of bells and the booming of minute-guns from three batteries that had been brought into the city, and from each of the many forts about Washington. The day was cloudless, and the sun shone brilliantly upon cavalry, infantry, artillery, marines, associations, and societies, with draped banners, and accompanied in their slow march by mournful dirges from numerous military bands. The Ninth and Tenth Regiments of Veteran Reserves headed the column; next came a battalion of marines in gorgeous uniforms; then the Sixteenth New York and the Eighth Illinois Cavalry Regiments; then eight pieces of United States light artillery in all the pomp and panoply peculiar to that branch of the service; next several mounted major-generals and brigadiers, accom- panied by their staffs; then army and naval officers on foot by the hundred, more mounted officers, and pall-bearers in car- riages; then the funeral car, a large structure canopied and covered with black cloth, somewhat like the catafalque which had been erected in the White House. The casket rested on a high platform eight or ten feet above the level of the street. As it passed many shed tears, and all heads were uncovered. The car was inclosed in a hollow square formed by a guard of honor consisting of mounted non-commissioned officers of various light artillery companies from Camp Barry, among them being the Independent Pennsylvania (Hampton's) Artillery, and the First West Virginia Battery, and the company of cavalry known as the President's bodyguard; then came the carriages for the family, and then the President, the Cabinet, the diplomatic corps, both houses of Congress, and others.

One noticeable feature of the procession was the appearance of the colored societies which brought up the rear, humbly, as was their wont; but just before the procession began to move, the Twenty-Second United States Colored Infantry (organized in Pennsylvania), landed from Petersburg and marched up to a position on the avenue, and when the head of the column came up, played a dirge, and headed the procession to the Capitol. The coffin was taken from the funeral car and placed on a catafalque within the rotunda of the Capitol, which had been darkened and draped in mourning.

The coffin rested in the rotunda of the Capitol from the nineteenth of April until the evening of the twentieth. During that time many thousands of people from every part of the United States paid to the dead form of the beloved President their last tearful tribute of affection, honor, and respect. The center of the building was temporarily in charge of the military, Congress not being in session, and the arrangements were admirable for the preservation of order, while all who came were allowed every reasonable facility in the carrying out of their melancholy errand. Guards marshaled the vast procession of sight-seers into a double line which separated at the foot of the coffin, passed on either side, was reunited again, and was guided out by the opposite door, which opened onto the great portico of the building on its east front.

While this solemn pageant was passing, I was allowed to go alone up the winding stairs that lead to the top of the great dome of the Capitol. Looking down from that lofty point, the sight was weird and memorable. Directly beneath me lay the casket in which the dead President lay at full length, far, far below; and, like black atoms moving over a sheet of gray paper, the slow-moving mourners, seen from a perpendicular above them, crept silently in two dark lines across the pavement of the rotunda, forming an ellipse around the coffin and joining as they advanced toward the eastern portal and disappeared. When the lying in state at the Capitol was over, the funeral procession from Washington to Springfield, Illinois, began, the cortège passing over the same route which was taken by Abraham Lincoln when he left his home for the national capital to assume the great office which he laid down only with his life.

It would be superfluous now to dwell on the incidents of that historic and most lamentable procession, or to recall to the minds of the present and passing generation the impressiveness of the wonderful popular demonstration of grief that stretched from the seaboard to the heart of Illinois. History has recorded how thousands of the plain people whom Lincoln loved came out from their homes to stand bareheaded and reverent as the funeral train swept by, while bells were tolled and the westward progress through the night was marked by campfires built along the course by which the great emancipator was borne at last to his dreamless rest.

THE DOOM OF THE CONSPIRATORS

The court-room in which were tried in May, 1865, the eight conspirators arraigned for being concerned in the plot against the lives of the heads of the Government, was a place of fascinating and perhaps morbid interest. The trial was arranged to be secret, but it was finally opened to those who could procure

passes from the president of the court. The room in which the
trial was held is a part of the great United States Arsenal
establishment, attached to which is the penitentiary in which
the conspirators were confined. It is on the banks of the Potomac,
in the suburbs of the city. Entering an old-fashioned brick
building, one was shown into a large, bare room on the ground
floor, where sat a couple of staff-officers receiving the credentials
of those who applied for admission; they sent these up to the
court, where an officer inspected them, and returned them, if
satisfactory, with the desired card of admission. A narrow flight
of stairs brought the visitor to a small chamber in the second
story, where a knot of orderlies were lounging about, and an
officer inspected one's pass; after another flight of stairs, another inspection of the pass permitted one to enter the court-
room, which was in the third story. It was an apartment about
twenty-five feet wide and thirty feet long, the entrance being at
the end opposite the penitentiary. Looking into the room, one
saw that it was divided lengthwise into two parts, the portion
on the right being occupied by the court, sitting around a long,
green-covered table, General Hunter at one end, and Judge-
Advocate-General [Joseph] Holt with his assistants at the other.
The part of the room which was not occupied by the court was
railed off, and was taken up with a few seats for reporters and
spectators generally, who were crowded confusedly about, and
rested as best they could against the bare, whitewashed walls of
the room. At the farther end of the apartment was a wooden
railing, behind which, on a narrow, raised platform, sat the
accused men, all in a solemn row, with an armed soldier sitting
between every two persons. At the left-hand corner behind them
was a heavy iron door opening into the corridor along which
were the cells of the prisoners. Each one of the accused was
manacled hand and foot, and sat grimly against the wall, facing
the court and the witnesses, the witness-stand being a raised
box in the center of the room.

On the left, in the line of prisoners, sat Mrs. [Mary] Surratt, deeply veiled, with her face turned to the wall, slowly and constantly fanning herself, and never raising her head except when ordered to show her countenance for the purpose of identification by witnesses. She was a dark-looking, fleshy, placid, and matronly woman, apparently about forty-five years of age. She was accused of being privy to the plot, assisting both before and after the assassination, and secreting in her house the arms and other implements to be used in carrying out the conspiracy.

Next to the guard who sat by Mrs. Surratt's side was [David E.] Herold, a small, dark man, about twenty-five years old, with a low, receding forehead, scanty black hair and whiskers, a stooping figure, protruding teeth, and a vulgar face. This man was Booth's intimate companion, and left him only when he was burned out in the Maryland barn.

Next was [Lewis] Paine, the assassin detailed for the murder of Seward. He sat bolt upright against the wall, looming up like a young giant above all the others. Paine's face would defy the ordinary physiognomist. It certainly appeared to be a good face. His coarse, black hair was brushed well off his low, broad forehead; his eyes were dark gray, unusually large and liquid. His brawny, muscular chest, which was covered only by a dark, close-fitting "sweater," was that of an athlete. He was apparently not much over twenty-four years old, and his face, figure, and bearing bespoke him the powerful, resolute creature that he proved to be. It was curious to see the quick flash of intelligence that involuntarily shot from his eyes when the knife with which he had done the bloody work at Seward's house was identified by the man who found it in the street near the house in the gray dawn of the morning after that dreadful night. The knife was a heavy, horn-handled implement, with a double edge at the point, and a blade about ten inches long, thick at the back, but evidently ground carefully to a fine point. This knife was subsequently given to Robinson, the faithful nurse who saved the life of Seward, and who was afterward made a paymaster in the Army of the United States.

Next in order sat [George A.] Atzerot, who had been assigned, it was believed, to the murder of Vice-President Johnson, but whose heart failed him when the time came to strike the blow. This fellow might safely challenge the rest of the party as the completest personification of a low and cunning scoundrel. He was small and sinewy, with long, dark-brown hair, dark-blue and unsteady eyes, a receding, narrow chin and forehead, and a generally villainous countenance. It was observed that when any ludicrous incident disturbed the gravity of the court, as sometimes happened, Atzerot was the only man who never smiled, although the others, Paine especially, would often grin in sympathy with the auditors.

[Michael] O'Laughlin, who was supposed to have been set apart for the murder of Stanton or Grant, had the appearance of the traditional stage villain. He had a high, broad forehead, a mass of tangled black hair, a heavy black mustache and chin-whiskers, and his face was blackened by a rough, unshaven beard. His large eyes, black and wild, were never still, but appeared to take in everything within the room, scanning each new arrival at the door, watching the witnesses, but occasionally resting on the green trees and sunny sky seen through the grated window on his left. He often moved his feet, and the clanking of his manacles would attract his attention; he would look down, then back and forth at the scene within the courtroom. A Californian vigilance committee in 1849 probably would have hanged him "on general principles." He was accused of being in league with both Surratt and Herold, and was seen at Stanton's house on the night of the murder, asking for General Grant.

[Edward] Spangler, the stage-carpenter of Ford's Theater, was about forty, heavily built, sandy in complexion, slovenly in appearance. He held Booth's horse at odd times, kept clear the way to the rear of the theater, and was suspected of being his lackey. The poor creature, more than any other, appeared to be under the influence of imminent bodily fear. His hands were incessantly moving along his legs from knee to thigh, his bony fingers traveling back and forth like spiders, as he sat with his eyes fixed on each witness.

Dr. [Samuel] Mudd, the companion and associate of Booth, who received the flying assassin into his house on the night of the murder, and set his fractured limb, in appearance was about thirty-five years of age, and had mild blue eyes, a good, broad forehead, ruddy face, hair scanty and thin, a high head, and a sanguine temperament. He sat in his shirt sleeves, with a white handkerchief knotted loosely about his neck, and attentively regarded the proceedings with the air of a man who felt sure of himself.

Last in the row, and looking out of the window upon the pleasant sky and tree-tops beyond, was [Samuel Bland] Arnold, the "Sam" of Booth's correspondence, who, writing from Hookstown, Maryland, informed the assassin that he had concluded to "give up the job," and was tired of keeping up appearances. This man was as uneasy as a caged whelp. He leaned his head on the rail before him, or looked out of the window, or lounged against the wall, or rested his chin on his breast, and generally was absolutely inattentive to everything that went on. He had retreated from the conspiracy, and was caught at Fort Monroe, where he had gone to get out of the way until suspicion had passed. It then appeared that he figured only in the original plan of abducting Lincoln, and was to have caught him on the stage when the rest of the villains had thrown him over from the box.

The appearance and demeanor of the court, it must be admitted, were neither solemn nor impressive. The members of the commission sat about in various negligent attitudes, and a general appearance of disorder was evident. Many ladies were present, and their irrepressible whispering was a continual nuisance to the reporters, who desired to keep track of the evidence. The witnesses were first examined by the Judge-Advocate, the members of the court putting in a question now and then, and the counsel for the prisoners taking up the cross-examination, each counselor attending only to the witness whose testimony affected his own client. The witnesses were brought in without regard to any particular criminal, all being tried at once. Occasionally an attorney for one prisoner would "develop" the witness under examination in such a manner as to injure the cause of another of the defendants, and then a petty quarrel would ensue between the different counsel.

Of the eight prisoners at the bar, Paine, Atzerot, Herold, and Mrs. Surratt were declared by the court guilty of murder, and were hanged on July 7, 1865. O'Laughlin, Arnold, and Dr. Mudd were found guilty of being accessory to the conspiracy, and were sentenced to imprisonment at hard labor for life. Spangler, who impressed most people as being a weak creature, unaware of being concerned in any real crime, was sentenced to six years' imprisonment, and, with O'Laughlin, Arnold, and Mudd, was sent to the forts of the Dry Tortugas. Dr. Mudd was pardoned by President Johnson in February, 1869, and Arnold and Spangler about a month later in the same year. O'Laughlin died of yellow fever while in prison at Fort Jefferson, Florida. John H. Surratt, who was at first believed to have been the would-be assassin of Mr. Seward, escaped from Washington immediately after the tragedy, and fled to Canada; thence he went to Italy, where he enlisted in the Papal Zouaves, but was traced by the sleuth-hounds of the United States detective force, and was brought back to this country on an American frigate in December, 1866, and tried, but not convicted. [He settled in Maryland, worked as a clerk, and lived until 1916.]

A painful and depressing feature of this tragical business

was the ease with which many well-meaning but unreasonable people not only appeared to forget the awfulness of the crime committed, but made objection to the findings of the court as well. Judge John A. Bingham, who assisted the judge-advocate in the trial, was unjustly, even wickedly, pursued by some of these wrong-headed persons for the part he took in the conviction of Mrs. Surratt. All the evidence in her case pointed unerringly to her guilt as an intelligent accomplice of the assassins. And the fact that Paine sought her house as a place of refuge after his murderous assault upon Seward, was only one of many more conclusive evidences of her active share in the great conspiracy. Her sex appears to have confused the judgment of many who did not follow the trial with attentiveness.

It was natural, but to a lover of Lincoln almost surprising, that while the lifeless form of the martyr was being borne home to Illinois, the newly installed President, Andrew Johnson, was surrounded, courted, and flattered by eager crowds of courtiers and office-seekers in Washington. If Johnson had just been inaugurated, after a political campaign in which he had defeated Lincoln, and was expected to overturn everything that remained of his predecessor's work, the appearance of things would not have been different from what it was. Multitudes from every part of the country rushed upon Washington, some with windy and turgid addresses to the new President, and many more with applications for official favor. To a thoughtful man this exhibition was disgusting beyond description.

Nor was one's respect for a pure democracy heightened by the habitual pose of President Johnson. It was a remarkable illustration of the elasticity and steadiness of our form of government that its machinery moved on without a jar, without tumult, when the head was suddenly stricken down. But the vulgar clamor of the crowds that beset Johnson, the boisterous ravings of the successor of Lincoln, and the complete absorption of Washington quidnuncs in speculations on the "policy" of the new head of the Government, saddened those who regarded this ignoble spectacle with hearts sore with grief for the loss of him who was yet unburied.

All these petty details are but a small part of our history; but they do belong to history. Posterity is already making up its verdict. We must be content to leave to posterity the final adjustment of all things. Smaller men are passing out of human memory. In the words of one who knew him well, Lincoln "belongs to the ages."

IX

Life in the White House

BROOKS's friendship with the family in the Executive Mansion enabled him to be one of the few to observe Mrs. Lincoln and Tad as well as the President. It is not unlikely that some of the spirit of Lincoln's youthful son existed in Brooks's juvenile books. He dedicated his book, *Abraham Lincoln and the Downfall of Slavery* (1888), to the memory of Tad. Mrs. Lincoln leaned on the young newspaperman in Washington both before and after her husband's death. Two letters from Mrs. Lincoln to Brooks, written in 1865 and 1866, and now held by Francis Whiting Hatch of Castine, Me., called upon Brooks to perform some small favors, and reported on the health and mental framework of the former First Lady and her "little Taddie." Mrs. Lincoln closed one with, "My husband was so earnest a friend of yours, that we will always remember you, with the kindest feelings & will always, be pleased to hear from you"; the second went, "I am well aware of the deep sympathy you feel for us, and the great affection and confidence, my husband cherished for you draws you very near to us."

The confidence permitted Brooks to see Lincoln in relaxed moments, making asides, scoring "hits" in personal meetings, commenting on the literary, theatrical and cultural tastes at the time, including his own. In all this Brooks stands modestly in the background, as a good reporter, observing his subject and the world around him. He hears Lincoln describe the semi-colon in punctuation as "a very useful little chap." He watches Lincoln studying nature, preferring the naked trees to those in leaf because then "their anatomy" could be seen. And he notes that Lincoln stored away all his impressions carefully and then applied them in future discussions and talks as parables and anecdotes.

Mr. Lincoln's simple habits in Washington startled many people. One summer morning, Brooks remembered, while passing the White House at an early hour, he saw the President standing at the gateway, looking anxiously down the street. In reply to a salutation, he said, "Good morning, good morning! I am looking for a newsboy. When you get to that corner I wish you would start one up this way." In an article in *Harper's Magazine* a month after Lincoln's assassination (the article appears in full in the editor's press biography of Lincoln, *Lincoln As They Saw Him*, Rinehart & Company, 1956), Brooks recalled this story and added: "There are American citizens who consider such things beneath the dignity of an official in high place."

P ROBABLY no family that ever lived in the Executive Mansion was so irregular in its methods of living as were the Lincolns. Naturally, Mr. Lincoln was methodical in his habits; he was scrupulously exact in all the details of his office, and his care for written documents was sometimes carried to an extreme; he appeared to have the Chinese reverence for a written paper. But the exigencies of those stormy times prevented him from being regular in his manner of life in the White House; and the example of the head of the family could not fail to affect all of the other members. Never very attentive to the demands or the attractions of the table, his incessant cares, his anxieties, and the engrossing calls upon his time (which he had not the skill to parry), left him with very little opportunity to attend to the simplest duties of the head of a family. Of his personal comfort he was so absolutely neglectful as to require constant prompting from other members of his household.

When Mrs. Lincoln, whom he always addressed by the old-fashioned title of "Mother," was absent from home, the President would appear to forget that food and drink were needful for his existence, unless he were persistently followed up by some of the servants, or were finally reminded of his needs by the actual pangs of hunger. On one such occasion, I remember, he asked me to come in and take breakfast with him, as he had some questions to ask. He was evidently eating without noting what he ate; and when I remarked that he was different from most Western men in his preference for milk for breakfast, he said, eying his glass of milk with surprise, as if he had not before noticed what he was drinking, "Well, I do prefer coffee in the morning, but they don't seem to have sent me in any." Who "they" were I could only guess.

For many years before Lincoln became President, there had been no children living in the White House. Buchanan was unmarried, and Pierce was childless when he took up his residence in the Executive Mansion. Although the great house, of which a large part was surrendered to public uses and inspection, never could be made to assume an air of domesticity, the three boys of the Lincoln family did much to invest the historic building with a phase of human interest which it did not have before.

THE BOY OF THE WHITE HOUSE

The youngest lad, Thomas, better known by his nickname of "Tad," was the irrepressible spirit of fun and mischief which, through the whole of his father's term, gave the life in the White House its only comic element. This lad, the complete embodiment of animal spirits, may be called one of the historic boys of America. His name is closely identified with that of his father in the minds of all who were admitted to the inner precincts of the White House; and thousands who never saw the home apartments of that gloomy building knew the tricksy sprite that brightened the weary years which Lincoln passed in Washington.

When the Lincoln family took up their abode in the White House, Robert, the eldest of the three children, was not quite eighteen years old. He had been admitted to Harvard College in 1860, and was away from home during a greater part of the time thereafter; and his subsequent successful career as Secretary of War, Minister to England, and lawyer is familiar in the mind of the reader. [Robert lived until 1926. His father's private papers were turned over to the Library of Congress.] The second son, Willie, a bright and cheery lad, greatly beloved by his parent, was a little past ten years old when the family entered the White House. He died in February, 1862, while the black shadows rested on many another American home. Tad was eight years old when he was taken to Washington with the rest of the family. He had a curious impediment in his speech which rather heightened the effect of his droll sayings; and the difficulty which he had in pronouncing his own name gave him the odd nickname by which he was always known. After his father's death, Tad was taken abroad by his mother, and, by judicious schooling, he overcame the defect of which I have spoken. Returning home with his mother in 1871, he was prostrated by a severe illness; and, after enduring with marked fortitude several months of suffering, he died in July, 1871.

Perhaps it was heaviness of grief at the loss of Willie that made it well-nigh impossible for Lincoln to treat Tad's innumerable escapades with severity. While the family lived in Washington, the lad was allowed his own way almost without check. His father was to the last degree indulgent, although when he chose to exercise his paternal authority, the boy was readily amenable to discipline or reproof. Much of the time it was impossible that he should not be left to run at large. He was caressed and petted by people who wanted favors of his father, and who took this way of making a friend in the family, as they thought; and he was living in the midst of a most exciting epoch in the country's history, when a boy in the White House was in a strange and somewhat unnatural atmosphere. But I am bound to say that Tad, although he doubtless had his wits sharpened by being in such strange surroundings, was never anything else, while I knew him, but a boisterous, rollicking, and absolutely real boy. He was not "old for his years," as we sometimes says of precocious children, nor was he burdened with care before his time. He was a big-hearted and fresh-faced youngster, and when he went away from the White House, after his father's tragic end, he carried with him, from the midst of sorrows and associations that are now historic, the same boyish frankness and simplicity that he took into it.

Very soon after he began life in the White House, Tad learned what an office-seeker was. All day long, unless the President was absent from the building, the office-seekers lined the upper corridors and passages; and sometimes the lines extended all the way down the stairs and nearly to the main entrance. When other diversions failed him, Tad liked to go around among these waiting place-hunters and institute inquiries on his own account. He would ask what they wanted, how long they had been there, and how much longer they proposed to wait. Some of these men came day after day, and for many successive days; with these Tad became acquainted, and to them he would give much sympathetic advice in his own whimsical but sincere way. Once he mounted guard at the foot of the public staircase, and exacted toll of all who passed up. "Five cents for the benefit of the Sanitary Fund," he explained to the visitors, who were not unwilling to have a friend at court for so small a price.

He organized for himself, after the custom of the day, a Sanitary Fair. Beginning with a little table, which he set in the grand corridor of the White House and stocked with small purchases of fruit and odds and ends begged from the pantry

of the house, he extended his operations in a second venture.
He secured from a carpenter a pair of trestles and a wide board,
on which he spread the entire stock of an old woman who sold
apples, gingerbread, and candy, near the Treasury building,
bought out with the lad's carefully saved pocket-money. This
"fair" was set up just within the portico of the White House,
where the place-seekers, whose patronage the shrewd boy catered
for, would be sure to pass on their way to the fountain of power.
Tad's enterprise was highly successful, but the proceeds of his
sales were speedily dispersed by his open-handed generosity. Before night, capital and profits had been spent, and the little
speculator went penniless to bed.

Everything that Tad did was done with a certain rush and
rude strength which were peculiar to him. I was once sitting
with the President in the library, when Tad tore into the room
in search of something, and, having found it, he threw himself
on his father like a small thunderbolt, gave him one wild, fierce
hug, and, without a word, fled from the room before his father
could put out his hand to detain him. With all his boyish rough-
ness, Tad had a warm heart and a tender conscience. He abhorred falsehood as he did books and study. Tutors came and
went, like changes of the moon. None stayed long enough to
learn much about the boy; but he knew them before they had
been one day in the house. "Let him run," his father would
say; "there's time enough yet for him to learn his letters and
get pokey. Bob was just such a little rascal, and now he is a
very decent boy."

It was curious, however, to see how Tad comprehended
many practical realities that are far beyond the grasp of most
boys. Even when he could scarcely read, he knew much about
the cost of things, the details of trade, the principles of me-
chanics, and the habits of animals, all of which showed the ac-
tivity of his mind and the odd turn of his thoughts. His father
took great interest in everything that concerned Tad, and when

the long day's work was done, and the little chap had related to the President all that had moved him or had taken up his attention during the daylight hours, and had finally fallen asleep under a drowsy cross-examination, the weary father would turn once more to his desk, and work on into the night, for his cares never ended. Then, shouldering the sleeping child, the man for whom millions of good men and women nightly prayed took his way through the silent corridors and passages to his boy's bed-chamber.

On an occasion of issuing a presidential proclamation for a national fast, Tad expressed some curiosity as to what a fast-day could possibly be. The result of his investigations filled him with dismay. An absolute fasting for one whole day, such as he was told to expect, was dreadful. Accordingly he established a food depot under the seat of a coach in the carriage-house. To this he furtively conveyed savings from his table-rations and such bits of food as he could pick up about the larder of the White House. Nobody suspected what he was doing, until a servant, one day, while cleaning the carriage, lighted on this store of provision, much to the rage and consternation of the lad, who stood by watching the gradual approach of the man to his provision depot. The President related the incident with glee, and added, "If he grows to be a man, Tad will be what the women all dote on—a good provider."

Tad accompanied his father and mother on the visit to the Army of the Potomac, spoken of in a previous chapter, and although he was greatly delighted with the bustle, animation, and brilliancy of the reviews during those memorable days, he was anxious for home when night and darkness came on, and there was nothing to engage his restless mind. Then he would begin to coax his father to go back to Washington. The President, although slightly annoyed by the boy's persistence, apologized for him, saying that there was a new pony at home waiting to be tried under the saddle by Tad, who had finally compassed a darling project of his own. Finally, to bribe the lad to cease his importunities, Lincoln offered to give him a dollar if he would not pester him with further inquiries about going home. The boy accepted the bargain, but he did not keep his agreement very well; and on the last day of our stay he shyly reminded his father that he needed that dollar very much. Lincoln thoughtfully took out of his pocket-book a dollar bill, and, looking in the boy's eyes, said: "Now, Taddie, my son, do you think you have earned this?" The lad hung his head, and answered not a word. "Well, my son," said the indulgent father, "although I don't think you have kept your part of the bargain, I will keep mine, and you cannot reproach *me* with breaking faith, anyway."

On the way from headquarters to the railway station at that time, there was an immense amount of cheering from the soldiers, who, as usual, seemed wild with delight at seeing the President. Occasionally we heard them cry, "Three cheers for Mrs. Lincoln!" and they were given with a will. Then, again, the men would cry, "Three cheers for the boy!" This salute Tad acknowledged, under instructions from his mother, and entirely unabashed by so much noise and attention. One soldier, after the line through which we were passing had given three cheers "for the next fight," cried, "And send along the greenbacks!" This arrested the attention of Tad, who inquired its meaning, and, when told that the army had not been paid for some time, on account of the scarcity of greenbacks, he said, with some indignation, "Why doesn't Governor Chase print 'em some, then?"

There are several interesting photographs of Tad now extant. One of these represents him dressed in the uniform of a lieutenant. In a moment of sportiveness, Secretary Stanton gave the boy a lieutenant's commission, and "Tad" managed to get together most of the articles of clothing and equipment suitable to his unexpected rank. He actually attempted to exercise military authority over the guards at the White House; but his elder

brother, Robert, interposed to relieve the men from duty after
Tad had placed them on sentry. That night, it is recorded, the
Executive Mansion was left unguarded. A well-known picture
of Tad and his father, engraved for the *Century Magazine* some
years ago, represents the boy standing by his father's side, looking over the pages of a large book. [The engraving, adapted
from an early Brady photograph, appeared in *Harper's Monthly*
early in 1865.] Lincoln explained to me that he was afraid that
this picture was a species of false pretense. Most people, he
thought, would suppose the book a large clasped Bible, whereas
it was a big photograph album which the photographer, posing
the father and son, had hit upon as a good device to use in this
way to bring the two sitters together. Lincoln's anxiety lest
somebody should think he was "making believe read the Bible
to Tad," was illustrative of his scrupulous honesty.

THE GETTYSBURG SPEECH AND OFFICE-SEEKING

One November day—it chanced to be the Sunday before the
dedication of the national cemetery at Gettysburg—I had an
appointment to go with the President to [Alexander] Gardner,
the photographer, on Seventh Street, to fulfil a long-standing
engagement. Mr. Lincoln carefully explained that he could not
go on any other day without interfering with the public business
and the photographer's business, to say nothing of his liability
to be hindered by curiosity-seekers "and other seekers" on the
way thither. Just as we were going down the stairs of the White
House, the President suddenly remembered that he needed a
paper, and, after hurrying back to his office, soon rejoined me
with a long envelop in his hand. When we were fairly started,
he said that in the envelop was an advance copy of Edward
Everett's address to be delivered at the Gettysburg dedication
on the following Tuesday. Drawing it out, I saw that it was a
one-page supplement to a Boston paper, and that Mr. Everett's

address nearly covered both sides of the sheet. The President expressed his admiration for the thoughtfulness of the Boston orator, who had sent this copy of his address in order that Mr. Lincoln might not traverse the same lines that the chosen speaker of the great occasion might have laid out for himself. When I exclaimed at its length, the President laughed and quoted the line:

"Solid men of Boston, make no long orations,"

which he said he had met somewhere in a speech by Daniel Webster. He said that there was no danger that he should get upon the lines of Mr. Everett's oration, for what he had ready to say was very short, or, as he emphatically expressed it, "short, short, short." In reply to a question as to the speech having been already written, he said that it was written, "but not finished." He had brought the paper with him, he explained, hoping that a few minutes of leisure while waiting for the movements of the photographer and his processes would give him a chance to look over the speech. But we did not have to wait long between the sittings, and the President, having taken out the envelop and laid it on a little table at his elbow, became so engaged in talk that he failed to open it while we were at the studio. A disaster overtook the negative of that photograph, and after a very few prints had been made from it, no more were possible. In the picture which the President gave me, the envelop containing Mr. Everett's oration is seen on the table by the side of the sitter, recalling the incident and Lincoln's quotation of Boston's "long orations."

It was a curious illustration of the pertinacity with which the office-hunters pursued the President, that even Sunday's sanctity was not respected by them. When we returned that day to the White House, one of these was waiting to intercept him at the entrance with a paper covered with indorsements. "Office-hunting was in the air," Lincoln said.

When a certain prominent comedian of the time was playing in Washington during Lincoln's administration, the President saw his representations with great delight, and was so
pleased that he expressed himself in warm terms to the player
through the medium of the manager. Thereupon the actor sent
the President a book in which he inscribed some pleasant words
by way of dedication to Lincoln, who acknowledged the gift in
a kindly little note. Not long after this, going to the President's
cabinet on a summons from him very late at night, I noticed
this man waiting alone in the corridor outside the President's
door. Lincoln asked me if any one was waiting without, and
when I told him that I had seen the actor sitting there, he made
a gesture of impatience and regret, and said that the little
courtesies which had passed between them had resulted in the
comedian applying to him for an office. I have forgotten what it
was, but I think it was an English consulate which the old man
wanted. Lincoln almost groaned as he said that it seemed impossible for him to have any close relations with people in
Washington without finding that the acquaintance thus formed
generally ended with an application for office.

One of the best things he ever said about the office-seeking
that consumed so much of the precious time which should have
been given to more important matters was that he was like a
man who was so busy renting out rooms at one end of his house
that he could not stop to put out the fire that was burning the
other end. On another occasion, he said that it sometimes seemed
to him that each one in the unending stream of place-hunters
that approached him seized and took away a bit of his vitality.
No wonder the harassed President was often so worn and spent
with his day's labors, in the midst of tremendous cares of office,
that he sunk into a semi-conscious state, his eyes fixed on
vacancy, and became so deeply abstracted that it was with difficulty that he could be roused by the friend, or member of his
own household, who stood over him.

Returning from a visit to the Army of the Potomac, when its depots were at City Point, I gave an account of my visit to the President, as he had sent me with a special pass to Grant's headquarters. He asked, jocularly, "Did you meet any colonels who wanted to be brigadiers, or any brigadiers who wanted to be major-generals, or any major-generals who wanted to run things?" Receiving a reply in the negative, he stretched out his hand in mock congratulation, and said, "Happy man!" Afterward, an officer who had been attentive to our little party did come to my lodgings and complain that he ought to be promoted, urging, among other things, that his relationship to a distinguished general kept him down. I told the incident to the President, after recalling his previous questions to me. Lincoln fairly shrieked with laughter, and, jumping up from his seat, cried, "Keeps him down? Keeps him down? That's all that keeps him up!"

A Western Senator who had failed of a reëlection, brought his successor, one day, and introduced him to the President. Lincoln, in reply, expressed his gratification at making the acquaintance of a new Senator. "Yet," he added, "I hate to have old friends like Senator W—— go away. And—another thing —I usually find that a Senator or Representative out of business is a sort of lame duck. He has to be provided for." When the two gentlemen had withdrawn, I took the liberty of saying that Mr. W—— did not seem to relish that remark. Weeks after, when I had forgotten the circumstance, the President said, "You thought I was almost rude to Senator W—— the other day. Well, now he wants Commissioner Dole's place!" Mr. [George W.] Dole was then Commissioner of Indian Affairs.

LINCOLN'S STORY-TELLING

Lincoln very seldom invented a story. Once he said to me, "You speak of Lincoln stories. I don't think that is a correct phrase. I don't make the stories mine by telling them. I am only a retail dealer." Numberless stories were repeated to him as being from him, but he once said that, so far as he knew, only about one sixth of all those which were credited to him had ever been told by him. He never forgot a good story, and his apt application of those which lay in his mind gave them peculiar crispness and freshness. Here is a case in point: In 1863, a certain captain of volunteers was on trial in Washington for a misuse of the funds of his company. The accused officer made only a feeble defense, and seemed to treat the matter with indifference. After a while, however, a new charge—that of disloyalty to the Government—came into the case. The accused was at once excited to a high degree of indignation, and made a very vigorous defense. He appeared to think lightly of being convicted of embezzling, but to be called a traitor was more than he could bear. At the breakfast-table, one morning, the President, who had been reading an account of this case in the newspaper, began to laugh, and said, "This fellow reminds me of a juror in a case of hen-stealing which I tried in Illinois, many years ago. (The writer is not certain, now, whether Mr. Lincoln told this story out of his own experience, or at second hand. The application, of course, was his own.) The accused man was summarily convicted. After adjournment of court, as I was riding to the next town, one of the jurors in the case came cantering up behind me, and complimented me on the vigor with which I had pressed the prosecution of the unfortunate hen-thief. Then he added, 'Why, when I was young, and my back was strong, and the country was new, I didn't mind taking off a sheep now and then. But stealing hens! Oh, Jerusalem!' Now, this captain has evidently been stealing sheep, and that is as much as he can bear."

Scripture stories and incidents were also used by Lincoln to illustrate his argument or to enforce a point. Judge E—— had been concerned in a certain secret organization of "radical"

Republicans, whose design was to defeat Lincoln's renomination. When this futile opposition had died out, the judge was pressed by his friends for a profitable office. Lincoln appointed him, and to one who remonstrated against such a display of magnanimity, he replied, "Well, I suppose Judge E——, having been disappointed before, did behave pretty ugly; but that wouldn't make him any less fit for this place; and I have scriptural authority for appointing him. You remember that when the Lord was on Mount Sinai getting out a commission for Aaron, that same Aaron was at the foot of the mountain making a false god for the people to worship. Yet Aaron got his commission, you know."

Lincoln particularly liked a joke at the expense of the dignity of some high civil or military official. One day, not long before his second inauguration, he asked me if I had heard about Stanton's meeting a picket on Broad River, South Carolina, and then told this story: "General Foster, then at Port Royal, escorted the secretary up the river, taking a quartermaster's tug. Reaching the picket lines on the river, a sentry roared from the bank, 'Who have you got on board that tug?' The severe and dignified answer was, 'The Secretary of War and Major-General Foster.' Instantly the picket roared back, 'We've got major-generals enough up here—why don't you bring us up some hard-tack?'" The story tickled Lincoln mightily, and he told it until it was replaced by a new one.

Anything that savored of the wit and humor of the soldiers was especially welcome to Lincoln. His fondness for good stories is a well-accepted tradition, but any incident that showed that "the boys" were mirthful and jolly in all their privations seemed to commend itself to him. He used to say that the grim grotesqueness and extravagance of American humor were its most striking characteristics. There was a story of a soldier in the Army of the Potomac, carried to the rear of battle with both legs shot off, who seeing a pie-woman hovering about, asked, "Say, old lady, are them pies sewed or pegged?" And there was another one of a soldier at the battle of Chancellorsville, whose regiment, waiting to be called into the fight, was taking coffee. The hero of the story put to his lips a crockery mug which he had carried, with infinite care, through several campaigns. A stray bullet, just missing the coffee-drinker's head, dashed the mug into fragments, and left only its handle on his finger. Turning his face in that direction, the soldier angrily growled, "Johnny, you can't do that again!" Lincoln, relating these two stories together, said, "It seems as if neither death nor danger could quench the grim humor of the American soldier."

When I had been at some pains, one day, to show the President how a California politician had been coerced into telling the truth without knowing it, he said it reminded him of a black barber in Illinois, notorious for lying, who, hearing some of his customers admiring the planet Jupiter, then shining in the evening sky, said, "Sho, I've seen that star afore. I seen him 'way down in Georgy." Said the President, "Like your California friend, he told the truth, but he thought he was lying."

In considering Lincoln's story-telling habit, it should be borne in mind that he never told a story for the sake of the telling; the tale came into his mind as an apt illustration of what was at that moment under discussion. Thus the cry for reinforcements that came from a Union general whose whereabouts had been anxiously debated, reminded him of an Illinois woman who, when she heard the wail of one of her offspring in the underbrush near her cabin, thanked God that there was "one who wasn't dead yet." And when Hood's Army in Tennessee was destroyed by Thomas, in December, 1864, the President told this story, which has since been often related: "A certain rough, rude, and bullying man in our county had a bull-dog, which was as rude, rough, and bullying as his master. Dog and man were the terror of the neighborhood. Nobody dared to touch either for fear of the other. But a crafty neighbor laid a plan to dispose of the dog. Seeing Slocum and his dog plodding along the road one day, the dog a little ahead, this neighbor, who was prepared for the occasion, took from his pocket a junk of meat in which he had concealed a big charge of powder, to which was fastened a deadwood slow-match. This he lighted, and then threw into the road. The dog gave one gulp at it, and the whole thing disappeared down his throat. He trotted on a few steps, when there was a sort of smothered roar, and the dog blew up in fragments, a fore-quarter being lodged in a neighboring tree, a hind-quarter on the roof of a cabin, and the rest scattered along the dusty road. Slocum came up and viewed the remains. Then, more in sorrow than in anger, he said, 'Bill war a good dog; but, as a dog, I reckon his usefulness is over.' " The President added, with a twinkle of his eye, "Hood's Army was a good army. We have been very much afraid of it. But, as an army, I reckon its usefulness is gone."

SOME OF HIS LITERARY TENDENCIES

It does not seem that Lincoln had a nimble fancy; his imagination was not fertile; if it was, he took pains to keep it under; but there was a vein of poetic sentiment which appears in many of his earlier writings and speeches. When the poetical tastes of Lincoln are mentioned, immediately there comes to mind that depressing and bilious poem, "Oh, why should the spirit of mortal be proud?" Those verses, with their lugubrious refrain, undoubtedly affected Lincoln strongly on the tragic side of his nature; but they have received a somewhat fictitious value as an expression of his literary taste. It is true, however, that he inclined toward the poetry inspired by sad and pathetic themes. It has been said that this was a sort of prophetic indication of the tragical ending of his own life; and some have thought that they detected in "the far-away look of his eyes" the gaze of one who was destined to a violent death. It is not likely that such thoughts occurred to any of us while he was yet alive; they are, however, the most natural of afterthoughts.

Like many men who have a keen sense of humor, Lincoln was easily moved by the pathos which is so nearly allied to jocularity. This is the reason, I suppose, why he liked best the minor poems of Thomas Hood and Oliver Wendell Holmes. Few men ever passed from grave to gay with the facility that characterized him. He liked, too, sad and pensive songs. I remember that, one night at the White House, when a few ladies visiting the family were singing at the piano-forte, he asked for a little song in which the writer describes his sensations when revisiting the scenes of his boyhood, dwelling mournfully on the vanished joys and the delightful associations of forty years ago. It is not likely that there was anything in Lincoln's lost youth that he would wish to recall; but there was a certain melancholy and half-morbid strain in that song which struck a responsive chord in his heart. The lines sunk into his memory, and I remember that he quoted them, as if to himself, long afterward.

Lincoln seldom quoted poetry in his letters or speeches, although in conversation he often made an allusion to something which he had read, always with the air of one who deprecated the imputation that he might be advertising his erudition. Occasionally, as in his farewell speech to his neighbors and friends in Springfield, he employed a commonplace quotation, with due credit to the unknown author. In that address he said, "Let us believe, as some poet has expressed it, 'Behind the cloud the sun is still shining.'" In a speech in Congress, on so unpromising a theme as internal improvements, then one of the issues of the time, he quoted Robert Herrick's lines:

"Attempt the end, and never stand to doubt;
Nothing's so hard but search will find it out."

Another example occurs in an address made to a delegation of colored men who had waited on him to obtain an expression of opinion on the subject of colonization. The President spoke at some length, and concluded by saying that he hoped that his visitors would consider the matter seriously, not for themselves alone, nor for the present generation, but for the good of mankind, and he added:

> "From age to age descends the lay
>   To millions yet to be,
> Till far its echoes roll away
>   Into eternity."

Amid all his labors, Lincoln found time to read the newspapers, or, as he sometimes expressed it, "to skirmish" with them. From their ephemeral pages he rescued many a choice bit of verse, which he carried with him until he was quite familiar with it. I am bound to say that some of these waifs would not receive the hospitality of a severe literary critic; but it was noticeable that they were almost invariably referable to his tender sympathy with humanity, its hopes and its sorrows. I recall one of these extracts, which he took out of his pocket one afternoon, as we were riding out to the Soldiers' Home. It began:

> A weaver sat at his loom,
>   Flinging his shuttle fast,
> And a thread that should wear till the hour of doom
>   Was added at every cast.

The idea was that men weave in their own lives the garment which they must wear in the world to come. I do not know who wrote the verses; but the opening lines were fixed in my mind by their frequent repetition by the President, who seemed to be strongly impressed by them. During the evening, he murmured them to himself, once or twice, as if in a soliloquy.

I think it was early in the war that some public speaker sent Lincoln a newspaper report of a speech delivered in New York. The President, apparently, did not pay much attention to the speech, but a few lines of verse at the close caught his eye. These were the closing stanzas of Longfellow's "Building of the Ship," beginning with:

> Thou too, sail on, O Ship of State!
> Sail on, O Union, strong and great!

To my surprise, he seemed to have read the lines for the first time. Knowing the whole poem as one of my youthful exercises in recitation, I began, at his request, with the description of the launch of the ship, and repeated it to the end. As he listened to the last lines:

> "Our hearts, our hopes, our prayers, our tears,
> Our faith triumphant o'er our fears," etc.,

his eyes filled with tears, and his cheeks were wet. He did not speak for some minutes, but finally said, with simplicity: "It is a wonderful gift to be able to stir men like that." It is quite possible that he had read the poem long before the war for the Union gave to the closing portion that depth of meaning which it held for him and now holds for us.

WRITING AND COMPOSITION

Lincoln always composed slowly, and he often wrote and rewrote his more elaborate productions several times. I happened to be with him often while he was composing his message to Congress, which was sent in while Sherman was on his march through Georgia. There was much speculation as to where Sherman had gone, and the secret was very well preserved. The President hoped, from day to day, that Sherman would be

heard from, or that something would happen to give him an
opportunity to enlighten "and possibly congratulate the country," as he put it. But December came, and there were no tidings from Sherman, though everybody was hungry with expectation, and feverish with anxiety. The President's message was
first written with pencil on stiff sheets of white pasteboard, or
boxboard, a good supply of which he kept by him. These sheets,
five or six inches wide, could be laid on the writer's knee, as he
sat comfortably in his arm-chair, in his favorite position, with
his legs crossed. One night, taking one of these slips out of his
drawer, with a great affectation of confidential secrecy, he said,
"I expect you want to know all about Sherman's raid?" Naturally I answered in the affirmative, when he said, "Well, then,
I'll read you this paragraph from my message." The paragraph,
however, was curiously non-committal, merely referring to
"General Sherman's attempted march of three hundred miles
directly through the insurgent region," and gave no indication
whatever of the direction of the march, or of the point from
which news from him was expected. Laying the paper down, and
taking off his spectacles, the President laughed heartily at my
disappointment, but added, kindly, "Well, my dear fellow, that's
all that Congress will know about it, anyhow."

He took a simple-hearted pleasure in considering some of
his best "hits." Occasionally, he would tell his more intimate
friends of a sharp saying that he had uttered during that day;
and once he wrote out for publication an account of an interview
which he had just had with two ladies who had come to him
with a request for the liberation of their husbands, held as prisoners of war in Federal camps. He thought he "had got the best
of the argument," he said, although he granted the petition of
the ladies. In that writing, I remember, he did not use capital
letters when he mentioned the days of the week; and he said
that with him punctuation was a matter of feeling, not of edu-
cation. But his punctuation, it may be added, was always good,

and he was addicted to what the printers call "close punctuation." Once he alluded to the semi-colon, which so few people use with intelligence and confidence, as "a very useful little chap."

As a rule, Lincoln wrote his most important letters with his own hand. Some of these—perhaps most of them—were read over to confidential friends and were corrected, or modified, before being sent. He kept copies of all letters of moment, and even some of these copies he made himself with painstaking care. In his office in the public wing of the White House was a little cabinet, the interior divided into pigeonholes. The pigeonholes were lettered in alphabetical order, but a few were devoted to individuals. Horace Greeley, I remember, had a pigeonhole by himself; so did each of several generals who wrote often to him. One compartment, labeled "W. & W.," excited my curiosity, but I never asked what it meant, and, one night, being sent to the cabinet for a letter which the President wanted, he said, "I see you looking at my 'W. & W.' Can you guess what that stands for?" Of course it was useless to guess. "Well," said he, with a merry twinkle of the eye, "that's Weed and Wood—Thurlow and Fernandy." Then he added with an indescribable chuckle, "That's a pair of 'em!"

Though Lincoln does not appear to have used much imagery in his letters and speeches, his innumerable good sayings were pregnant with meaning; as Emerson has said, his fables were so wise that in an earlier time he would have been a mythological character, like Æsop. His parables were similes. His figures of speech, used sparingly, were homely and vigorous, the offspring of an uncultivated imagination, rather than of a mind stored with the thoughts of the great men of all ages. The simplest incidents of every-day life furnished him with similes. In one of his speeches in the famous campaign with Douglas, he said, referring to the suppression of political debate, "These popular sovereigns are at their work, blowing out the moral lights around us." This figure of blowing out the lights is not only a simple one, but highly suggestive of the homely incident which was in the mind of the speaker; an affected or fastidious person would have weakly said, "extinguishing." In the same way, Lincoln insisted on retaining in his first annual message to Congress the phrase "sugar-coated pills;" and when remonstrated with by the public printer, John D. Defrees, who was a personal friend, he defended his use of the figure by declaring that the time would never come when the American people would not know what a sugar-coated pill was.

His earlier addresses showed, perhaps, more use of figures of speech than did his later ones. Criticizing that part of President Polk's message which referred to the Mexican war, Lincoln, then a representative in Congress, compared it to "the half-insane mumbling of a fever-dream." In the same speech he described military glory as "the attractive rainbow that rises in showers of blood; the serpent's eye that charms to destroy." I do not now recall a more striking picture, drawn by Lincoln, than this description of the helpless state of the American slave in 1857. "They have him in his prison-house," said he. "They have searched his person and have left no prying instrument with him. One after another they have closed the heavy iron doors upon him, and now they have him, as it were, bolted in with a lock of a hundred keys, which can never be unlocked without the concurrence of every key; the keys in the hands of a hundred different men, and they scattered to a hundred different and distant places; and they stand musing as to what invention, in all the dominions of mind and matter, can be produced to make the impossibility of his escape more complete than it is."

Lincoln was a close observer of nature, as well as of men. He used natural objects to complete his similes. Into the alembic of his mind everything was received, to be brought forth again as aphorism, parable, or trenchant saying. In woodcraft, for example, he was deeply skilled, his habit of close observation leading him to detect curious facts which escaped the notice of most men. Riding through a wood in Virginia, he observed a vine which wrapped a tree in its luxuriant growth. "Yes," he said, "that is very beautiful; but that vine is like certain habits of men; it decorates the ruin that it makes." At another time, when we were in Virginia together, just after a fall of snow, I found him standing on the stump of a tree, looking out over the landscape. He called attention to various subtle features of the view, and said, among other things, that he liked the trees best when they were not in leaf, as their anatomy could then be studied. And he bade me look at the delicate yet firm outline of a leafless tree against the sky. Then, pointing to the fine network of shadows cast on the snow by the branches and twigs, he said that that was the profile of the tree. The very next day, somebody was discussing with him the difference between character and reputation, when he said,—with a look as if to remind me of what he had been talking about the day before,—perhaps a man's character was like a tree, and his reputation like its shadow; the shadow is what we think of it; the tree is the real thing.

Perhaps his exceeding plainness of speech detracted somewhat from the real depth of his thought, but he was acute rather than profound; and I am inclined to think that those who were nearest him during the last years of his life were impressed by the swiftness and the correctness of his intuitions, rather than by the originality and profundity of his reasoning. Some of the more radical members of his party were impatient with his "exasperating slowness"; but I never heard any one criticize him for lack of speed in arriving at a rational conclusion when he had once undertaken an argument on any subject whatever.

We were once talking about woodcraft, and the President said that, although he had had undue credit for rail-splitting, he did know how to fell a tree; and he gave an entertaining disquisition on the art, illustrated by examples before us. He said that he did not remember splitting many rails in his life. In fact, rail-fences were not in his line at all; but he was proud, he said, of his record as a woodsman. Somebody reminded him that he had authenticated some rails as of his splitting, during the Lincoln and Hamlin campaign. "No, I didn't," he replied. "They brought those rails in where I was, with a great hurrah, and what I did say was that if I ever split any rails on the piece of ground that those rails came from (and I was not sure whether I had or not), I *was* sure that those were the rails."

In private conversation Lincoln manifested a singular reluctance to speak of himself as President, or to mention the office with any sort of personal reference to himself. He always used the phrase, "since I came into this place," instead of saying, "since I became President." The war he usually spoke of as "this great trouble," and he seldom alluded to the enemy as "Confederates," or "the Confederate Government," but he used the word "rebel" in his talks and in his letters.

LINCOLN, EVERETT, AND AGASSIZ

There was, sometimes, a curious inconsistency between Lincoln's public and private utterances. Not long after Edward Everett's death, he referred to that event as a public loss. On the evening of the day when the news of the death reached Washington, I was at the White House, and the conversation naturally fell upon that topic. Lincoln said, "Now, you are a loyal New Englander,—loyal to New England,—what great work of Everett's do you remember?" I was forced to say that I could not recall any. The President persisted and wanted to know if I could not recollect any great speech. Not receiving satisfaction, he said, looking around the room in his half-comical fashion, as if afraid of being overheard, "Now, do you know, I think Edward Everett was very much overrated. He hasn't left any enduring monument. But there was one speech in which, addressing a statue of John Adams and a picture of Washington, in Faneuil Hall, Boston, he apostrophized them and said, 'Teach us the love of liberty protected by law!' That was very fine, it seems to me. Still, it was only a good idea, introduced by noble language."

Continuing his discussion of Everett, he referred to his celebrated address on Washington, which was delivered through the South, as if in the hope that the rising storm of the rebellion might be quelled by this oratorical oil on the waters. Lincoln recalled a story told of Everett's manner. It was necessary, in his Washington oration, to relate an anecdote accompanied by the jingle of coin in the lecturer's pocket. This was done at each of the five hundred repetitions of the address, in the same manner, and with unvarying accuracy. When gold and silver disappeared from circulation, Mr. Everett procured and kept for this purpose a few coins with which, and a bunch of keys, the usual effect was produced. "And I am told," added Lincoln, "that whenever Mr. Everett delivered that lecture, he took along those things. They were what, I believe, the theatrical people would call his 'properties.' "

While this talk was going on, the cards of Congressman Hooper and Professor Agassiz were brought in by a servant. "Agassiz!" exclaimed the President with great delight, "I never met him yet, and Hooper promised to bring him up to-night." I rose to go, when he said, "Don't go, don't go. Sit down, and let us see what we can pick up that's new from this great man."

The conversation, however, was not very learned. The President and the savant seemed like two boys who wanted to ask questions which appeared commonplace, but were not quite sure of each other. Each man was simplicity itself. Lincoln asked for the correct pronunciation and derivation of Agassiz's name, and both men prattled on about curious proper names in various languages, and odd correspondences between names of common things in different tongues. Agassiz asked Lincoln if he ever had engaged in lecturing in his life. Lincoln gave the outline of a lecture which he had partly written, to show the origin of inventions, and prove that there is nothing new under the sun. "I think I can show," said he, "at least, in a fanciful way, that all the modern inventions were known centuries ago." Agassiz begged that Lincoln would finish the lecture some time. Lincoln replied that he had the manuscript somewhere in his papers, "and," said he, "when I get out of this place, I'll finish it up, perhaps, and get my friend B—— to print it somewhere." The fragment, for it is little else, was found among his papers after his death, and was printed by his literary executors, Messrs. Nicolay and Hay.

X

The Last Grand Review

THE victory parade of the Union Army in May, 1865, following the obsequies for the murdered President, a month before, marked the triumphal end of the war. Noah Brooks was there. A few days before the Army of the Potomac and the Army of the Mississippi marched down Pennsylvania Avenue, past the covered wooden stands near the White House erected for President Johnson and other high-ranking officials, Brooks had filed a dispatch to the *Sacramento Union*. "It is hard to realize that he is gone," Brooks wrote, "that we shall no more see his commanding form, hear his gentle voice or touch his pure and honest hand, with its well-remembered earnestness." The high point of victory had been attained by Lincoln in another form: when groups of Negroes, in conquered Richmond, had thanked him for their freedom.

Now, in the reviewing stand, the President, Secretary of War Stanton and General Grant stood up to catch the salutes of the lowered flags and swords. The regiments marched by in proud blue lines, sixty abreast on the broad avenue, bayonets fixed and glistening under a sky filled with sunshine. Washington watched as Sheridan's cavalry clopped steadily for more than an hour. They saw a scarfed General Custer in buckskin breeches, galloping and swinging his saber; the men of the corps and regiments and companies carrying battle flags reading Shiloh, Vicksburg, Chattanooga, Atlanta, Savannah—the long road to Appomattox; General Sherman, horse and rider decked out in flowers, leading his troops while the band played "Marching Through Georgia."

The rutted roads of Washington, so much a part of the vision of the capital in war-time, had been cleared and the dust settled by two days of rain. Across Pennsylvania Avenue from the President's reviewing stand, the lesser dignitaries were grouped, including the newspapermen. Brooks trained his field-glasses on the scene before him. He watched as General Sherman saluted the President on the reviewing platform but refused to shake hands with Secretary of War Stanton; Sherman's surrender terms with Confederate General Joseph Johnston had not been recognized until modified in Washington.

"In a few weeks this army of two or three hundred thousand men melted back into the heart of the people from whence it came," Brooks said, "and the great spectacle of the Grand Army of the Republic on review disappeared from sight."

Brooks himself hung around Washington for a few months. The capital had returned to its own almost-pastoral look, Lincoln gone, the war excitement gone, only the difficult job of reconstruction, and bitterness, remaining. The stories for a great war-time reporter were now beyond Washington, and Brooks moved on to California, as he had done once before, from Castine.

THE city of Washington, so often wrung with grief, and so often delirious with hope and joy, during those memorable years of war, saw a noble and inspiring sight on the twenty-third and twenty-fourth days of May, in 1865. This was when we witnessed the farewell march through the National capital of more than one hundred and fifty thousand soldiers, who were welcomed with an enthusiasm impossible of description, as they passed through the city which for the time being might have been regarded as being the heart of the nation. It was a noble sight to see; and it is not altogether certain that the pride and joy of the soldiers ready to be mustered out at last were any greater than the pride and joy of the citizens who regarded with affectionate admiration this brave array. On the first day was reviewed the Army of the Potomac, General Meade commanding; and the second day saw the march-past of the famous Army of the Mississippi, commanded by General Sherman.

It was a notable event, and people came from every part of the United States to look upon the passing pageant. Never in the history of Washington had there been such an enormous influx of visitors as at that time. For weeks there had been so vast a volume of applications for accommodations at the hotels and boarding-houses that every available nook and corner had been taken. Governors and other state functionaries, congressmen, and private citizens from even distant cities desired to look at last upon the grand armies now about to dissolve. So great was the number of visitors that many were obliged to spend the night in the open air, sleeping on park benches, or walking the streets. The mild summer weather of Washington softened these discomforts to the houseless and determined patriots.

Along the route of the great march stands were built by the Government or by the District authorities, and in some instances by private individuals; so that, from the Capitol to the White House, Pennsylvania Avenue presented a well-nigh unbroken mass of seats, rising rank above rank along the line of march, decorated with the national colors, and filled with joyful and enthusiastic crowds of men, women, and children. The city had ordered a closing of the schools for these two days, and one of the charming features of the great occasion was the massing of the children, in gay attire, on the steps and platforms of the massive porticos and terraces of the northern end of the Capitol. The little folks greeted the returning soldiers with bursts of patriotic song and the waving of miniature flags, to which the men in the ranks responded with cheers, many a father doubtless looking up with moistened eyes to the childish throngs with thoughts of homes to which they were now returning after long absences in perilous campaigns.

The main point of attraction was the part of Pennsylvania Avenue which is nearest the White House. There were built several covered stands for the comfortable accommodation of some ten or fifteen thousand people; the central space being designed for the President of the United States, members of his cabinet, heads of departments, military officers of the highest rank, and the diplomatic corps. On the opposite side of the avenue were stands for use of congressmen, the Federal judiciary, the press, and invited guests. A commodious stand had been built near here, too, by a public-spirited Bostonian, at his own expense, for the exclusive use of crippled and convalescent soldiers. These disabled heroes filled the structure, and it was impossible to regard without emotion the continual exchange of cheers between the scarred veterans and their returning comrades.

The weather was absolutely perfect on both the days of the grand review; all the conditions, barring the painful memories which even this inspiring sight recalled to many minds, were complete for the full enjoyment of the people's holiday. Two days of rain had cooled the air and laid the dust; and the streets of Washington, not always clean, were pleasant to march through. The air was bright, clear, and invigorating; as far as the eye could reach along the wide avenues through which the armed hosts moved with measured tread there was a blaze of color. Flags, banners, streamers, and all imaginable forms of patriotic device were lavishly spread to the air. The home-coming of the armies had been the signal for the removal of the somber badges of mourning that for more than a month had marked the grief of the city over the death of the beloved Lincoln. Looking over the canopy of the reviewing stand opposite that in which I sat, one could see that the flag on the White House, for the first time since the fifteenth of April, was no longer at half-mast.

In the center of the reviewing stand nearest the White

House grounds was seated President Andrew Johnson; on his
right were Secretary Stanton, General Grant, and Attorney-
General Speed; and on his left were General Meade, Secretary
Welles, Postmaster-General Dennison, and Generals Sherman,
Barnard, and Meigs. Behind these were Secretary McCulloch,
Secretary Harlan, and a group of military notables. On the
higher platform behind were the members of the diplomatic
corps in full ceremonial costume, and in the stands at the right
and left of that occupied by the President and other dignitaries
were military, naval, and civil functionaries by the hundreds.
Among these one noted the fine figure and handsome face of
General W. S. Hancock; he was often recognized and cheered
by the passing soldiery, as well as by civilian spectators. As
each Army corps passed the President's stand, the commander
of the corps took his seat by the side of President Johnson. The
cavalry, a mighty cavalcade, occupied a full hour in passing.
The clatter of hoofs, the clank of sabers, and the shrill call of
bugles resounding on the air invested this favorite arm of the
service with something of that romance with which our people
usually regard it. And a striking incident ushered in the march
past of the corps. Suddenly dashed upon the scene, while the
pavement was clear and the spectators were watching for the
first appearance of General Wesley Merritt's forces, a splendid
blooded charger, covered with foam, wildly plunging and galloping, and ridden by a young major-general. His stirrups were
loose, his empty scabbard clattered behind him, his long yellow
curls were flying in the wind, but his saber was gallantly carried
at salute as he fled by. This was the dashing Custer, whose horse,
frightened at a tremendous wreath of flowers flung over his head
by some indiscreet admirer, was for a few minutes beyond the
control of his rider. There was an irrepressible burst of cheers
from the spectators as the scared steed flashed past, and "Custer!" "Custer!" "Custer!" flew from lip to lip. Shortly, curbing
his horse, the gallant young cavalryman rode back again—a

beautiful figure, lithe, graceful, and every inch a soldier, saluting again as he repassed the President and took his place at the head of his division, which now came up and passed in review. General Merritt commanded the cavalry corps, General Sheridan having departed to his new command in the Southwest.

After the cavalry, which made a picturesque and brilliant spectacle, came the mounted artillery of the regular army, nine batteries in all, Colonel Robertson commanding. The glitter of their equipments, the gleam of their polished cannon, the champing and tramping of their fine horses, and the soldierly appearance of the men, made this an impressive feature of the great parade. Next came the Provost-Marshal's guard,—two regiments of cavalry, and the Third and Tenth United States Infantry, General Macy commanding. The Engineer Brigade, commanded by General Benham, was a corps that roused the enthusiasm and gratified the curiosity of the multitudes as it marched past, with pioneers bearing the implements of their branch of the service, and hauling with them the pontoons, boats, and other appliances required on the march to battle, but seldom seen in a holiday military show.

The Ninth Corps of the Army of the Potomac, formerly Burnside's, was headed by General John G. Parke. This corps was one of the most splendidly equipped and best drilled in the first day's parade; the regiments appeared in fine order, marching "company front," with arms at right-shoulder-shift until just before reaching the President's stand, when they were brought to shouder-arms with a military precision that evoked a great roar of applause from the admiring thousands who looked on. Each brigade of infantry was accompanied by six ambulances, three abreast, and the rear of the corps was brought up by a brigade of artillery. Almost no break occurred in the line of march, and the passing troops were halted but once, and that for a brief moment in front of the main reviewing stand.

After the Ninth came the Fifth Corps, General Charles Griffin in command. Many of the spectators turned their eyes involuntarily toward Warren, who had only recently been relieved of his command, and who was seen, recognized, and uproariously cheered by the men of the Fifth as they marched by. The affection and admiration of those cheers were unmistakable, whatever may have been thought of the infraction of military discipline which was thus committed. A vivid bit of color, giving a pictorial effect to the show, was the appearance of four regiments of Zouaves in the First Brigade, Second Division, of this corps. These were the One Hundred and Fourteenth Pennsylvania, the Fifth New York, the One Hundred and Forty-sixth, and the One Hundred and Fortieth New York. They were splendid in appearance; their marching was perfect, and the men were all well formed and muscular; their gay uniforms and unique dress gave a pleasant relief in the general monotony of color that pervaded the ranks of the marching armies. The Second Corps, commanded by General A. A. Humphreys, brought up the rear of the Army of the Potomac, the Sixth, under General H. G. Wright, not being near enough at hand to take part in the review. It was, however, reviewed separately June 8, 1865. The First, Second, and Third Divisions of the Second Corps were commanded by Ramsey, Barlow, and Mott respectively: and in the First Division was the famous Irish Brigade, Nugent commanding, composed of the Sixty-ninth New York, the Twenty-eighth Massachusetts, the Eighty-eighth New York, the Fourth New York Artillery (equipped as infantry), and the Sixty-third New York. Every soldier and every officer wore a sprig of green in his hat, and the regimental colors had the emerald-green ground, the sunburst, and the harp of Erin. These emblems and the men who bore them were loudly cheered all along the line; we could hear the great roar of the people long before the regiments reached us. Generally speaking, it was noticeable that the applause and the cheering were less frequent at the grand stands where the dignitaries were assembled than at other places along the line where the multitude was enjoying itself in its own free-and-easy fashion.

On the stand where I sat it was entertaining to watch the movements of many Governors of States, who made it their business to "rally" whenever a regiment from their own prideful community came marching by. Governor John A. Andrew of Massachusetts was one of those who, bubbling over with enthusiasm, started volleys of cheers for regiments from the Eastern States; and Governor Fenton of New York was always prepared to "give a hand" to the boys in blue who represented by the thousands the Empire State in the Army of the Potomac. There was an occasional good-humored laugh when a New York militia officer, who never saw service in the field, put himself conspicuously in evidence with his elaborate uniform and military gear, proposing cheers for favorite regiments.

It was noticeable that the commanders of divisions and corps were not, for the most part, men of an elderly appearance. Meade, Benham, and Humphreys were the only exceptions to this rule; almost all the other general officers being youthful of look. Another notable feature of the parade was the fewness of the field officers; companies were commanded by lieutenants who had taken the places of captains temporarily commanding regiments; and colonels led brigades. This was an expressive reminder of the sorrowful mortality that had laid low so many gallant officers leading their men in desperate charges on the field of battle.

There were many inquiries why there were no colored troops in line; at that time the Negro troops were being massed at City Point, Virginia, preparatory to being sent to Sheridan's new command in the Southwest. Those troops would doubtless have had a rousing welcome in Washington; for in those days men recognized in the tardily enlisted freedmen something very like the last hope of the distraught and long-harassed republic.

The general regret that Sheridan was not "on view" with the other famous generals was marked, and significant of his vast popularity. Sherman's appearance on the grand stand was the signal for a tremendous outburst of applause from those who gazed upon the brilliant group, with cheer upon cheer. The redoubtable warrior returned these salutes with grim composure. At that time the public was agog over the dispute that had arisen between the General and the Secretary of War on account of Sherman's terms of agreement for the surrender of the Confederate forces under General Jos. E. Johnston. People who disliked Stanton (and these were many) had hoped and expected that Sherman would treat him with marked disrespect when they met. I sat in the stand opposite that of the presidential party, between Senator Conness of California and Senator Wilson of Massachusetts; and when Sherman, removing his hat, emerged upon the platform from the crowd near the President, Senator Wilson excitedly said: "Now let us watch Sherman; people think he will affront Stanton, whom he hasn't met yet." We trained our field-glasses on the group and saw Stanton extend his hand to Sherman, who, after saluting the President, approached the Secretary of War. At our distance from the party in the grand stand, we could not hear whether any words were spoken; but we could see that Sherman, declining Stanton's greeting, firmly placed his right hand by his side with a very slight gesture. Stanton's face, never very expressive, remained immobile. Sherman, as he turned his attention to the troops passing by, looked grimmer than ever, and a dark-red scar, the mark of a recent slight accident, imparted to his visage a certain sinister expression which rather heightened the effect of this little episode. Some have said that Sherman put his hands behind him, and at the same time made a curt remark as he put aside the greeting proffered by Stanton.

The Army of the Potomac, on its grand review, left outside of the city a great number of men in charge of camps, and many unarmed and dismounted men; but there were in line on that beautiful May day eighty thousand fighting men. There were twenty-nine regiments of cavalry, thirty-three batteries of artillery, one hundred and eighty regiments of infantry, and numerous brilliant staffs of division and corps commanders.

On the second day of the review, the Army of the Mississippi made its first and last appearance in Washington: its victorious leader, Sherman, the idol of the hour, and more than ever admired after his bout with the great War Secretary, stood, at last, in the city whose political atmosphere he so much abhorred. The divisions of his army were the Army of the Tennessee, which formed the right wing, and was commanded by General John A. Logan, who had lately succeeded General O. O. Howard, the newly appointed chief of the Freedmen's Bureau, and the Army of Georgia, or the left wing, commanded by General H. W. Slocum. Of these grand subdivisions, the Army of the Tennessee was composed of ninety-four regiments of infantry; that of Georgia had eighty-six regiments, and a full complement of artillery, and a smaller contingent of cavalry. These forces aggregated about seventy thousand. The Army of the Ohio, made up of the Tenth and Twenty-third Corps, commanded by General John M. Schofield, had been left in North Carolina, and did not participate in the review.

With military precision, as the church clocks chimed nine in the morning, General Sherman appeared at the head of his armies, accompanied by General O. O. Howard, the gorgeously arrayed staffs of the two generals streaming out behind them, a shining spectacle. Sherman was a skilful horseman, but his spirited steed, a powerful beast, gave him all he could do to manage him. The commander saluted the President with impassive face, and Howard, who guided his horse by the stump of his amputated arm, did the same; then the two officers, having passed the reviewing stand, dismounted, and took up their stations with the reviewing party. There was something almost fierce in the fever of enthusiasm roused by the sight of Sherman. Volleys of cheers, prolonged and loud, rose from the crowd; a multitude of small flags waved from the reviewing stands, and wreaths and bouquets of flowers flew thick and fast through the air. In the group of notable men on the grand stand, Sherman was certainly the most notable in appearance. His head was high and narrow, his hair and whiskers were sandy in hue, his moustache stiff and bristling, and his eyes keen and piercing. He was very tall, walked with an immense stride, talked rapidly and nervously, and would be picked out in any assemblage as a man of distinction. All eyes were fastened upon his striking countenance, the vast multitude gazing with a certain rapture at the famous man whom they now saw for the first time.

There was, of course, a great deal of popular curiosity to see the Western soldiers who had marched from Atlanta to the sea, and through the Carolinas and Virginia to Washington. Everybody welcomed with glad acclaim to the national capital these heroes who now, for the first time since they had been in the military service of the country, saw its seat of government. Comparisons between the Eastern and the Western men were made at once. It was observed that the Western men wore a more free-and-easy uniform, generally adopting the loose blue blouse and the sugar-loaf-shaped felt hat, rather than the close-fitting coat and natty French *kepi* of the Eastern soldiers who had marched before us in the Army of the Potomac. But nothing could be more perfect than their marching order, each rank stepping out as one man. As a rule, the Westerners were of larger build than their brothers in the Army of the Potomac; and they were so allotted in the ranks that each company front presented a line of uniform height, the tallest men in the front.

As each brigade reached the President's stand, its band and drum corps swung around opposite the reviewing officer, who had taken his place by the President, and played until the rear came up, and then fell in, giving place to the next brigade band. In this way, there was always good marching music at the reviewing stand, adding greatly to the fine effect of the military spectacle of passing troops. Great praise was given to the Fifteenth Corps of the Army of the Tennessee, commanded by General W. B. Hazen, and made up of troops from Iowa, Missouri, Minnesota, Michigan, Illinois, Indiana, and Ohio. This magnificent body of men was generally regarded as comprising some of the very best types of Western fighting man; their free, swinging stride, their boldness of bearing, and their powerful physique, were certainly highly impressive, and extorted the unstinted admiration of the onlookers, who saw many regiments and brigades made famous during the long struggle in the Southwest long before the review in the national capital was even so much as thought of.

The Seventeenth Corps, which immediately followed the Fifteenth, was composed of troops from the States above mentioned, and included one regiment from the State of New Jersey. In this corps, too, were many Wisconsin men—splendid specimens of humanity, tall, well-made, and marching with the stride and cadence step which were so marked a feature of the Westerners. The long legs and the long marches of Sherman's men, it was said, gave the Army that peculiar and impressive appearance in the line of parade. General Frank P. Blair, Jr., rode at the head of this noble corps; and he looked stouter and browner than when he was in Congress. He was frantically cheered by the populace as soon as he was recognized, riding there with a certain military grace and alert manner that were characteristic of his admirable soldierly reputation. The good-humored crowds laughed and cheered when they saw in the rear of each brigade of these two corps some of the typical "Sherman's bummers," of whose exploits they had heard so much. These were accompanied by jacks and mules, laden with camp

equipage and the spoils of foraging expeditions, and attended
by grinning darkies; chickens, roosters, goats, dogs, young rac-
coons, and camp pets of various species were all mixed in
motley array. The plantation of Jeff Davis had been laid under
tribute, and two small white jacks of a fancy stock were among
the trophies of one regiment.

Between the Armies, as they marched past, and occasionally between the individual corps, were gaps of distance across
which the sovereign people on the outer lines would run to gaze
upon the notables in the reviewing stand. Sometimes a great
throng of people would collect in front and cheer lustily for
Grant, Sherman, Howard, or some other military favorite, not
omitting President Johnson; and each would rise with manifest
unwillingness to make his bow to the multitude. Then the guards
on duty would rush in and ungraciously force back the sovereigns in most admired disorder, a great show of glittering bayonets being made. But, for the most part, the streets were kept
clear for the marching men, and good order was preserved.
Toward the end of the second day's parade, popular respect for
the military guards on duty seemed to have abated somewhat,
and there were frequent irruptions of spectators into the lines,
and civil and military confusion most inextricable followed.

Like the Army of the Potomac, the corps of the Army of
the Mississippi had adopted distinctive badges; and it was an
interesting novelty to see in Washington some of the totems of
the great forces that had opened the navigation of the Father
of Waters, split the Confederacy into fragments, and finally
marched to the sea. People gazed with admiring curiosity upon
the Fifteenth's cartridge-box, set transversely on a square field,
with the legend, "Forty rounds," the Seventeenth's arrow, the
star of the Twentieth, and the acorn of the Fourteenth. Looking
at these novel emblems of military prowess (for they were novel
to us), one could realize how far apart had been the two great

Armies fighting in the defense of the Union. The brave men who bore these badges had hewed their way from the Mississippi to Washington, and on their battle-flags they carried the magical names of "Atlanta," "Lookout Mountain," "Chickamauga," and a host of other titles that symbolized and immortalized their valor and their successes. They were still brothers in blood with their comrades in the Army of the Potomac, and with the dense multitudes that cheered and cheered again as the strangers passed. One must needs recall with grateful heart the mighty achievements and the self-denying sacrifices of these marching men, whose victories had so often given occasion for national thanksgiving as the tide of victory ebbed and flowed and the day of peace at last drew nearer and more near.

Now on every pennon, flag, and guidon fluttered a black streamer; the hilt of every victorious saber wore a band of crape. These were the tokens of that national mourning over the last illustrious martyr, whose death left a pang of sorrow, even in this hour of jubilation, in every patriot's heart. Nor could the thoughtful spectator restrain a sigh for the thousands who should have marched with these triumphant cohorts, but who fell, a sacrifice for the cause of the Union for whose defense they had risked and lost their lives. They were not forgotten in that hour of triumph—they who had fallen out of the ranks now marching past, although they slept their last sleep in the bayous and marshes of the Southwest and had made the South all billowy with graves. One could almost imagine, as the glittering, cheered, and cheering columns passed by, redundant with life and vigor, that another host, spectral and shadowy, but as numerous and as vividly characterized and marked, moved with and over them with silent tread in the viewless air—two armies, one living and one dead.

The pageant faded. The men-at-arms who had spent their years and lavished their energies in camps or on fields of battle went from the national capital to their own homes, to take up once more the arts of peace and the cares and joys of sweet domesticity. In a few weeks this army of two or three hundred thousand men melted back into the heart of the people from whence it came, and the great spectacle of the Grand Army of the Republic on review disappeared from sight.

APPENDIX

A Column by "Castine"

THE following news column did not appear in the original edition of *Washington in Lincoln's Time* but is included here to show how a correspondent reported and wrote in the raw during the Civil War. It is an interesting example of one of Noah Brooks's 258 newsletters from Washington because it includes such twentieth-century topics as Congressional maneuvering; electioneering; inactive Army generals; sanitation and the looks of the District of Columbia; revenue laws and the national finances, and filibustering. The main subject under discussion here is the Conscription Bill. This "Letter From Washington" appeared in the lead columns on page 1 on Saturday morning, March 28, 1863, of the *Sacramento Daily Union*. The signature, as usual, was simply "Castine."

—EDITOR

LETTER FROM WASHINGTON
[From Our Special Correspondent.]
Washington, February 26th.

The Conscription Bill.

IT has been the endeavor of your correspondent to keep the readers of the *Sacramento Union* well posted upon the history of the debate upon the important bill for the enrollment and calling out of the national forces, introduced in the Senate by Henry Wilson of Massachusetts, and passed by that body without a division. But, at the risk of being tedious, let us make a brief résumé of the main characteristics of this exciting and interesting debate, which was listened to, day after day and night after night, by an attentive audience, which crowded the spacious galleries of the House of Representatives during the whole progress of the debate. This audience, by the way, was a sore grief to the Copperheads, for they could not but feel the unpopularity of their sentiments when they saw that occasional and spontaneous outbursts of patriotism and expressions of determination to vigorously prosecute the war were always received with applause by the irrepressible and impressionable galleries. All demonstrations of applause or dissatisfaction by the lookers-on or by the members are out of order and contrary to rule; but now and then their feelings will get the better of their wholesome dread of the rules of order, and it has become an indulgent custom for the Speaker to tolerate such rare ebullitions of the sentiment of the sovereign people in the galleries. The fact is that the galleries of the House are now very generally frequented by the soldiers who are quartered in and around the city. They have usually permission to go into the city during the hours of daylight, and during the day session they show their interest in national affairs and their intelligent appreciation of the importance of present legislation by visiting the Capitol.

The principles of the bill are correct, according to the estimation of the best jurists, and the severity of the measures proposed are warranted by the terrible exigency into which we have fallen. The people have not sufficiently realized the imminence of the public danger, but have, with great unconcern, left the management of the rebellion to the care of an undefined central power which they have thought existed somewhere, and was responsible for all failures and all reverses. They have seemed to forget that the tone and temper of the people mainly determines that of the Army, and have allowed their own querulousness, fault-finding and ironical criticism and unmilitary insubordination to infect that portion of the people which has been temporarily recognized as the military arm of the country. While the nation has been struggling for its own existence, the people have been buying, selling, marrying and given in marriage, prospering in business and undisturbed by the din of wasting war, save when death upon the battlefield brought mourning and grief to individual hearts without touching the general welfare.

By the provisions of the Conscript Bill, as it is called, all this is changed. Its far-reaching and searching characteristics will touch every household in the land; its severity and thorough measures will bring home to every man, woman and child in the loyal States the awful consciousness that we have now reached the final crisis of the great rebellion, when we must do or die. Upon this point I cannot do better than to note the remarks of B. F. Thomas, the eccentric Massachusetts Unionist, who votes against the Administration usually. Yesterday, just before the passage of the bill, he said that it was truly a terrible bill, and was warranted only by the terrible exigency upon which the country has happened. He said that the duty of crushing out the rebellion was the most onerous which had ever been thrust upon any government which the world had ever seen, and that the National Government, to preserve itself, had the undoubted right, under the Constitution, to take in its inexorable right hand every subject of the Government, white or black, bond or free, of every condition, and use him for its own righteous purposes; and that it also had the right to strike through State rights everywhere. After all our experiments in the policy of confiscation, emancipation and other abstractions, we have come back to the point from where we started, and are now about to pass a bill which, in effect, declares that nothing but the mailed right hand of power can save the nation.

The right of the Government to make arbitrary arrests naturally came up for debate, and was defended by Unionists, who demanded that the National Government be intrusted with powers to defend itself, which should not have the interference of any undefined State rights, a prolific source of heresy and mischief. In other words, coercion or surrender have become necessary, and Congress, acting as the representative of the people, has made the choice, and if the people will repudiate their action and rise against it, all has been done that can be done, and henceforth the result is left with the sovereign people, with whom all power originates and to whom it must be returned for legitimate exercises. The line of argument pursued by the Opposition was defective and superficial, being chiefly drawn from a sincere desire to retard the progress of the war, hamper the Administration and impede legislation, the expediency and necessity of which were so apparent to the more candid that many of the Border States and conservatives, who were shy on the earlier votes on the bill, went solid for its final passage.

Amending the Bill.

Yesterday being by common consent the amendment day of the bill, and the last of the fight, was opened at the beginning of the session of the House by the offering of several verbal amendments by Olin of New York, Chairman of the Military Committee, the conductor of the Conscription Bill. The most important amendment is that which provides that spies found within our lines, or arrested while lurking about our fortifications, shall, upon conviction by a court-martial, suffer death. The amendment was adopted, and Vallandigham offered an amendment to the twenty-fifth section, which embodies some of the most objectionable features of the bill, as considered by the submissionists, as it vests all of the arresting and judicial power of the proposed law in the hands of Provost Marshals. The amendment offered by Vallandigham provided that deserters, persons who hinder the draft, persons guilty of treasonable practices, etc., shall be arrested by warrants issued by civil officers or civil courts having competent jurisidiction, on oath or affirmation setting forth the charge. Upon this amendment the ayes and noes were demanded, and it was lost by 57 ayes to 107 noes—a large vote for the military law, and considered as a test of the principle, as understood in the House.

Diven of New York offered an amendment providing that if from any unavoidable cause the draft cannot take place upon the time assigned for it, it shall occur as soon as is possible. The amendment was adopted. Cox of Ohio offered an amendment to limit the conscription to white citizens. Rejected. Thaddeus Stevens tried to amend the bill to exempt Quakers and those having conscientious scruples against bearing arms, but the House refused to make the exemption, wisely concluding that if they could not fight they must pay, and if they have conscientious scruples against paying they can leave property lying around loose in such manner as to enable the officers of the Government to seize that which their consciences will withhold from a deliberate sacrifice. The next amendment offered was that of old man Wickliffe, who called the ayes and noes upon the following: That the men thus called into service be by the Governors of their respective States organized and officered, according to the provisions of the Constitutions and laws of such States. This brought up the State rights conflict, and was voted down by 104 noes to 55 ayes. Holman of Indiana moved to strike out the thirteenth section of the bill, which provides that drafted men may furnish substitutes, or, in lieu thereof, pay for such procuration an amount not to exceed three hundred dollars. This amendment was lost by 66 ayes to 88 noes. He then offered a

substitute for the bill, which differs only from the original bill
in that it provides for the enrolling of the militia subject to
draft by State authorities, exempts a greater variety of persons,
excludes the "treasonable practice" clause, and limits the draft
to white persons. The substitute was lost by 44 ayes to 108 noes.

The Passage of the Bill.

The hour for the final passage of the bill arrived while
the vote was being taken upon Holman's substitute; and as soon
as it was rejected the air was filled with loud calls for more
amendments, more time, a few moments more of grace; but the
House inexorably refused to listen to any appeals for more
indulgence of debate. Scores of members arose in their seats,
swinging their resolutions or amendments in the air, bawling,
"Mr. Speaker! Mr. Speaker!" Dawes of Massachusetts and
Biddle of Pennsylvania vainly begged and implored for "just
a half hour," five minutes even, but it was a waste of breath,
and the bill was read *in extenso* as amended, occupying three
quarters of an hour. The members scattered during the reading;
but as soon as it was over came back to their seats in a crowd,
and eagerly watched the progress of the vote as each member
answered aye or no to the roll call of the Clerk. The bill was
passed by a full vote of 115 ayes to 49 noes. [This vote has been
published in the *Union,* with a classification of the politics of
the members.—EDS., *Sacramento Union.*] When the vote was
announced there was an involuntary throb of suppressed applause in the crowded galleries, whence hundreds of people were
looking, with absorbed interest, upon the proceedings, but the
Speaker's hammer held them in awe and the wholesome terror
of having the galleries cleared restrained them. The bill was
finally passed, and the law has become substantially a fixed fact,
for the concurrence of the Senate in the House amendments and
the necessary signature of the President are considered as fore-

gone conclusions. So the crowds of people, who for four days and nights have filled the galleries of the House during this long debate, arise and pour along the passages, convinced that the awful exigency of the times is now about to come nearer the people than ever before. As they pass out they smile cheerfully. We accept the omen.

Congressional Elections to Come Off.

As the time for the adjournment of this Congress draws near, public attention is directed toward the Congressional elections of the several States which have not yet chosen their Representatives to the Thirty-eighth Congress. New Hampshire elects three Representatives on the second Tuesday in March; Rhode Island two, on the first Wednesday in April; Connecticut four, on the first Wednesday in April; Kentucky nine on the first Monday in August; Vermont three on the first Tuesday in September; California three on the first Thursday in September; Maryland five in November. West Virginia will send three members; Old Virginia one or more; Louisiana two or more, and Tennessee will send two or more.

Of course from all these States we may expect a fair share of positive anti-Administrationists, but the indications are that the average will afford a fair working majority in the House for the Lincoln Administration. Such, at least, is the general belief here among friends of the Union. Great efforts are to be made by the Copperheads to carry New Hampshire and Connecticut. The former State will be canvassed by Richardson of Illinois, and Cox is going into Connecticut what time he can spare from the gubernatorial contest in Ohio. The nomination of Tom Seymour, a notorious Peace Democrat, as Governor of Connecticut, is deemed a fatal stroke of policy for the Copperheads, who dare and cannot consistently try the same deceitful game which was so efficacious in the last election, by which

peace men were returned to Congress upon a war policy platform. But a vigorous canvass is being made in the State. The
result in New Hampshire is now considered to be more doubtful
than that in Connecticut, as the issue in the latter will be as
between peace and war. Kentucky, of course, will send a delegation of the same mixed character as that in the present Congress
—men who are opposed to the war being partially assisted by
those who are sound on the main question, but unreliable so far
as any moral support to the Government is concerned.

The Army of the Potomac.

The accounts from this Army are of the most encouraging
character. Notwithstanding the severity and inclemency of the
weather, the Army has steadily progressed in its reorganization
and re-moralization, and it is generally agreed, by those whose
experience and candor entitle them to credit, that at no time
since its organization has the Army of the Potomac possessed so
high a degree of efficiency as now. The indomitable Hooker has
infused his own courageous and bold spirit into the ranks of the
soldiery, while recently inaugurated stringency in dealing with
officers guilty of insubordination has had the salutary effect
to compact and invigorate an Army which we hope once more
to see accomplish great things.

The Inactive Generals.

No disposition is yet made of the large number of "retired"
major-generals at present out of active service. We are daily
treated with rumors concerning the future commands of these
generals, which frequency of rumors is indicative of the popular
desire to see the commanders taken from their *otium cum digni-
tate* to actual service. The murmurings are frequent, and just
now the popular grumble is against that policy which detains in

inactivity so efficient and capable a man as General Butler. It is generally understood that the opposition of Secretary Seward is the principal bar to the reinstatement of Butler to the Louisiana command. As for the other generals nothing reliable is now known of their whereabouts. Frémont's latest rumored command is said to be in Texas, and Shields has gone to California on his own account.

National Arms for California.

The California delegation in the House of Representatives have been steadily besieging the Secretary of War to send out arms and munitions of war to the Pacific Coast, believing that the danger of aggressive demonstrations upon that line of coast, in case of a foreign war, is too imminent to be risked any longer. He has just agreed to send ten thousand stand of arms to California forthwith, and will send some heavy ordnance as soon as the gunboats now in process of completion are got rid of. The speech of Senator McDougall upon the French attitude toward the United States has attracted considerable attention here, and has, perhaps, had the salutary effect to hasten the action of Secretary Stanton, who appears to be alive to the dangers of the situation.

Aboriginal Visitors.

Washington just now has a delegation of some thirty Chippewa from Lake Superior and Northern Minnesota. These representatives of a fading race are here for the purpose of securing their rights to certain lands and funds, which they claim under treaty from the United States. They have been presented to the President, and have had several interviews with Commissioner Dole, at the Indian Bureau. They are mostly ignorant of the English tongue, and go about the streets, attended by an interpreter, all clad in semi-savage rig, and gaping with an envious interest at the novel sights of the capital city. They have attended the theaters and other places of amusement in the city, where they are said to enjoy the divertisements very highly. The display of legs at the Canterbury Ballet—a sort of Washington Belle Union—is reported to have been extremely gratifying to these children of nature, who probably think, with more sophisticated people, that the more you see of the natural figure the better for the observer.

A Muddy City.

At this present writing the city of Washington, the capital of the nation, is probably the dirtiest and most ill-kept borough in the United States. It is impossible to describe the truly fearful condition of the streets; they are seas or canals of liquid mud, varying in depth from one to three feet, and possessing, as geographical features, conglomerations of garbage, refuse and trash, the odors whereof rival those of the city of Cologne, which Coleridge declared to be "seventy separate and distinct stinks." At some points, where a street has a sloping intersection with another, I have seen a torrent of thick, yellow mud flowing in unruffled smoothness over the concealed crossing, bearing on its placid surface the unconsidered trifles which have been swept out of saloons, shops and houses. Through such masses as this labor the unfortunate animals which are condemned to drudge their miserable life in such a wretched vocation as falls to the lot of a Government-contract horse. Numbers of these unfortunate animals, near to death, are turned out at large to wander in the bone through the scenes which they knew in the flesh, until they drop their frames in some soft spot and are carried off by the city carrion cart—a peculiar vehicle which has an apparatus for hoisting the carcasses into its embrace, the stiff legs of the departed equines shaking helplessly in the air as they

are hauled off. Everybody has heard of the great corruption of
the city of Washington, but I will venture to say that its moral
corruption is far exceeded by the physical rottenness of its
streets.

Congressional Fillibustering.

I suppose that everybody knows that the above term refers
to the system of tactics by which a minority in a deliberative
body defeat legislation by all sorts of irrelevant motions and
frivolous measures. This has always been a part of the defensive
warfare of a minority which may be opposed to any pending
measure in Congress, but it has been particularly a feature in
this present Congress, where the minority are more than usually
factious, and desire to stave off all important legislation with
the hope that an extra session may be called, when, as they believe, they will have the whip hand on the Administration in
the House of Representatives. I have had frequent occasion to
allude to this favorite resource of the Opposition in the House,
and I note it again, that Californians may know to whom they
will be indebted for the failure of such bills as affect their interests and are likely to go over to another Congress from the present House of Representatives. The Copperheads will fillibuster
upon the Missouri Emancipation Bill, and last night when the
bill to indemnify the President for the suspension of the Habeas
Corpus Act came up in the House for concurrence in the Senate
amendments, they went into fillibustering forthwith, and kept it
up until two o'clock in the morning, when a compromise was
effected by conceding the Opposition the privilege of debate
upon the amendments during the session of this evening, the
vote to be taken on the bill at one o'clock, March second. It is
very probable that when important bills are pending at the last
hour of Congress the Copperheads will commence their usual
practice of calling the ayes and noes upon unimportant motions,

and have the session end by the law during a roll call. Should that be the case, it is possible that the question may arise as to the possibility of the expiration of Congress during a pending roll call, as it has been decided that an adjournment cannot take place under such circumstances.

Revenue Law Amendments.

The work of amending the Internal Revenue Law has proved to be a considerable task, as there are so many conflicting interests to be considered. Yesterday the whisky tax was discussed at considerable length in the House, and the Ohio representatives were swift to oppose the proposed rise of tariff upon that indispensable article. Holman of Indiana said that only one third of the whisky manufactured in the Northwest was drunk "straight"; the rest went into the manufacture of various articles, and was used in many of the arts besides the art of making beasts of men. Among other amendments adopted, is one creating the office of Deputy Commissioner of Internal Revenue, at a salary of three thousand dollars, and a Cashier, at a salary of twenty-five hundred. This is demanded by the enormous increase of business at the Bureau of Internal Revenue.

The National Finances.

This is a rather formidable caption for a brief item, for the limits of this long letter forbid anything more than a brief allusion to the fact that the public credit is just now imperiled by the failure of Congress to agree upon a system of national finance. We are now within three days of the close of the session, and the Senate and House Committees of Conference have not yet agreed upon the differences of the two branches of Congress upon the Ways and Means Bill. The radical point of difference is the bank-tax clause and the legal-tender sections.

The House is afraid of the banks, and the Senate is not; but in the meantime financial matters are in a muddle, and gold goes up to fabulous figures, being at 172 to-day. There is not a very encouraging prospect ahead; but the telegraph will anticipate all of my speculations upon the financial aspect, so I will only say that most of the difficulty which now surrounds the question is due to the determination of the bank men on their part to oppose all taxation and undesirable legislation, and of the Copperheads on the other to create all of the factious opposition and discussion upon such vital measures as they are able to.

Senator McDougall on the Rampage.

During an unimportant debate last night in the Senate, upon a railroad bill, it was incidentally mentioned that Secretary Stanton had written a letter upon the subject to somebody. This brought McDougall on his feet instanter, and he said that "the person" at the head of the War Department was a base man, and that he (McDougall) had promised the President, in his own house, that he would denounce the Secretary of War. He thought that the President ought to be a President of the United States, and the people should know it. Morrill called the Senator from California to order for the irrelevancy of his remarks. The Chair decided the Senator to be out of order, but he proceeded to say that he was ready to declare in his seat in the United States Senate, and upon his own responsibility, that the man who is at the head of the War Department is a man who has wronged the country. The Chair called him to order again, whereupon the irate McDougall said that he should appeal from the decision of the Chair, and that he wanted to see if a Senator of the United States is equal to a Secretary of War. Trumbull asked him to withdraw his appeal, but the Senator replied that he would be d—d if he would, but he subsequently withdrew his appeal with a very bad grace. Upon this disgraceful scene it is hardly worth while to give any comment further than that the Senator from California was, as usual, very drunk, and that, under such circumstances, his assertion concerning the request of the President to him as to his remarks upon Secretary Stanton must be received with many grains of allowance.

CASTINE

Index